Michael SCHÜRMANN

Paris •
Movie
Walks

**Ten Guided Tours Through
The City of Lights!
Camera! Action!**

Paris Movie Walks:
Ten Guided Tours Through the City of Lights! Camera! Action!

Published by
The Intrepid Traveler
P.O. Box 531
Branford, CT 06405
http://www.intrepidtraveler.com

Copyright ©2009 by Michael Schürmann
First Edition
Printed in the U.S.A.
Cover design by Pascal Blua, mousedesign.fr
Interior design by Jana Rade, impactstudios.com
Cover photo ©Raymond Cauchetier, Paris. All rights reserved.
Interior photos (except pages 218 and 277) ©2009 by Michael Schürmann. All rights reserved.

ISBN: 978-1-887140-83-6
Library of Congress Control Number: 2009922202

10 9 8 7 6 5 4 3 2 1

Publisher's Cataloging-in-Publication
(Provided by Quality Books, Inc.)

Schürmann, Michael, 1957-
    Paris movie walks : ten guided tours through the city
of lights! camera! action! / Michael Schürmann. -- 1st
ed.
    p. cm.
    Includes index.
    LCCN 2009922202
    ISBN-13: 978-1-887140-83-6
    ISBN-10: 1-887140-83-2

    1. Paris (France)--Tours. 2. Walking--France--Paris
--Guidebooks. 3. Paris (France)--In motion pictures--
Guidebooks.   I. Title.

DC708.S38 2009   914.4'3610484
                           QBI09-600055

Photo Credits

Table of Contents

Maps

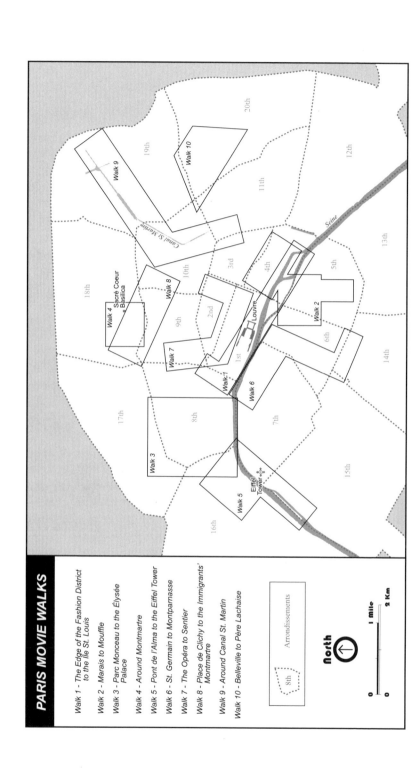

PARIS MOVIE WALKS

Walk 1 - The Edge of the Fashion District to the Île St. Louis

Walk 2 - Marais to Mouffle

Walk 3 - Parc Monceau to the Élysée Palace

Walk 4 - Around Montmartre

Walk 5 - Pont de l'Alma to the Eiffel Tower

Walk 6 - St. Germain to Montparnasse

Walk 7 - The Opéra to Sentier

Walk 8 - Place de Clichy to the Immigrants' Montmartre

Walk 9 - Around Canal St. Martin

Walk 10 - Belleville to Père Lachaise

north

Arrondissements

8th

0   1 mile
0   2 Km

Prequel

Paris, the world's number one tourist destination, has been explored and mapped more thoroughly than any other city on the globe. Yet it is full of "hidden" sights: street corners, cafés, and urban beauty spots where famous movie scenes were shot. Though often unremarkable in themselves, these sights have given many of us our first idea of the look and feel of the real Paris. And in the process, they have made us eager to follow Amélie, Zazie, Jason Bourne, and hosts of others to see the sights for ourselves.

This book will let you follow in their footsteps. It will also help you see some of the city's best-known landmarks with fresh eyes—the eyes of the movie-maker. Over the years, film directors and cinematographers from around the world, and especially Hollywood, have created some of the most memorable movie moments of all time by the banks of the Seine, along the Champs-Élysées, and in the shadow of Sacré-Coeur. Paris, after all, is Hollywood's favorite foreign destination. Whenever American directors feel they have to "go foreign" because domestic locations don't seem to provide the requisite romance, glamour or exoticism, Paris is their first port of call.

In effect, the city has become one giant stage where nearly every famous French and American movie star has made a mark. Matt Damon, Brad Pitt, and George Clooney; Jean-Paul Belmondo, Alain Delon and Gérard Depardieu; Julia Roberts, Meg Ryan, and Michelle Pfeiffer; Juliette Binoche, Audrey Tautou, and Catherine Deneuve; Gary Cooper and Cary Grant; Jean Gabin, Yves Montand and Simone Signoret; Audrey Hepburn and Ava Gardner; Paul Newman and Marlon Brando; Harrison Ford and Jack Nicholson; Fred Astaire and Gene Kelly, or any of those other famous "Americans in Paris" or French stars you've enjoyed watching.

The walks in this book follow the movie-makers and take in all the major sights of Paris. On the way, you'll also learn a few things about the sights and the city itself—occasionally even about modern French life and culture in more general terms. But I can promise you one thing: there will be no endless lists of French monarchs and their annoying mistresses, no stories about poets and painters about whom you know little and care even less. If you are interested in finding out more about 17th century tapestry and the intricacies of the Bourbon succession, you have come to the wrong place.

Instead, you'll find ten walks, divided into three categories:

- Category 1 includes four walks that cover the "essential sights" of Paris, both in terms of movie sites and general importance—the center of the old city with the Louvre and Notre-Dame Cathedral, the area around the Champs-Élysées, and the main sights in Montmartre and on the Left Bank (i.e., south of the Seine).
- Category 2 walks stray further afield. These four walks include some parts of town that, while still picturesque, interesting, and full of sights, may be less familiar to the overseas visitor—Montparnasse, the Opéra quarter, and the areas at the foot of the Montmartre hill and the Eiffel Tower, respectively.
- Category 3 consists of two walks—along the banks of Canal Saint-Martin and through the adjacent quarters of Belleville and Ménilmontant. These are a little different in nature from the sites you'll visit in the other walks. There are fewer "hard sights" here from Hollywood movies. Instead, the visitor is invited to take a gentle stroll through some of the town's legendary working-class neighborhoods, the so-called *quartiers populaires*. These walks will let you take in the old-style Paris of Maurice Chevalier and Édith Piaf that is celebrated in the French movies of the 1930s and '40s.

I follow the walks with a "Further Afield" chapter that features locations that allow you to explore some of Paris's flea markets, green spaces, suburbs, and other areas of interest to visitors and moviemakers.

Each of the ten walks starts and ends at a Métro station. Most will take a minimum of three hours and could become a full day's activity if you stop to shop or step in to visit museums or galleries instead of just passing them by. The Montmartre (Walk 4) and Belleville (Walk 10) itineraries include a few stairways and some hills, but on the whole, there is nothing in this book that could or should scare anybody in near-average physical condition. Just take your time. If you feel you need a break, there is always a street café nearby where you can rest your weary bones for a few minutes. It may be a good idea, however, to put your newly acquired stiletto-heeled designer pumps back into their box for the time being and go for that comfy old pair of walking shoes.

At which point you may well ask: Must I have seen all the movies men-tioned in a tour to enjoy it? Well, clearly it would help if you have seen one or two. For the others, you can do it the other way round: see the sights first and, if you like what you see (and read) about the movie, put it on your

Netflix list, rent it, or buy the DVD. Then see if you can recognize the spots you visited. If, on the other hand, you are still in the process of planning your visit, you may want to include some movie viewing in your preparations. In that case, consult my notes on "What to Watch" at the end of the book.

A book like this can never be fully comprehensive, intentionally. While I have done my best to cover all of Hollywood's "Paris" movies (and will be grateful to readers who take the time to email me—schuermann.michael@gmail.com—about omissions of films and scenes). I have limited the French movies to films that received a major international release. Never forget one thing: Visiting a foreign city should be a joy, not an ordeal. You've come to Paris to have *fun*. So go out and experience the sights, the sounds, and the smells of the city. Feel its buzz. Explore. As someone who knew a lot more about Paris than I once said: "Paris is a moveable feast." Enjoy it.

A note about Arrondissements and Métro Lines: Paris is divided into 20 districts (arrondissements) that spiral clockwise from the center of the city near the Louvre museum to its eastern boundary. I've included arrondissement and Métro line information for each walk to help you pinpoint the areas and stations quickly on city and Métro maps. The Walk Locator map on page 8 will help you visualize precisely which areas of the city each walk covers, and you'll find maps of each walk in the appropriate chapters. Most have been divided into two parts for convenient reference. A Métro map appears on page 278.

Dining in Paris

One of the best things about Paris is the food, whether purchased in a market stall, a shop, or enjoyed in a restaurant or café. Here are some tips for dining in cafés and restaurants, whether they have a movie theme or not:

First, learn to distinguish among them. *Restaurants* by and large serve only food, often in somewhat formal surroundings, *Brasseries* are less formal and often extremely busy dining establishments. *Cafés* mostly offer only a limited variety of dishes, often not much more than a *plat du jour* and snacks like the ubiquitous *croque monsieur*, a slice of ham and cheese on toast.

Second, be aware of French dining habits. Outside of general lunch and dinner hours—lunch from noon till about 2:30 or 3:00 p.m., dinner from about 7 p.m.—it may be difficult to get any food at all at a dining establishment, even in a café. The French observe regular hours for dining out, and that is that. If, on the other hand, all you want is a cup of coffee, the regular lunch and dinner hours may not be your best bet. Most *cafés* reserve most or all of their tables for diners (clue: napkin, fork, and knife on the table) and you may have to take your coffee at the bar, standing. This is something you can do all day long—provided the place has a bar, of course. Some *brasseries* do, some don't; *restaurants* generally do not.

If all you want is a coffee or a quick snack to just chase those hunger pains away, you may do best by avoiding cafés and restaurants altogether. Most bakeries offer sandwiches and slices of quiche or pizza to go—and they can heat them for you, too.

Third, if you have your heart set on eating at one of the city's gourmet temples, you will have to play by their rules, I am afraid. Always remember, it is a mix of going to church and a special type of theater where you are spectator and stage actor at the same time—very much like the scene in Luis Bunuel's *The Discreet Charm of the Bourgeoisie* where hosts and guests at an upper middle-class dinner party sit down to dine—only to see the curtains rise and give way to a packed theater auditorium. This is also when they discover that the roast chickens on their plates are actually made of plastic—a point at which the analogy to a French restaurant breaks down, thankfully.

Many things could be said here, most of them obvious, so I shall send you on your way with three cardinal rules:

- Make a reservation. At the very least, phone a few minutes in advance to ask whether they still have a free table. This also makes it more difficult for the head waiter to turn you away simply because he does not like the way you look. Think about it.
- Dress appropriately. Chances are you may already feel a little bit nervous. You don't want to exacerbate that by attracting attention by being the only guy in the place without a proper coat or in trainers. And let us not even mention shorts.
- Choose lunch over dinner. Your bank account will thank you for it. The businessman's lunch menu in a luxury restaurant will, on average, set you back $70 to $100 a head without wine. Dinner—à la carte only—can easily cost you twice that much and more.

ARRONDISSEMENTS: 1, 4, and a bit of 8 and 6.
DURATION: 3½ hours—longer if you'd decide to do any of the possible "side" excursions

Walk 1

The Edge of the Fashion District to the Île-St-Louis

The Church of the Madeleine to the place de la Concorde, the Louvre, and—across the pont des Arts and the pont Neuf—the Île-de-la-Cité (with Notre-Dame Cathedral) and the Île-St-Louis.

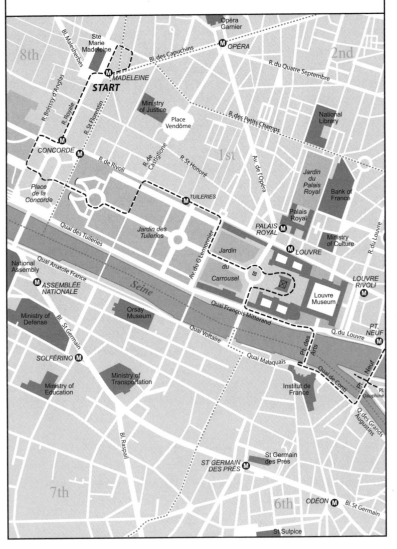

WALK 1 - PART 1

The Edge of the Fashion District to Ile St. Louis

Start: Métro Madeleine (Lines 8, 12, 14)
End: Métro Sully-Morland (Line 7)

	Walking Route
Ⓜ	METRO STATION
	Landmark
8th	Arrondissement

North
↑

0 — ¼ Mile
0 — ¼ — ½ Km

Opéra Garnier
Ⓜ OPÉRA

8th

Ste Marie Madeleine
Ⓜ MADELEINE
START

Bl. Malesherbes
Bl. des Capuchins
R. du Quatre Septembre

2nd

Ministry of Justice
Place Vendôme
R. des Petits Champs

National Library

R. Boissy d'Anglas
R. Royale
R. St Florentin

Ⓜ CONCORDE
R. de Rivoli
R. de Castiglione
R. St Honoré
1st
Av. de l'Opéra

Jardin du Palais Royal
Bank of France

Place de la Concorde
Ⓜ TUILERIES

Palais Royal

Quai des Tuileries
Jardin des Tuileries
Av. du G Lemonnier
Jardin du Carrousel

PALAIS ROYAL Ⓜ
Ⓜ LOUVRE

Ministry of Culture

R. du Louvre

National Assembly
Quai Anatole France
Ⓜ ASSEMBLÉE NATIONALE

Seine
Quai François Mitterand

Louvre Museum

LOUVRE RIVOLI Ⓜ

Ministry of Defense
Bl. St Germain
Orsay Museum
Quai Voltaire
Quai Malaquais
Pl. des Arts
Q. du Louvre

PT. NEUF Ⓜ

SOLFÉRINO Ⓜ
Ministry of Transportation
Institut de France
Quai de Conti
Pl. Neuf
Pl. Dauphine

Ministry of Education
Bl. Raspail
Q. des Grands Augustins

7th
ST GERMAIN DES PRÉS Ⓜ
St Germain des Prés

6th
ODÉON Ⓜ Bl. St Germain

St Sulpice

Go to the Métro station Madeleine (Lines 8, 12, 14) and take exit No. 2, "Église." Turn left out of the exit into the boulevard de la Madeleine.

Don't be surprised if the first person you run into is a six-foot-two supermodel who looks like a million dollars. This is, after all, the part of Paris where many of the city's most famous fashion designers have their offices and design facilities. The house to your left, no. 14, on the corner of rue Vignon, for instance, houses the offices and design facilities of Karl Lagerfeld.

Cross rue Vignon and turn left into the rue Godot-de-Mauroy.

You are about to meet models of a different kind—higher heels and lower hourly rates—for you are now entering one of the city's many small red-light districts. These are often only a block or so long and, like this one, are frequently located in the immediate vicinity of rather respectable, even up-market, shops and restaurants—something that rarely fails to amaze or amuse visitors from more neatly laid out cities in the Anglo-Saxon world. It is here, at the corner of rue Godot-de-Mauroy and rue de Sèze, that Nathalie Baye "crawls the curb" in the multi-award winning cop thriller **La balance**, one of the best and coolest French movies of the 1980s.

Turn left into rue de Sèze, leaving the windows of Fauchon (the most famous, and most expensive, Parisian deli and grocery) to your right—and behind you (Fauchon has locations on both sides of the street)—as you walk to the far corner on the eastern side of the place to the temple-like building that occupies the traffic island in the middle of the square.

Nowadays known as the Église de la Madeleine, this building was originally conceived by Napoleon as a Victory Temple. But, like so much else in Paris, it was only completed decades later during the so-called Deuxième Empire (1852-1870) of his nephew, Napoleon III.

Continue walking along the far side of the church to the western porch and climb the stairs to the main entrance.

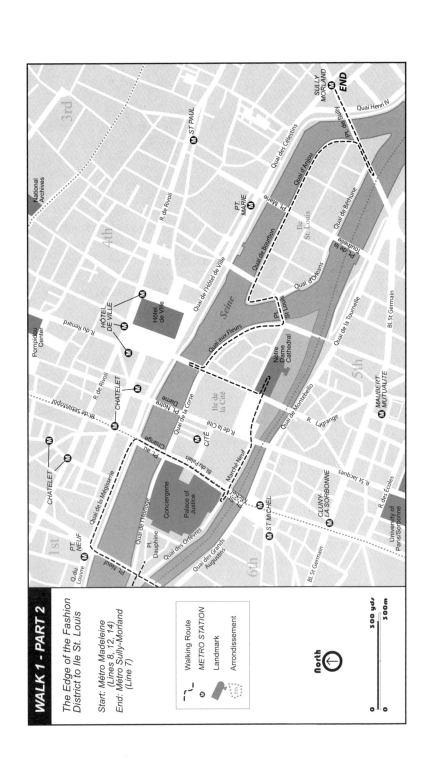

WALK 1 - PART 2

The Edge of the Fashion District to Ile St. Louis

Start: Métro Madeleine
(Lines 8, 12, 14)
End: Métro Sully-Morland
(Line 7)

Legend:
- Walking Route
- METRO STATION
- Landmark
- Arrondissement

north

500 yds
500m

Map labels:

3rd

National Archives

Pompidou Center

CHATELET

R. de Rivoli

R. du Renard

HÔTEL DE VILLE

Hôtel de Ville

Bd de Sébastopol

CHATELET

R. de Rivoli

4th

M ST PAUL

R. de Rivoli

PT. MARIE

Quai des Celestins

Quai d'Anjou

Quai de Bourbon

Pt. Marie

Ile St. Louis

Quai de Béthune

SULLY MORLAND

END

Quai Henri IV

Pt. de Sully

Quai de l'Hôtel de Ville

Seine

Quai aux Fleurs

Quai d'Orléans

Pt. de la Tournelle

PL. St Louis

PT.

Notre Dame Cathedral

Quai de la Tournelle

5th

Pt. au Change

Pt. Notre Dame

Ile de la Cité

R. de la Cité

Quai de la Corse

CITÉ

Marché Neuf

Quai de Montebello

R. Lagrange

Bl. St. Germain

MAUBERT MUTUALITE

Q. du Louvre

PT. NEUF

Pt. Neuf

1st

Quai de la Mégisserie

PL. Dauphine

Conciergerie

Palace of Justice

Quai de l'Horloge

Quai des Orfèvres

Quai des Grands Augustins

PL. St. Michel

ST MICHEL

6th

Bl. St Germain

CLUNY-LA SORBONNE

R. St Jacques

R. des Écoles

University of Paris/Sorbonne

Bl. St Germain

The flashback wedding scene in **Trois couleurs: Blanc / Three Colors: White,** the middle part of Krzysztof Kieslowski's masterful *Three Colors* trilogy, was shot here. Note the view (below) of the place de la Concorde as you look out from the top of the stairs.

Now walk back down the stairs and cross the square in front of you to the right side of the street—the rue Royale—which leads towards the places de la Concorde.

Depending on the traffic density, your nerve, and your physical fitness (how fast can you run?), you may find it more prudent to cross via the series of traffic lights to your right, rather than trying to dash straight across the square.

Either way, once you reach it, walk down rue Royale past the shopfronts of Cerrutti and Gucci. Cross rue St-Honoré—more posh shops to your left and right—and keep going until you come to Maxim's. You'll reach it just before you get to the Concorde itself.

This famous eating and entertainment establishment opened toward the end of the 19th century, during the so-called Belle Époque (the decades just before and after the turn of the 20th century). Paris was booming like mad then, awash with new money—much like London or New York one hundred years later—and Maxim's was a hot spot for the rich and famous. Truth to tell, however, its food has not been on a par with the hautest of the Parisian haute cuisine for some time, and certain high priests in the High Church of French Cookery have always held it in a bit of contempt—not least because of its cheek in mixing the sacred (food) with the profane (entertainment such as singers and a band). It is also revealing that Aristotle Onassis took Jackie Kennedy to the extremely posh Le Grand Véfour when he was wooing her, reserving the more "vulgar" Maxim's for dates with his long-time mistress Maria Callas.

But Maxim's had undoubted snob appeal, at least until 1981, when it became a mere subdivision of Pierre Cardin's empire of luxury brands. It has since become the prototype for half a dozen franchised "Maxim's" restaurants around the globe. The final boot was put in a few years ago in an English newspaper when some batty old toff wrote himself all red in the face about the decline in the quality of some starter or another. Maxim's has never quite recovered from that indictment. Imagine the shame: to be hauled over the coals for the quality of your food—by an Englishman!

Because of its Belle Époque credentials, Maxim's is often used in period movies as shorthand for their protagonists' lifestyle. For example, Louis Jourdain takes **Gigi** to dine here, and we know immediately what a cad he is. In **Moulin Rouge**, Jose Ferrer's Toulouse-Lautrec is shown to entertain his entourage at Maxim's. (Of course we already knew what a cad he was from his smutty pictures). In more recent times, Eli Wallach sweet-talks Audrey Hepburn here in **How to Steal a Million**—until Peter O'Toole intervenes from an adjoining table. And bon vivant David Niven takes his party (including a desperately bored Jean Seberg) to Maxim's to dine in **Bonjour tristesse**.

For those of you who are too cheap to shell out €35 for the pleasure of a *mousse au chocolat* and a glimpse of the immaculately maintained period interiors, there is a guided tour through Maxim's Art Nouveau museum (not the restaurant itself). Even that, however, comes at the rather hefty price of €15.

Continue straight ahead into the place de la Concorde. Turn immediately to your right and keep going until you reach rue Boissy-d'Anglas. Then stop and turn left.

The curb at the corner of the park (straight ahead of you as you look toward the "classical Greek temple" of the Palais Bourbon (a.k.a., the Assemblée Nationale) in the distance) is the place where Jet Li—who has been hiding under the chassis—lets go of the escape car in **Kiss of the Dragon** and then proceeds to wash his face in the central fountain (of which more anon). He's seen from the front door of the Hôtel Crillon (behind you) with the distant jardin des Tuileries as a backdrop. The heavily guarded building in front of you, across rue Boissy-d'Anglas, is the American Embassy. It's the setting for some key shots in **Charade** and the backdrop for that film's final twist, where Cary Grant reveals to Audrey Hepburn who he really is.

Now turn left towards the nearest of several traffic islands in the middle of the Concorde, walking in the direction of the antique temple (the Assemblée Nationale) at the far side of the square, which mirrors the Madeleine opposite. (The Assemblée was actually there first, and the mirroring was Napoleon's idea.)
Walk past the statue that represents the French town of Rouen. (One such statue adorns every corner of the place de la Concorde, indicating what provincial town you would reach if you journeyed in the corresponding direction; Rouen stands for the northwest.) Then proceed—across the section of the street that's been closed to traffic—to the next island, the one with the statue for the French city of Brest (west). From here, turn left and cross over at the traffic lights to reach the central traffic island, on which you'll find the famous Concorde fountain and the obelisk.

At the end of **The Devil Wears Prada**, Anne Hathaway tosses her mobile phone—and the life of a professional fashionista it represents—into the fountain, while Meryl Streep searches for her assistant. Seemingly, Streep is only a few steps away, in the entrance of the Hôtel Crillon—or so the setting implies. Actually, the actress didn't make the trip to Paris with the rest of the crew: the hotel where she greets the press is located in LA.

The fountain also serves as the centerpiece for the final tableau of the great dance sequence in **An American in Paris**. That movie, however, was shot entirely on an MGM sound stage in California, and all Parisian locations in it are more or less authentic reconstructions rather than the real thing. (More of this way of "shooting on location" later on.)

Take a look around you before you move on. You are now pretty much in the center of contemporary Paris, which shows how fast the city has grown in the past 150 years. Until the middle of the 19th century, the Concorde essentially marked the western border of the town.

From where you stand, you can catch most of the famous Parisian landmarks in one sweeping glance: the Eiffel Tower, the Arc de Triomphe (if you move a few steps to stand at the foot of the obelisk), and the Louvre (on your left). But the Concorde somehow doesn't spell "Paris." Instead, words like "vast," "empty," and "forlorn" spring to mind. Maybe that is the reason why—despite its central location and its history (this is, after all, where King Louis XVI was beheaded during the French Revolution)—place de la Concorde is almost never used as an establishing shot. The exception is Ernst Lubitsch's **Ninotchka**, which opens with a shot of the Concorde as seen from the other side of the square, to the left of the Parliament building. That's almost the only angle from which you can avoid getting any of the more typical Parisian landmarks into the picture.

Continue by turning (left if you are facing the Assemblée Nationale) into the jardin de Tuileries, the gardens of the Louvre.

A giant Ferris wheel was erected in front of the main entrance in 1999 as part of the Parisian millennium celebrations. It stood there for roughly two years. You can catch a glimpse of it in **Kiss of the Dragon**. It also puts in an appearance in **The Truth About Charlie** when Tim Robbins takes Thandie Newton for a Ferris-wheel ride (faintly echoing Orson Welles in *The Third Man*).

Before you enter the Tuileries, cast a last glance back over the Concorde in the direction of the Assemblée Nationale. This view across the square is seen both in **The Man Who Cried**—for the shot of the deportees leaving Paris—and in Bille August's version of **Les Misérables** where you see the ambulance with Marius (accompanied by Liam Neeson's Valjean) cross the *place*. You may also envision—again from **The Man Who Cried**—Christina Ricci and Johnny Depp entering the square from the rue de Rivoli (she on a bicycle and he on a white horse).

Enter the park.

As you walk into the gardens between the two large buildings flanking the entrance, take a look at the one on the left. This is the Jeu de Paume, so named because in the days when the Louvre was still used as a royal residence, the kings of France played an early form of tennis (called "jeu de paume") in the building. It is now a museum—the very one the paintings saved by Burt Lancaster in the thriller **The Train** come from. All the scenes outside of the museum were shot on location.

Walk further into the park, right up to the octagonal basin (below).

The great French movie actor Jean Gabin—obviously enjoying his break from impersonating powerful "men of substance," such as gangster bosses and industrialists—takes a bath in the buff here as the title character in **Archimède le clochard**.

Walk past the basin into the broad tree-lined path that stretches straight ahead of you and turn left at the first intersection.

You're following in the footsteps of Jane Fonda and Maximillian Schell in **Julia** (where Schell asks her to smuggle $50,000 out of the country).

Pass the carousel on your left and leave the park through the gate that leads straight into rue Castiglione (and then on to the place Vendôme). We'll visit place Vendôme in Walk 2; so instead of continuing on, leave the triumphal column of the Vendôme to your left and turn right into rue de Rivoli under the colonnades.

One of the first buildings to your left is the Hôtel Meurice (at no. 228), which served as the HQ of the German High Command during WWII. The hotel puts in cameo appearances (playing itself) in **Paris brûle-t-il? / Is Paris Burning?** as well as in Alain Resnais' **On connaît la chanson / Same Old Song**, which won multiple *Césars*, the French Oscars. (The tour guide explains the history of the building to her group right at the beginning of the movie.) It is also the place where Jane Fonda stays in **Julia**.

Incidentally, the Meurice also served as the Parisian address of Salvador Dali. He stayed there for at least one night every month for a period of 30 years. The staff of the Meurice had to procure flies for him, caught in the nearby Tuileries, and bring him little furry animals which he then proceeded to shoot dead—or so the legend has it.

Just past the Meurice, you will find the coffee shop Angelina, renowned worldwide for its rich, thick chocolate. If you like that kind of thing, believe me, you'll like it here. And if you think you have already walked long enough to deserve a treat, this is the place to take a break from the relentless task of strolling the streets of Paris.

Continue down the colonnades …

… following—more or the less—the path of the mailman in the French cult classic **Diva**, who escapes his pursuers on his scooter, wildly slaloming between shoppers, tourists, and stallholders.

After a couple of blocks, just before you arrive at the place des Pyramides with its equestrian statue of Jeanne d'Arc ...

... you may recognize—on your left—the spot where Matt Damon and Franka Potente plot their next moves in **The Bourne Identity**, after Matt has discovered that the Hôtel Regina on the other side of the square may hold some information about his (forgotten) real identity. Franka Potente then walks inside the hotel to find out more. The Regina is also the hotel where Jet Li is set up in **Kiss of the Dragon** (and where he climbs underneath the chassis of the chief baddie's car in order to escape).

Follow now in the footsteps of Matt Damon and Franka Potente, who cross the rue de Rivoli (on the near side of the square, before the statue) ...

... to make a call from a phone booth at the corner of Rivoli and the path to the Louvre, the rather grandly named avenue du Général-Lemonnier. (The phone booth was only placed here for the movie.)

Continue in the direction of the museum, with the Tuileries to your right and the jardin du Carrousel (the garden on the near side of the Louvre) to the left. At the first intersection, turn left into the central road inside the park, keeping the distant Arc de Triomphe at your back and walking towards its kid brother. (More mirroring: the French just love this kind of thing!)

The "little" Arc de Triomphe just in front of the place du Carrousel provides the setting for one of the fashion shoots in **Funny Face** (Audrey Hepburn in bell-shaped frocks and elbow-length gloves). It is filmed from the museum side of the structure with the "big" Arc de Triomphe visible through the main arch.

The large building straight ahead of you is, of course, the Louvre—once a royal palace, nowadays (since the French Revolution) the largest and most famous museum in the world. Ironically, practically everything you see from here—the sights that now spell Paris—was built during or after the late 19th century, long after the heydays of both royals and revolutionaries.

This is the moment of truth. You have to ask yourself this question: Are you really interested enough to go inside? (Well, are you, punk?)

If the answer to that is yes, I recommend a movie-inspired itinerary, by which I do not necessarily mean that you should follow the example of Anna Karina and her criminal friends in Jean-Luc Godard's **Bande à part / Band of Outsiders**, who dash through the Louvre to "beat the American record" (then standing at 9:47 minutes).

Works in the Louvre which have put in appearances in major motion pictures include:

- the Venus de Milo - Toulouse sermonizes about her beauty for the benefit of his lady friend in John Huston's **Moulin Rouge**.
- the "Winged Victory" - another backdrop for Audrey Hepburn to display some frocks and her fine bone structure in **Funny Face**.
- the "Raft of the Medusa" and "The Death of Sardanapalus" - admired by Joanne Woodward and Paul Newman in **Mr. and Mrs. Bridge**.
- the Louvre's self-portrait of Rembrandt - as seen by Juliette Binoche (she breaks into the Louvre to steal one last private look at her favorite picture

before she goes totally blind) in the grandiose **Les amants du Pont-Neuf / The Lovers on the Bridge**, famous for going artistically and financially overboard (more of this story a little later on).

* the Mona Lisa - The scenes in **The Da Vinci Code** where the museum's curator is being killed in front of his most famous painting and, later, where Tom Hanks and Audrey Tautou escape from the French police, were partly shot in the Louvre and partly on a sound stage in London, depending on what level of property damage the scene required (the scene with the defaced Mona Lisa obviously falling into the latter category).

If you want to spare yourself the trouble of queueing up and schlepping through the Louvre, you may want to see if you can at least soak up a bit of the atmosphere by walking around in the museum's front courtyard (in the spirit of the tourists who visit Stratford-upon-Avon in the apparent belief that you can best understand the Bard's works by banging your head against some low-hanging Elizabethan woodwork).

Start by walking clockwise around the Pyramid itself.

This is the place where **The Da Vinci Code** concludes when Tom Hanks makes a nocturnal visit to the Louvre Museum, having finally discovered the answer to the Grail mystery.

Continue clockwise immediately to the left of the Pyramid …

… where Marcello Mastroianni steps in dog shit in Robert Altman's **Prêt-à-Porter**. This is, by the way, probably the only place in Paris where this is unlikely to happen!

A few yards farther down (photo opposite) is the place where Kim Basinger's hapless TV journalist—again in **Prêt-à-Porter**—does another of her foot-in-mouth straight-to-camera takes.

If you'd like to call it a day now, go back to the pyramid and turn right across the plaza and then right again on rue de Rivoli to reach the Palais-Royal-Musée du Louvre Métro station (Lines 1, 7). If you are up for more walking:

Leave the front courtyard of the Louvre by turning left towards the Southern Wing, which bears the inscription "Pavillon Lesdiguières."

In Bille August's **Les Misérables**, you see Liam Neeson's coach leave the Louvre through these arches.

Follow in his track and, once outside the building complex, cross to the other side of the street. Turn left and keep walking until you come to the next bridge.

This bridge is the wooden pont des Arts, which provides one of the most glorious 360-degree-views in Paris. It takes in both banks of the Seine as well as the Île-de-la-Cité with the Cathedral of Notre-Dame. Consequently, it is a sight that few Paris-based movies seem ready or willing to miss. Audrey Hepburn in **Funny Face** is shown on the pont des Arts. Amélie Poulain chooses the bridge to cross the river on her sojourn to the Left Bank (to deposit the toys in the phone box) in **Le fabuleux destin d'Amélie Poulain / Amélie**. Harrison Ford kisses Julia Ormond here in the final scene of Sydney Pollack's 1995 re-make of **Sabrina**, and—on a less romantic note—the eponymous **American Werewolf in Paris** gets his first wolfish hunger pangs here. The pont des Arts also provides the backdrop for the scene in the remake of **The Pink Panther** where Jean Reno sums up the facts of the case for Steve Martin's Inspector Clouseau.

British visitors of a certain age, however, will forever associate the pont des Arts with the image of art historian Kenneth Clark pontificating (in the opening scene of the ground-breaking TV series *Civilisation*), about how easy it is to recognize "civilization" and how difficult to define (falling just short of drawing the—for him, at least—slightly risky conclusion that one panoramic view says more than thirteen 60-minute TV episodes).

Now look ahead as you cross the bridge.

The church-like building in front of you is the Institut de France, home of the Académie Française, a sort of semi-official "Supreme Court" for all issues concerning French culture and language. The building appears in **Jefferson in Paris** as Gwyneth Paltrow's convent (run, incidentally, by Tony Soprano's mother, the character actress Nancy Marchand). The movie's interior scenes were shot about 30 miles north of Paris at the Panthémont Abbey and the Lycée de St-Vincent in Senlis; so now you know.

At the end of the bridge, turn right into the quai de Conti and then walk only as far as the traffic light opposite the far corner of the Académie Française.

The buildings on the other side of the quai were recreated for the set of the 1930s' French film classic **Boudu sauvé des eaux / Boudu Saved from Drowning** (later remade in Hollywood as *Down and Out in Beverly Hills*). Have a look into the premises of no. 7 (until recently a bookshop, as in the film, but now a fashion boutique) and the adjacent café, which also puts in a cameo appearance.

The entire site was rebuilt in the studio—that was how the French movie industry operated at the time—with the buildings shifted slightly to the left so that the bookseller's drawing room window would look straight into the pont des Arts.

Retrace your steps, past the Académie again …

… in the spirit of Audrey Hepburn and Cary Grant in **Charade**, whose riverboat journey passes the Académie Française twice in 20 seconds.

Cross the quai de Conti at the next set of traffic lights and continue along the left side near the river. Just before you reach the bridge, look down at the small path directly by the riverside.

This is where Charlize Theron and Stuart Townsend discuss fate, predestination, and lesbian love in **Head in the Clouds**. The church on the other side of the Seine whose turret you see across the roofs to the right of the Louvre is St-Germain l'Auxerrois, where NBA star Tony Parker—who is a French citizen—and "Desperate Housewife" Eva Longoria were married in July 2007, the "wedding of the year" for France's tabloids.

Turn left onto the bridge, oddly enough called the pont Neuf (new bridge), although it is the oldest in Paris. Cross over to the right side, to the island in the Seine known as Île-de-la-Cité. Turn right through the narrow street in the middle of the island (rue Henri-Robert). This street leads you straight into the place Dauphine.

One of Paris's hidden treasures, place Dauphine provides the backdrop for the WWII victory parade in **Surviving Picasso**.

Walk on the left side of the square, following the route of the U.S. soldiers, to the end of the place Dauphine where the Parisians burn the Nazi flag. Then turn around, walking back on the other side.

In **The Pink Panther**, we see Steve Martin's Inspector Clouseau (on his first full day on the job) and Jean Reno walk across place Dauphine from no. 17, the restaurant Le Caveau (right canopies, photo opposite), to no. 16 on the other side. Here Martin warns Reno that he may attack him at any moment, just to test his reactions—and finds that Reno's reactions are painfully excellent.

Return via rue Henri-Robert and cross the pont Neuf to the left of the equestrian statue.

Look down from here on to the Seine and to the riverboats moored by its banks. This is the view Paul Newman enjoys on his nightly walk in **Mr. and Mrs. Bridge**.

Now walk down the stairway behind the statue into a charming little garden, the square du Vert-Galant, at the tip of the Île-de-la-Cité. Some wit once called this leafy garden "the pubic hair of Paris between the thighs of the Seine." (Oh, the French: Do they ever think of anything else?) Turn right towards the boats and proceed counterclockwise.

The boat immediately in front of you was used for the wedding scene of Albert Finney's son in Tim Burton's **Big Fish** (exterior shots only, i.e. the conversation between father and son; the actual reception was shot on board the larger "L'Excellence," which you will see later on). A few steps further down, Sam Waterston and his kids see a boat arrive in **Le divorce** and, still on the same side, the saxophone player enchants the Parisian night with his

moody solo in **Forget Paris**. At the very tip of the island, Juliette Binoche paints the face of her boyfriend, Alex, in **Les amants du Pont-Neuf / The Lovers on the Bridge,** and on your return to the stairway that leads you back to the bridge you may recognize some of the places frantically searched by Faye Dunaway, who has lost her kids in **La maison sous les arbres / The Deadly Trap** (a.k.a. *Death Scream*).

> *Climb the stairway back up to the bridge and continue along the pont Neuf in the direction of the La Samaritaine department store.*

This part of the bridge (which connects the Île-de-la-Cité with the Right Bank) is the home of Alex in **Les amants du Pont-Neuf / The Lovers on the Bridge,** although—bizarrely—director Leos Carax had the entire site reconstructed in the South of France and shot the scene there. Actually, it wasn't entirely by choice. It was clear from the beginning that it would not be possible to shoot the entire film on location because that would have required closing the bridge to traffic for three months. So the moviemakers initially decided to shoot the night scenes on a simplified model and the day scenes in Paris. The model had to be upgraded for daytime use when one of the actors was injured—while repairing a shoe, of all things—forcing Carax to miss his two-week slot for the on-location shoot. Things got seriously out of hand at this point and, in the end, it took Carax about 18 months, several producers, and four times the original budget to finish his film.

As you walk toward the end of the bridge …

… you may recognize the spot where Faye Dunaway is momentarily distracted by a flower seller in **La maison sous les arbres / The Deadly Trap**, giving her kids the opportunity they've been looking for to escape and leave "Mommie Dearest" in the lurch.

Stop for a moment just before the bridge joins the Right Bank.

The left side of this spot is the place where Matt Damon's former boss is waiting in **The Bourne Identity** for his ex-agent to contact him. The other half of the scene, meanwhile, unfolds in the building opposite you, or—to be more precise—on its roof. That's where Matt Damon has positioned himself to look out onto the street below to check whether his former boss has laid a trap for him. The building in question is the department store La Samaritaine, traditionally the most downmarket of Paris's four largest department stores. (It was the first to introduce an installment payment scheme to attract working class customers.) More recently it was acquired by a group of investors set on repositioning it as a luxury retailer. This may explain why the free viewing platform on the top floor, which for decades had provided the best view over Central Paris, was closed to make way for an overpriced cafeteria. Go there anyway, just to spite them. Pretend you are looking for someone—or tell them the truth: that you are an amnesiac CIA hitman hiding from your murderous former employers—and enjoy the splendid views across the Conciergerie, Notre-Dame and, of course, the pont Neuf.

Turn into the quai de la Mégisserie—left if you are coming out of La Samaritaine.

Stroll past the booksellers in their wooden stalls, the so-called bouquinistes, and the passersby browsing their wares, as Joanne Woodward does in **Mr. and Mrs. Bridge**. Also note the lively and picturesque market for exotic plants and all types of pets that begins more or less right past the first corner on the left side of the street.

In **National Lampoon's European Vacation**, the restaurant where the waiter insults Chevy Chase and his family in the rudest of terms was set up at the corner of quai de la Mégisserie and rue Édouard-Colonne. You may remember the scene: the waiter smiles and appears exceedingly polite while ripping the family apart verbally, and they have no clue to what's going on because they don't speak a word of French. ("In America, you could never have a waiter as friendly as that," they agree.)

Step briefly into the place du Châtelet at the next corner.

Movie fans will be chiefly interested in the two theaters flanking the square. On the near side, we have the Théâtre du Châtelet where the final scene of **Diva** (the concert) was shot. On the far side, you can see the Théâtre de la Ville / Sarah Bernhardt which—with Gianni Esposito on its roof—provides the location for the most famous shot of director Jacques Rivette's Nouvelle Vague classic **Paris nous appartient / Paris Belongs to Us**.

Continue by crossing the bridge to your right and returning to the Île-de-la-Cité. As you step onto the bridge, look to the right.

This is the spot where we first see Woody Allen in **Everyone Says I Love You**, with the thick walls and turrets of the Conciergerie in the background. Once a palace and later a prison, the Conciergerie is the place many members of the French aristocracy, including Marie Antoinette, passed their last weeks and hours during the heyday of the French Revolution. It lends its gloomy presence to many period movies. The title character in **Danton** (played by Gérard Dépardieu), for example, is brought here to await his execution.

Continue straight into the boulevard du Palais, leaving the turrets of the Conciergerie to your right.

The well-guarded building just past the Conciergerie is the Palais de Justice. In the first scene of **Trois couleurs: Blanc / Three Colors: White**, Julie Delpy divorces her Polish husband here, having brought all his personal belongings to court in a suitcase for him to take away so that he need never come back, which is, of course, exactly what he does—with a vengeance.

Walk on to the quai des Orfèvres at the riverside and turn right into it. After passing only three doorways (no. 14 is immediately followed by no. 32) …

… you will find the door with the legendary address, "36 quai des Orfèvres." This is the home of the "Special Brigade Against Crime," established by the police in 1924 (on the third and fourth floors, stairway A—since you ask). It's adroitly used by director Jean-Pierre Melville in **Le cercle rouge**. We see Alain Delon (in his usual role as the Angel of Death) come out of the building, button up his trench coat, and rearrange his hat—an image every bit as iconic as Clint Eastwood pulling a couple of .44s from beneath his poncho.

Retrace your steps to the corner of the quai des Orfèvres and the boulevard du Palais and continue along the quai, with the Seine to your right.

Cast a glimpse down to the river walkway. This is the stretch of the Seine where Jeanne Moreau jumps into the river during the nightly walk with her two lovers in François Truffaut's **Jules et Jim / Jules and Jim**, expecting—rightly, as it turns out—that the film's two eponymous heroes will fight for the right to save her. (It would have been a far, far better movie if they had let her drown and, say, joined Gary Cooper's Beau Geste in the Foreign Legion—or better still: Stan Laurel and Oliver Hardy.)

Continue on to the corner of the quai and the cathedral courtyard (which will be right in front of you).

If you look around, you may recognize this area as the main battleground of **Paris brûle-t-il? / Is Paris Burning?**, the 1960s' epic about the liberation of Paris (scripted by Francis Ford Coppola and Gore Vidal, no less). The big building on your left is the HQ or "Préfecture" of the Parisian Police, occupied and fiercely defended in the movie by the forces of the French

Résistance, while on the bridge to your right (the Petit-Pont), a German patrol comes under fire (a ferocious battle ensues when the patrol is reinforced by tanks and more troops) and the Résistance forces gather on the left side of the Cathedral courtyard to storm the HQ. After liberation, the victorious Résistance members see the French flag being hoisted on Notre-Dame through a first floor window of the Préfecture, one of the movie's key shots.

Now walk straight into the Cathedral courtyard, the so-called place du Parvis-Notre-Dame, towards the home—of course—of movie history's most famous **Hunchback.**

None of the story's many versions was actually filmed on location, mainly, I guess, because the dense network of narrow lanes that must have once contributed at least as much as the church itself to the Île's medieval atmosphere were flattened by Baron Haussmann in his wholesale reinvention of Paris during the 1840s.

And before any of you asks: The cathedral scenes in **An American Werewolf in Paris** were not shot here either, but in Luxembourg instead. A permit thing, apparently. Why didn't they call it "An American Werewolf in Luxembourg" then? Well, I leave that for you to ponder.

The Charlemagne statue on the right of the churchyard also puts in an appearance in **Paris brûle-t-il? / Is Paris Burning?** when a Molotov cocktail is thrown from here straight into the turret of a German tank thirty yards or so away—a spectacular Michael-Jordan-style three-pointer. (It will not have escaped your attention, meanwhile, that Charlemagne hardly looks his most majestic here, more Olaf the Slayer from an early Schwarzenegger movie than Defender of the Faith.)

Now is the time to take a look at the interior of Notre-Dame ...

... following in the footsteps of James Fox's hitman in **The Day of the Jackal**, who inspects the cathedral as a potential site for killing Général Charles de Gaulle. Walk in through the main entrance, preferably through the Portal of Ste-Anne on the right-hand side. It features some of the most glorious high medieval bas-relief sculptures to be found anywhere in the world, underneath a gallery of near-lifesized statues that represent Knute Rockne's unbeaten 1919 Notre-Dame football team. (Only kidding.)

On leaving Notre-Dame, turn immediately to your right into rue d'Arcole. Continue straight on to the bridge, the pont d'Arcole, and stop about halfway down on the left-hand side.

You are now standing in more or less the exact spot on the pont d'Arcole where Jack Nicholson, on his nightly walk in **Something's Gotta Give**, finally admits—first to himself, then to Diane Keaton, who arrives as if on cue—that he has finally and for the first time in his life, fallen in love. The ornate building in front of you on the Right Bank is the City Hall, the "Hôtel de Ville," and if you turn to your left, you will be looking at the Conciergerie (building with turrets in photo on page 14). This is the direction Old Nick is facing during his tearful monologue.

Walk back to the Île-de-la-Cité. Turn left on to the quai aux Fleurs and look for house no. 9.

This is known as the "House of Abélard and Héloise," visited by Daniel Day-Lewis and Winona Ryder on their honeymoon in **The Age of Innocence**. The house (built in 1849) is obviously of a much later date and was only erected *in the place* where the star-crossed medieval lovers once met for their trysts. But it is nonetheless worth taking a look into the rue des Ursins to the right. Most of its houses may be newish, but the street pattern has remained unchanged since the days of Abe and Elly, Esmeralda and Quasimodo. So a glance will give you a pretty good idea of what the Île (and much of the rest of the city besides) must have looked like before Haussmann gave Paris its present appearance.

Continue down the quai to the pont St-Louis. On your right …

… you'll pass the cathedral garden, where Peter Coyote and Emmanuelle Seigner promise each other to meet again in Roman Polanski's **Bitter Moon**.

Turn left onto pont St-Louis and cross into the Île-St-Louis, the more residential of the two islands in the Seine.

The square on the far side of the bridge is shared by no less than four brasseries. We, however, are only interested in the one on the extreme left. This is the Brasserie Île-Saint-Louis where in the 1995 **Sabrina** Julia Ormond reads her father's letter. While you are here, you might as well sit down for a while and take a little refreshment before the final stage of this walk, a rather leisurely stroll around the picturesque Île-St-Louis. Why not seize the opportunity to sample the excellent Berthillon ice cream which is famous all over France and originated right on this little island in the Seine?

When you feel refreshed, start your journey around the Île-St-Louis by following the quai de Bourbon, the island's "outer ringroad," clockwise to your left.

The next corner, where the quai de Bourbon bends sharply to the right, is the place where Johnny Depp seeks refuge on the cobblestones after the fire in **The Ninth Gate**.

Continue through the bend and follow the quai to the corner of rue des Deux-Ponts, the pont Marie on your left.

In **The Ninth Gate**, Depp is being closely observed as he eats his dinner in the restaurant Au Franc Pinot, which was located on the right corner until recently, when the building was sold. You'll find the stairway where Depp has to face and fight his pursuer a little further down quai d'Anjou (which is the continuation of the quai de Bourbon) opposite no. 35.

Continue along quai d'Anjou.

Towards the end of the island, at 17 quai d'Anjou, you'll see one of the oldest and most beautiful buildings on the Île-St-Louis, the Hôtel de Lausun, built in 1657 and used in **The Ninth Gate** as the home of the Kessler Foundation.

At the end of the Île, take a right turn into boulevard Henri-IV.

The house on your right, at the corner of the quai d'Anjou and rue St-Louis-en-l'Île, is the Parisian residence of the Rothschild family.

At the traffic lights, cross over to the left side of the bridge (the pont de Sully) and walk about halfway across.

Look towards the docks on the left-hand side (the port Henri-IV) and the large white boat, "L'Excellence." It was used by Tim Burton for the wedding reception in **Big Fish**. Now raise your eyes above the docks to the quai Henri-IV. In **Before Sunset**, Ethan Hawke and Julie Delpy finish their boat ride on the quai when he decides to take her home.

Walk to the other side of the bridge now and take a good look over to your right.

Search for the next bridge downstream, the pont de la Tournelle, and take a look at the third house from the corner (no. 11 quai de la Tournelle, although you can't see the address from here). In the 2006 re-make of **The Pink Panther**, we see Kevin Kline (on his hospital bed) shoot out from one of its windows into the Seine. They must have given him the mother of all mighty pushes, because from the window to the water—across a busy three-lane street, wide sidewalks, and quite a lot of ground down by the river—is a distance of a good 100 yards.

Now let your eyes stray a bit further to no. 15 quai de la Tournelle, the building two houses down on the same side of the street at the corner of the bridge. On its top floor, you can see Paris's most distinguished (and most expensive) restaurant, the Tour d'Argent, which—apparently—counts Robert De Niro and Woody Allen among its regulars. It puts in an appearance in **Count Your Blessings**, when Maurice Chevalier's duke—at a corner table, the Eiffel Tower in the background—tries to talk Rossano Brazzi into seeking a reconciliation with his wife, Deborah Kerr. For you and me, however, this—a view from the bridge—is probably as close as we are ever going to get to the Tour d'Argent.

This is the end of the walk. If you are looking for the next Métro, you will have to walk back across the tip of the Île-St-Louis to the Right Bank and the station Sully Morland (Line 7).

If, however, you are absolutely determined to sample the delicacies of the Tour d'Argent, you should not miss the opportunity of ordering the house specialty, called *Canard au sang* (literally "duck in its own blood"), a recipe developed by the Tour's cooks in 1890 (also, incidentally, served on board the Titanic—to passengers in the Kate-Winslet-Class only, of course). Every *Canard* is individually numbered (number one million was served in 2003), and the restaurant keeps a Golden Book where some famous diners are listed together with the numbers of their ducks. No. 328, for instance, was munched by the Prince of Wales, later King Edward VII, in 1890, No. 147,844 by his grandson, the Duke of Windsor (Edward VIII) in 1938, and No. 185,397 by the young Princess—later Queen—Elizabeth in 1948.

To wash it down, we strongly recommend searching the wine list from the top down. The Tour has bottles in its cellar you could only afford by re-mortgaging your house, and this is no mere figure of speech: The most expensive bottle on the list, the 1945 Romanée-Conti, is a steal at a mere—are you ready for this?—$200,000. But, as it says at the bottom of the Tour's menu, alcohol abuse is dangerous for your health, consume with moderation. So don't get carried away and always remember: one bottle is enough.

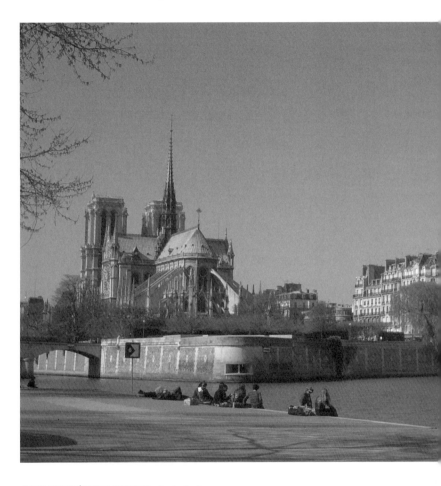

ARRONDİSSEMENTS: 3, 4, 5, 6
DURATION: Count on at least 3 hours.

Walk 2

Marais
to Mouffle

*From the Centre Pompidou through the Marais to the Latin Quarter, where we meet **An American in Paris**, Hemingway's ghost, and the city's most picturesque street market.*

WALK 2 - PART 1

Marais to Mouffle

Start: Métro Rambuteau
(Line 11)
End: Métro Censier-Daubenton
(Line 7)

Walking Route
METRO STATION
Landmark
Arrondissement

north

0   500 yds
0   300m

Leave the Métro station Rambuteau (Line 11) through the exit "Centre Pompidou." Take the first street to your right (rue Rambuteau) and turn left at the kiosk into rue St-Martin.

The huge building, now to your left, with its color-coded pipes on the outside is the Centre Pompidou. Designed by the architects Richard Rogers and Renzo Piano, it's been hailed by some as a modernist masterpiece. The Café Georges on its top floor is the place where Thierry Lhermitte's charming, if slightly sleazy, politician invites Kate Hudson for lunch in **Le divorce**.

Turn left into rue St-Merri at the junction.

The fountain on your right with the grotesque sculptures by Niki de Saint-Phalle set against the backdrop of the Church of St-Merri was used to set the scene for the second fashion shoot in Sydney Pollack's 1995 remake of **Sabrina**. This is the shoot where Sabrina (Julia Ormond) begins to get things right and where the French photographer, played by the popular French singer Patrick Bruel, is starting to make eyes at her.

Cross rue du Renard at the corner and continue on rue St-Merri.

You have now entered the Marais, the oldest residential district in Paris and the only one with large numbers of buildings from pre-revolutionary times. In the past ten years or so, it's also become the city's gay quarter. It is therefore no. surprise that Gus Van Sant chose the Marais as the location for his contribution (a brief encounter between two gay men in an artists' workshop) to **Paris, je t'aime**. (You don't get to see a lot of the Marais in his episode, however. He just gives you an establishing shot of the neighboring rue des Francs-Bourgeois and a brief look at the place des Vosges, which lies a few blocks ahead.)

*Continue to walk down rue St-Merri. Cross rue du Temple and continue straight into rue Ste-Croix-de-la-Bretonnerie. Turn left into rue des Archives (Possible detour here for **Le divorce** fans, see page 242) and continue straight for three blocks to the corner of rue des Francs-Bourgeois, where you turn right.*

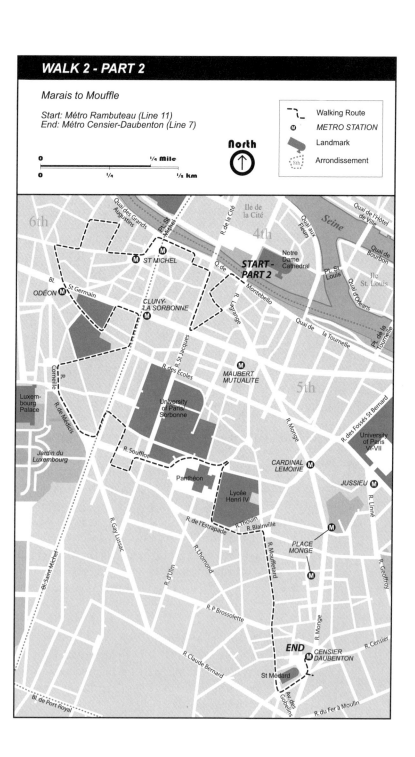

WALK 2 - PART 2

Marais to Mouffle

Start: Métro Rambuteau (Line 11)
End: Métro Censier-Daubenton (Line 7)

North

Walking Route	
Ⓜ	METRO STATION
	Landmark
8th	Arrondissement

0 — ¼ Mile
0 — ¼ — ½ km

The building on your left is the French National Archives, used in many movies as a "body double" for the Élysée Palace (the official residence of the French President) or, in **The Day of the Jackal**, for the Matignon (the official residence of the Prime Minister). This is where the politicians meet in *The Day of the Jackal* to discuss what to do after they have been informed of the plot to kill the President.

Continue down rue des Francs-Bourgeois.

Notice the old houses on either side of the street. Their archways and court-yards are just big enough for horse-drawn carriages to pass through and turn around.

When you reach rue des Hospitalières-St-Gervais take a right turn, walk to the end of the street, and then turn left into rue des Rosiers.

That's one small step for a city visitor, but a giant leap in almost every other way. The change in scenery and atmosphere as you turn the corner is as unexpected and drastic as they come, even for a city like Paris. It's rather like walking from the set of *La Cage Aux Folles* straight into *Fiddler on the Roof.*

For centuries, the rue des Rosiers has been the central thoroughfare of the city's Jewish quarter. Once the home of the Jewish working classes (who have, by and large, moved up the social ladder and out of the area), the rue des Rosiers has preserved its character by attracting some Jewish institutions and new waves of Jewish immigrants. Today, it presents the visitor with one of the more curious contrasts a modern city can offer, ultra-orthodox Jews rubbing shoulders (if not much more) with gay men.

The "rue des Rosiers"—at least that's what the street sign says—also provides the setting for the "grand parade" in the Louis de Funès caper **Les aventures de Rabbi Jacob / The Mad Adventures of Rabbi Jacob** where the ultra-orthodox inhabitants of the *quartier* have prepared a grand welcome for their guest of honour, a Hassidic wise man and miracle worker from New York. The street we see in the movie, however, is no. more the real rue des Rosiers than the man in the center of the parade is the real Rabbi Jacob. While the one is, of course, Louis de Funès in disguise, the other is a nondescript suburban street dressed up for the occasion.

Incidentally, the way we have just walked—from rue des Hopital-
ières into rue des Rosiers—is also the route that Kevin Kline takes in
French Kiss on his search for Meg Ryan (on a motorbike—that he has
just stolen, of course). In that scene, we can spot the blue double doors
of the passage des Singes at the end of the street and Sacha Finkelsztajn's
kosher bakery on the left just before Kline turns into rue des Écouffes
(on our right).

*Walk past the corner of rue Ferdinand-Duval and rue des Rosiers to
no. 7 rue des Rosiers.*

On the ground floor of the building at no. 7, you could, until recently, dine
at Jo Goldenberg's, Paris's most famous kosher restaurant. But in 2008,
the septuagenarian restaurateur became but the most recent in a long line
of Jewish businessmen to throw in the towel in the face of skyrocketing
property values and rents in the ever-more fashionable Marais. Along
with Goldenberg and his cosmopolitan crowd of diners, an important
reminder of a bloody episode in recent French history also disappeared:
On August 9, 1982, six people in and near the restaurant died when a
bunch of terrorists threw a grenade into the packed dining room and fired
indiscriminately into the crowd. Until recently, the bullet holes could
still be seen in the frames of the shop window. (On a lighter note, Ethel
meets her friend **Mina Tannenbaum**, in the French chick-flick of that
name, at Goldenberg's to tell her about her trouble with her overweight
boyfriend.)

*Continue on rue des Rosiers for another two blocks, crossing rue
Pavée and then turning right into rue Malher. At the end of rue
Malher, turn left into rue St-Antoine (leaving the baroque facade
of the Church of St-Paul to your right) and immediately to your
left again into rue de Sévigné.*
*Take the first street on your right, rue d'Ormesson. After a few
steps, you will find a little square on your left, the place du Marché-
Ste-Catherine. Look for house no. 2 and the second floor above
the residential entrance door between the two restaurants.*

Here you will find the Paris headquarters of Treadstone, a secretive sub-organization of the CIA, if the plot of **The Bourne Identity** is anything to go by. You can spot the drainpipe Matt Damon climbs on his way to the final reckoning with his old superiors.

Follow rue d'Ormesson through to its end a few short blocks ahead. Turn left into rue de Turenne and then right into rue des Francs-Bourgeois. After a few steps, you will reach the place des Vosges, one of the most beautiful squares in Paris. Turn into the colonnades on the right-hand side.

Alain Delon meets Leslie Caron here in **Paris brûle-t-il? / Is Paris Burning?** to discuss his plan for liberating her husband from the Nazis.

Follow the colonnades through the 90-degree left turn and leave the place des Vosges through rue de Birague on your right …

… following a lovelorn Jack Nicholson in a rare "I vant to be alone" moment on his nightly walk through deserted streets in **Something's Gotta Give**.

Continue to busy rue St-Antoine.

Fans of The Doors may want to make a little detour here:

Cross the street and continue straight into rue Beautreillis.

No. 17/19 on the right side of the street is the house where Jim Morrison spent the last months of his life and where he died, in the bathtub, on July 3, 1971. The flat is located on the fourth floor (two below the top floor) and occupies the first four double windows, counting from the street corner.

Turn right into rue St-Antoine (left if you've made the detour to Jim Morrison's flat and are coming from rue Beautreillis) and left into rue St-Paul, the calmer (and less gay) part of the Marais on the southern side of rue St-Antoine. After about 100 yards, you will spot an archway on the right side of the street that leads into rue Eginhard.

This is where Julie Delpy and Ethan Hawke emerge out of rue Eginhard and into rue St-Paul on their walk in Richard Linklater's **Before Sunset**—to look straight at the Pure Café (photo page 240). The moviemakers are playing tricks on us here. The café is located a mile to the east of the Bastille, and the Bastille is actually several blocks away from where you're standing. This is, of course, an example of the type of editing trickery that is the movie industry's stock in trade. So we shouldn't be too disappointed that a movie like **Before Sunset**, which prides itself so much—a trifle too much, maybe—on its emotional honesty, uses the same sleight-of-hand. At any rate, Julie's and Ethan's walk through Paris on either side of the Café consists of no fewer than four unconnected sections—each of them with real twists and turns—that the film editors have spliced together into one continuous walk. If you'd like to see Le Pure Café yourself, you'll find directions in the chapter *Further Afield*, page 261.

This stretch of Julie's and Ethan's walk leads the couple through one of the prettiest and most interesting parts of ancient Paris.
We follow the pair (in reverse direction actually, "rewinding" the scene) on their walk from rue Eginhard, through its 90-degree-turn to the left, to rue Charlemagne where we turn right and then left into rue des Jardins-St-Pauls, past attractive courtyards with restaurants and art galleries on your left. (Julie and Ethan leave them unexplored, but you should feel free to take a peek.)
Just before you get to the Seine, turn right into rue de l'Avé Maria and bear left around the splendidly medieval Hôtel de Sens into rue de l'Hôtel de Ville.

In about a block, where the rue de l'Hôtel de Ville meets the street leading to the next bridge, i.e. at 62 rue de l'Hôtel de Ville or 1 pont Louis-Philippe, you'll find an elegant little restaurant called Chez Julien. This is where William Hurt—sitting at the window facing the bridge—takes his lunch, alone, in **The Accidental Tourist**.

Pass the restaurant and turn right into the next street, the rue des Barres, walk up a couple of steps and pause.

At the foot of the gently descending stairs (below), Steve Martin's Inspector Clouseau has his flat (at no. 2) in the undeservedly reviled 2006 remake of **The Pink Panther**. Early on in the film, he almost kills a cyclist here by carelessly opening the door of his small car. It may not look very funny on the page, but it sure does on the screen. "Have you just said something?" a blissfully unaware Clouseau asks his driver. "I thought I heard you say aaaaaahhh …"

Turn around and head for the Seine and the left side of the nearby pont Louis-Philippe. Cross the Seine, the Île-St-Louis, and the Seine again (via pont St-Louis) to the Île-de-la-Cité and quai de l'Archevêché.

Pause here to enjoy one of the great picture postcard views of Paris. The Capitol-like building in front to your left is the Panthéon and the Notre-Dame-like building in front to your right is, well, Notre-Dame.

Continue along quai de l'Archevêché crossing pont de l'Archevêché to reach the south bank of the Seine …

… following in the footsteps of Billy Crystal in **Forget Paris**, who tells Debra Winger, first, that this is a very important spot for him and, second,

"It's very clear our love is here to stay." Why? And what does this mean for him? A bit of patience, please—all will be revealed in just a few minutes.

But first cross the street—the quai de la Tournelle—and turn right before taking the third street on your left, the rue du Haut-Pavé.

It is here that Anne Hathaway and her new boyfriend—the cold and calculating one—take a nightly walk in **The Devil Wears Prada** and she remarks that she has "totally lost all orientation" (that's Notre-Dame Cathedral behind you, you silly girl!) before showing us that she has at least kept her aesthetic standards by pointing out "how beautiful" Paris is.

Which, essentially, is the message conveyed by the scene in the 1995 **Sabrina** where Julia Ormond and Patrick Bruel (again these two—do we feel a romance blossoming maybe?) have a cup of coffee on the terraces of La Maison on the far side of the square just ahead of you.

Turn left into rue des Grands-Degrés and then right into the rue Maître-Albert. At the end of this street, cross the street (rue Lagrange) into place Maubert, walking past the little fountain and the café on the corner to position yourself between the advertising column and the entrance to the Métro station Maubert-Mutualité.

Now take a look at the big restaurant (the Village Ronsard) on the other side of the main street. This is the view Jean-Pierre Melville gives us in his brilliant heist movie **Le cercle rouge** to show us where Bourvil's inspector lives, facing the lively boulevard St-Germain with the Panthéon in the background (where we will see the inspector in action a little later on).

Turn left into the boulevard St-Germain, crossing the street again, and continue on boulevard St-Germain past rue de Bièvre ...

... now, as in the 1970s and earlier, a quiet residential side street. But in the 1980s and 1990s, a heavily armed police contingent would have welcomed you at this very spot. No. 22, about halfway up the street on your left, was the house in which President François Mitterrand kept his private apartments throughout his term of office.

Keep walking for a couple of blocks until you reach rue de Pontoise, then turn right.

The unbecoming brick building, a few steps into rue de Pontoise, houses the Piscine de Pontoise, the most beautiful of all Parisian indoor swimming pools, with stunning Art Deco period interiors. (If you left your swimming trunks at home, at least take a peek into the lobby, where they display a picture.)

This is the pool of deep blue where Juliette Binoche repeatedly tries to submerge the pain of having lost her loved ones in **Trois couleurs: Bleu / Three Colors: Blue**, the first film of Kieslowski's color-coded trilogy which is loosely based on the "liberté-égalité-fraternité" triad of the French revolution and the French flag. (In the movie, the "blue" represents freedom; the "white" of part two, equality; and the "red" of part three, brotherly affection. Kieslowski received an Academy Award nomination for best direction for the last.)

Retrace your steps to the boulevard St-Germain. Cross it and continue down rue de Pontoise to its end in quai de la Tournelle. Cross the quai about 50 yards to your right at the striped pedestrian crossing— although, truth be told, it doesn't make much difference where you cross. Parisian drivers are no. more likely to let a pedestrian escape unharmed at a pedestrian crossing than anywhere else.

If you have survived the experience …

… walk down to the river bank, taking the path to the right of the building in front of you, the Inspection Générale de la Navigation.

The view we get down by the river—the Île-St-Louis straight ahead and Notre-Dame Cathedral to our left—is the first sight we see of an early morning Paris in **The Bourne Identity**: Matt Damon waking up in Franka Potente's car, rubbing the sleep out of his eyes, and looking around. (It appears that Franka Potente has chosen this spot to park her car. Why—and who does she work for: the CIA? the Russians? Or is it the French tourism board?)

Continue to the left, past the stop for the riverboat service—the sign with the no. 6 on it.

Here Julie Delpy and Ethan Hawke board a boat in **Before Sunset**. They continue up the Seine, under the pont de la Tournelle and the pont de Sully, on your right, to the port Henri-IV on the Right Bank, where they disembark.

On the near side of the pont de l'Archevêché, Woody Allen and Goldie Hawn perform their dance routine in **Everyone Says I Love You**. A few steps further, on the other side of the bridge, Audrey Hepburn smears ice cream on Cary Grant's immaculately tailored suit in **Charade** while attempting to do a little dance. Both scenes echo the steps and movements of another couple who danced "in this very spot" before them, turning this small part of Paris into a shrine for movie fans from all over the world. Because this is where Gene Kelly and Leslie Caron meet for their nightly tryst in **An American in Paris**. Ironically, as it happens, they did so without ever stepping off their Hollywood sound stage.

Now, you may burst into song, following Billy Crystal—or, rather, George and Ira Gershwin: "in time, the Rockies may crumble, Gibraltar may tumble, they're only made of clay ..."

On second thought, this may be a good time to take a little breather and think about the practice of shooting movies on location:

Shooting on Location

Sit down for a couple of minutes on one of the stone benches and let the **An American in Paris** scene play through in your mind. Then ask yourself why the makers of **An American in Paris** felt it was okay to shoot the movie on a set in Hollywood and yet Woody Allen traveled halfway around the world to shoot the scene in **Everyone Says I Love You** that pays homage to the **An American in Paris** scene.

Wouldn't it have been a much more fitting tribute to shoot the dance sequence in **Everyone Says I Love You** on the same soundstage? What happened in the forty-odd years between the two films that would have made Allen (and us) dismiss this suggestion as ridiculous out of hand?

I personally think there were two different processes at work here, one aesthetic and the other market-driven and fueled by technological advances. It is important to remember that cinema did not fall from the sky one day as a fully fledged "seventh art." Its rules, aesthetics, and narrative structures developed over a number of decades. Therefore, much of what we see in early cinema—its acting styles, camera positions, sense of place and time—was derived from the conventions of

Continue alongside the port de Montebello down by the river. A few steps further, opposite the cathedral …

… we find the spot where the final confrontation between Liam Neeson and Geoffrey Rush (the latter killing himself) takes place in the 1998 version of **Les Misérables**, directed by Bille August. This is one of the few scenes in the movie that were actually shot in Paris. All the grand street battles and set pieces were filmed in the Czech Republic.

Which provides our location story with a nice little coda: nowadays, the technology is there to shoot almost everything on location, but commercial pressures of a different kind prevent the producers from doing so.

This very same spot alongside the port de Montebello also provides the background for the key scene in Pixar-Disney's brilliant animated feature **Ratatouille**. It is here that the kitchen boy Linguini and Remy the rat bond for the first time. A Pixar crew of five, including the director, production designer, and director of photography, visited Paris for a week to steep themselves in first-hand impressions of their locations. Most of these were later amalgamated into an ultimately fanciful whole, but a few landmarks were carefully re-created. Director Brad Bird specifically chose this dramatic

---

the theater. Whenever a film director wanted to take his audience to Paris for a scene in the old days, he used a kind of simple cinematic shorthand: a picture of the Eiffel Tower or the Arc de Triomphe, an (unconvincing) back projection of the Champs-Élysées, maybe a few bars of the "Marseillaise" on the soundtrack—and hey presto, there we were. All of these techniques are directly derived from the theatrical expectation that the audience will fill in the gaps through its suspension of disbelief.

The way Paris is introduced in the movie *Casablanca*, made in 1942, is a good ex-ample of these old-fashioned cinematic

conventions at work. Outside of Bogey's Parisian flat, all the houses seem to be about two stories high and the street looks like a dirt track—more Paris, Texas, than Paris *ville de lumière*.

For most Americans in the 1920s and 1930s, I suspect, Europe was a faraway place, not much closer than China or Africa. But World War II changed all that. People not only were likely to have seen pictures of the real places in the newsreels, they might even have been there. So they could no longer be fooled by scenes such as the one in *Casablanca*. More importantly—and taking us straight to the second process site by the Seine, with the soaring Notre-Dame Cathedral in the background, as the place where Linguini and Remy would establish their reluctant partnership.

The bridge just ahead of you is the pont au Double—used in many movies, one suspects, for the opportunity it offers of showing a riverboat picturesquely approaching Notre-Dame Cathedral through the bridge's round arches. Examples include scenes in **The Man Who Cried** and **CanCan**— where Shirley MacLaine chooses this spot to jump off the boat. In **Mr. and Mrs. Bridge**, Paul Newman and Joanne Woodward quite sensibly refuse to let a young man convince them that a watch of doubtful origin is the ideal Parisian souvenir.

Now walk up the stairway that's roughly even with the square tower of Notre-Dame and cross quai de Montebello. Turn right and walk past the square (square Viviani) on your left. Just past the square …

… the building at the corner, 37 rue de la Bûcherie, is the home of Shakespeare and Company, quite possibly the most famous second-hand bookstore in the world.

---

at work—there were new competitive pressures. The type of movie that had filled the cinemas in the 1930s and 1940s—more dialogue-based than visual, slow and theatrical, and also cheap to produce— would simply no longer do. People could watch this kind of stuff on their new TV sets, for free and in the comfort of their own homes. Hollywood needed to invest serious money to get them out of their living rooms and into the theater. That meant providing things TV couldn't: color, new widescreen formats, and exotic locations. So producers started, willy-nilly, to instill a certain sense of place into their movies, at first carefully and conscientiously reconstructing whole streets and neighborhoods (often after extensive research conducted on site) and, by the early 1950s, by actually filming on location.

New and lighter equipment was the key to going reconstruction one better. In 1949, the film version of the musical *On the Town* had been (partly) shot on location in New York City. Thanks to the new equipment, there was no reason Hollywood couldn't carry this one step further by crossing the Atlantic and using real locations for its foreign-based movies. Still, it didn't happen overnight. When, in 1951, MGM was

Shakespeare and Company's most glorious moment occurred in 1922: it published James Joyce's *Ulysses* when nobody else dared to release it. Back then, the shop was owned by Sylvia Beach and located near the Théâtre de l'Odéon at 12 rue de l'Odéon (about a mile from its current location). The German occupying forces closed that shop in 1941 and it never reopened. George Whitman opened the current "successor" establishment on rue de la Bûcherie in 1951.

Shakespeare and Company provides the location for Ethan Hawke's reading from his recently published novel in **Before Sunset**. He even tells Julie Delpy that he has spent the previous night in the bookstore's guestroom. It is, indeed, the policy of the store to provide all of its guests with shelter, and that may include students and ordinary book lovers as well as authors. It is said that some 50,000 people have slept at Shakespeare and Company at one time or another through the years. (Owner George Whitman—who may or may not be a descendant of the great American poet Walt Whitman—used to comment, "I run a socialist utopia that masquerades as a bookstore.")

Take a look inside the shop. As you leave, turn right and then immediately right again into rue St-Julien-le-Pauvre, with square Viviani

---

planning to make **An American in Paris**, Gene Kelly insisted—as he had done for *On the Town* two years earlier—on using real locations; in this case, to no avail. The reasons for MGM's refusal were less commercial—the studio spent more than half a million dollars on the final dance sequence alone (nearly equal to the average budget for an entire movie at the time)—than artistic: the production team as a whole obviously felt that dreamlike, semi-realistic settings for the Parisian street scenes would suit the movie better. And, on a practical level, shooting on a set would guarantee that the non-dance scenes would be in sync with the dance *tableaus* that had to be shot in a studio anyway.

There is no particular moment in time when it became imperative to shoot on location, although the *Casablanca* approach was already looking dated by the 1930s. But, as the 1950s progressed, the number of projects filmed (at least partly) on site steadily grew. It's my understanding that Paramount's **Funny Face** was the first major Hollywood film to be shot (in 1957) almost entirely on actual Parisian locations.

Time to move on now and to discover some more of these original Parisian locations on our own. ⬥

on your left and the shop on your right. Walk past the Church of St-Julien-le-Pauvre …

… where Jean Gabin's wise-cracking **Archimède le clochard** and his dog reside (in the part which is now fenced off) …

… into rue Galande on your left …

… following Julie Delpy and Ethan Hawke on the first part of their walk in **Before Sunset**, the one where they reconstruct the events from their last encounter in Vienna. Julie and Ethan break off this stage of their walk about halfway down rue Galande, to reappear in the Marais where we just have come from. So …

… we take a right turn into rue Dante and follow this street until we meet rue St-Jacques. Turn right into rue St-Jacques and then— shortly after the street has changed its name to rue du Petit-Pont (about three blocks)—turn left into rue de la Huchette, once famous for its large number of art galleries.

No. 3, the second house on your left, is the place where Jean Seberg's artist boyfriend has his exhibit at the very start of **Bonjour tristesse**.

Continue down this street and turn right into rue Xavier-Privas. Follow this narrow lane to its end. Rejoin the quai and turn left.

The building at the corner, no. 15 quai St-Michel, is the Hôtel Les Rives de Notre-Dame. In Jean-Luc Godard's groundbreaking debut feature **À bout de souffle / Breathless**, Jean Seberg rents a room here. It's also here that she washes her feet in the bidet—like all good American girls. The hotel—a fairly downmarket hostel called the Hôtel de Suède at the time the film was made—was also used as a make-do studio for some of the film's other interior shots. It's since been extensively renovated into the four-star boutique hotel you see before you. Belmondo's cocky street gangster Michel Poiccard, the anti-hero of *À bout de souffle / Breathless*, would have fired a salvo from his .44 into its tastefully arranged shop window.

Continue down the quai St-Michel until you reach place St-Michel. Turn left and cross the boulevard St-Michel at the traffic lights towards the Fontaine St-Michel (photo opposite).

You are now in the spot where the forces of the French Résistance fight a pitched battle with the German occupiers in **Paris brûle-t-il? / Is Paris Burning?**

Continue straight ahead past the fountain, then turn left, cross the street at the first crosswalk, and take a right into rue St-André-des-Arts. Turn right into rue Séguier and left at the first corner into rue de Savoie.

You are practically walking in the footsteps, or more precisely the bicycle tracks, of Natasha McElhone, whom we see pedaling to her tryst with Anthony Hopkins in **Surviving Picasso**.

Turn right on rue des Grands-Augustins.

The third house on your right (no. 7, with the gate) is the place where the real Picasso had an atelier from 1937 to 1967 and where he painted many of his greatest works, including *Guernica*. All the exteriors of Picasso's atelier in **Surviving Picasso** were shot here.

> *Turn around now and walk down rue des Grands-Augustins until you rejoin rue St-André-des-Arts. Turn right and follow the street almost to its end. At no. 61, pass through the archway into the Cour du Commerce St-André.*

This is one of the oldest and loveliest alleyways in Paris; it has almost totally preserved its pre-revolutionary character. Just past the iron gates on your right is the café Le Procope (est. 1686), proudly claiming to be "the oldest coffee shop in the world" (where many of the revolutionary and pre-revolutionary thinkers such as Rousseau and Voltaire regularly met and where Benjamin Franklin is said to have fine-tuned the American constitution). Directly opposite is the building that served as Patrice Chéreau's printing shop in the French movie **Danton**, which featured Gérard Dépardieu as the title character, a hero of the Revolution. In the movie, the shop is eventually closed down by the Revolutionary Guards.

Follow the lane down to its end at the boulevard St-Germain. Turn left, cross the boulevard at the crosswalk, and take a left into rue de l'École-de-Médecine.

Some of the student riots in Bernardo Bertolucci's **The Dreamers**—an epic about a later and far less bloody "French revolution," the uprisings of May 1968—were filmed here: the temple-like building at 12 rue de l'École-de-Médecine (the former Medical Faculty of the University of Paris, commonly known as the Sorbonne) stood in for the University's main administration building, which was occupied by left-wing students in May 1968 and was eventually stormed by the French riot police.

At the next corner, turn left into rue Hautefeuille then right to rejoin boulevard St-Germain. Go to the corner of boulevard St-Michel.

On the corner opposite you, on the far side of the boulevard, Klaus Maria Brandauer's left-leaning, but opportunistic actor experiences something like The Last Temptation of **Mephisto**. Should he stay in Paris, he wonders, a city whose spirit of liberty and tolerance he adores? Or should he return to the Germany of Hitler's brownshirts for whom he has nothing but contempt, but who are promising him riches, power, and respect beyond his wildest dreams? (In the end, it's an offer he can't refuse.)

*Turn right into boulevard St-Michel (possible detour for a **Pink Panther** site, see page 243.) and right again into rue Racine.*

The classical building that you see in the distance at the end of the street is the Odéon theater, another hallowed spot of the events of May 1968. It was occupied by left-wing students who turned the theater into an alternative Parliament—although this rather sober term somehow fails to capture the "happening" atmosphere of the event. Some students, for instance, plundered the theater's costume department and climbed the speaker's podium dressed as Julius Caesar or King Lear's fool.

Turn left in front of the theater into rue Corneille and then continue left down the main road, the rue de Médicis.

This street and the adjoining area further down, alongside the jardin du Luxembourg, provide the backdrop for the last battle between the U.S. forces and the Germans in **Paris brûle-t-il?** / **Is Paris Burning?**—the one where Anthony Perkins is felled by a sniper's bullet. This is also the location of the bookshop called "le Meilleur des Mondes" (the French title of Aldous Huxley's novel *Brave New World*) in Jean-Luc Godard's **Pierrot le fou**. We see Jean-Paul Belmondo purchase a copy of Élie Faure's *Histoire de l'Art* here. (Later, sitting in the bathtub at home, he reads aloud a particularly impenetrable passage on Velasquez to his five-year old daughter.) The bookshop's address in the film, however—27-43, rue de Médicis—does not exist: another of Godard's sly little jokes that I'm not sure I fully understand.

Where rue de Médicis meets place Edmond-Rostand …

… you'll find Le Rostand, Gérard Depardieu's restaurant in **Paris, je t'aime** (the one where Ben Gazzara and Gena Rowlands meet). If you feel like taking a little rest now and refuelling on fresh air before tackling the last part of this

---

May '68: The Modern French 'Revolution'

Let's start at the beginning: After the national humiliation of World War II, restoration of the old order was the *ordre du jour* in France. It was so successful that by the mid 1960s, the country was still stuck, in many ways, in the 1940s. Young French people resented the stuffiness of it all, and it was this all-pervasive smell of Grandpa's old socks, if you like, that they wanted to air out. The first protests in March, after all, were directed at Nanterre University's policy of banning male students from the female dorms after ten o'clock.

How did such a seemingly harmless and limited local protest evolve into a full-blown general strike only two months later?

It still seems incredible, but after the administration shut down Nanterre University on May 2, and students at the Sorbonne protested on May 3, things got out of hand. The Sorbonne was eventually shut down, too, and, on May 6, when about 20,000 students marched in protest towards the Sorbonne, they suddenly found riot police blocking their way. What followed was the first real pitched battle between student protesters and police, which was largely fought on and around the barricades the students had erected on nearby place Edmond-Rostand.

walk, why not take a breather in the jardin du Luxembourg to your right, where you will also find toilets.

You may also want to catch a performance of the Guignol here if the timing is right. This famous puppet theater features in François Truffaut's semi-autobiographical debut feature **Les 400 coups / The 400 Blows**. As we go to press, performances are Wednesdays, Saturdays, and Sundays at 3:00 and 4:30 p.m., but the schedule changes from time to time.

Alternatively, you may prefer to seek out a quiet place in the *jardin*, a stone's—or Molotov cocktail's—throw away from place Edmond-Rostand and rue Gay-Lussac, the scenes of some of the fiercest pitched battles between the left-wing students and the riot police in May '68. Sit down on one of the chairs by the octagonal pool in front of the Palais du Luxembourg (where Penelope Cruz gives Stuart Townsend the long and short of the Spanish Civil War in **Head in the Clouds**) and let me fill you in on (or refresh your memory of) the closest France came to a "real" revolution in the 20th century—and definitely the most exciting thing to have happened here in the past fifty years (see below).

Another big protest was scheduled for May 10 and was again stopped by the police. The next day, the two largest trade unions—which spotted the opportunity for making life difficult for a right-wing government they thoroughly detested—got into the act, declaring a "day of action" for the following Monday, May 13.

Faced with over a million protesters in the streets of Paris, the government buckled that day. The Sorbonne was reopened—and promptly occupied by students, who declared it a "people's university." Now the real fun started. Workers all over the country, encouraged by the government's apparent weakness, called wild-cat strikes and even occupied some factories, demanding big pay raises and longer holidays. Just when it seemed that the general order faced total collapse, President Charles de Gaulle appeared on national radio—the country's TV workers were all on strike—to dissolve Parliament. Somehow that, combined with some real concessions to the striking factory workers, took the wind out of the movement's sails. By the time the country went to the polls a few weeks later, on June 23, the "revolution" was, for all practical purposes, over.

Oh yes, and the Gaulists won those elections with an increased Parliamentary majority. Apparently, the French, bored and tired of the old political guard from the 1940s

It's time we moved on.

Walk back to the junction of rue de Médicis—where you passed the restaurant Le Rostand—and the boulevard St-Michel. (The impressive building ahead in the distance is the Panthéon.) Cross the boulevard with the fountain to your right, turn left up the boulevard, and then take the first street to your right, called rue Cujas.

No. 22 on your left was the "B-Burger" bar where Adam Goldberg, Julie Delpy's American boyfriend in **2 Days in Paris** (which Delpy also wrote and directed), meets a self-confessed fairy ("no, a real fairy") who tells him to patch things up with Delpy and then proceeds to set fire to the joint. The place is, as of now, being refurbished, so maybe the B-Burger company decided to let it go at that after the place burned down.

Continue down rue Cujas. Turn right at the next corner into rue Victor Cousin and continue straight—across rue Soufflot, the

---

and 1950s, felt that they had made their point. Having looked into the abyss of real social unrest, they now politely drew back.

Notwithstanding, "May '68" finished off the *ancien régime* and everything it stood for. Less than a year later, de Gaulle was forced to resign. And while the students may not have achieved much in concrete terms, there is a France before May '68 and a France after, and the two aren't the same. Whichever way you look at it, this isn't the worst way of defining a revolution.

These days, May '68 is, more than anything else, remembered as a big coming-of-age party for the baby boomers. Somehow it never quite lost the ambience of a playground confrontation. Which is one reason it is so

fondly remembered. Not enough credit for this is generally given to the government of Général de Gaulle which never demonstrated a will to end the conflict whatever the cost. The struggle was characterized all along by a strong undercurrent of "sons vs. fathers." At some stage, those fathers apparently decided that opening fire on their sons was totally out of the question.

One might even say that hidden somewhere in all of this is a profound insight into the ways things in general are handled in French society—there is always "a certain way" of doing things, an unspoken consensus of what is right and what is wrong. When de Gaulle was told by his police chiefs that it was time to arrest the philosopher Jean-Paul

Panthéon to your left—into rue le Goff (the continuation of rue Victor Cousin). At the next corner, turn left into rue Malebranche.

In Billy Wilder's **Love in the Afternoon**, Audrey Hepburn and Maurice Chevalier (as her dad) live in an apartment at no. 17, at the bottom of the stairs in front of you. In one scene, we see Gary Cooper drive down the street and jump out of his car to ask Chevalier—unaware that he is Hepburn's dad—where he can find the young woman he's in love with.

Turn left on rue Paillet and then right into rue Soufflot, walking towards the Panthéon …

… which was built (in the 1760s) as a church dedicated to the patron saint of Paris, Saint Geneviève, and converted after the Revolution into a shrine to the memory of the great and good, a sort of Hall of Fame for writers, artists, philosophers, and the like. For the final shot of Roman Polanski's **Frantic**, the camera pans up in front of the Panthéon with a view over the jardin du

---

Sartre, who was seen handing out Maoist leaflets near the university where he was supposed to teach, de Gaulle replied: "On n'arrête pas Voltaire"—you/one can't arrest Voltaire. This *"On"* ("one" or "a person") a kind of national superego, is very powerful in France. It defines the narrow band of acceptable behavior. This keeps parents from shooting at their sons—undoubtedly a good thing—but it also discourages people from straying from the acceptable and conformist norm in less dramatic and even potentially beneficial ways.

Think about it: the reason French women are generally so well dressed is also the reason that new fashions have, by and large, come from the Anglo-Saxon world over the past forty years. (The terms "ground-breaking" and "tasteful" are mutually exclusive!) Thus, the French "On" can be stifling and even oppressive. But while it discourages mavericks and independent spirits, and has had a correspondingly negative effect on recent French culture, in politics, one can at least argue the possible merits of such a national superego. Has this force of constraint, all things considered, been a force for the good? Whatever opinion you may have on this, it cannot be denied that in 1968, it led to a peaceful and restrained resolution of a serious conflict that could easily have turned bloody, sour, and very nasty indeed, as it did in neighboring Germany. ▲

Luxembourg to the distant Eiffel Tower—rather incongruously and so much out of context that one suspects Polanski found the shot on the cutting-room floor and didn't have the heart to throw it away. It is the mother of all crane shots.

Walk around to the left side of the Panthéon.

In **Le cercle rouge**, Bourvil's inspector has the schoolboy arrested in the parking area in order to put some pressure on his father. That suggests that the boy is a pupil of either the Lycée Louis-le-Grand to your left or the Lycée Henri-IV in back of the Panthéon, the two most exclusive and elitist high schools in France. Incidentally, **Le cercle rouge** is known as director Jean-Pierre Melville's masterpiece, and director-producer John Woo (*Face/ Off*)—one of its many admirers—has apparently been planning for some years to shoot a remake in Hollywood.

Now peek down rue de la Montagne-Ste-Geneviève, which veers off to your left just in front of the stylistically somewhat jumbled Church of St-Étienne-du-Mont.

In **The Sun Also Rises**, the bal musette (dance hall) where Tyrone Power meets Ava Gardner was set a little further down this street.

Behind the Panthéon, turn right into rue Clotilde. Walk to its end and turn left into rue de l'Estrapade. Walk straight across the picturesque little place Emmanuel-Lévinas into rue Blainville and then straight into the place de la Contrescarpe.

This is one of the prettiest squares in the whole of Paris—which is probably why Director Krzysztof Kieslowski chose it as the backdrop for Juliette Binoche's slow "awakening" in **Trois couleurs: Bleu / Three Colors: Blue**. (Even the icy soul of the Binoche character, we are given to understand, begins to thaw as she sits by the side of the Contrescarpe on a lovely sunny day.) This is also the place where Fanny Bryant barrages poor Julia Ormond with her cold existentialism in the 1995 **Sabrina**—life, loneliness, and man's place in it, neatly wrapped into a 20-second soundbite. Do Americans really think this is the way French people talk? No wonder they can't seem to take them seriously.

Place de la Contrescarpe was also one of Ernest Hemingway's favorite hangouts. Hem lived here for a while (a little less than one year), a few houses away at 74 rue du Cardinal-Lemoine. (If you want to pay the old boy's ghost a visit, the street runs directly from the Contrescarpe, and the house itself is the second on the left. Look for the tastefully named "Travel Agency Under Hemingway." Then return to the Contrescarpe.)

> *Head down rue Mouffetard, one of Paris's great tourist streets, from the southeastern corner of the square. (Turn right if coming out of rue de l'Estrapade, left if you come from rue du Cardinal-Lemoine.) The house numbers should get larger as you walk down the street.*

Rue Mouffetard is unquestionably pretty, if a little over the top, but just when you get tired of walking past the one-hundredth shop offering tasteful little African earrings and hand-made chocolats, "la Mouffe" has one last twist up her sleeve and surprises you with the liveliest and most colorful street market

in the whole town—off the corner of rue Mouffetard and rue de l'Arbalète to your right.

This is also where you'll find Le Mouffetard (below opposite), the brasserie where Juliette Binoche eats her ice cream in **Trois couleurs: Bleu / Three Colors: Blue** as she listens to the mysterious flute player, and where she later meets her lover. (In his—very positive—review of the movie, Roger Ebert says Binoche moves into an "obscure street in an anonymous corner of Paris." Which only goes to show that Roger Ebert knows his movies a whole lot better than his Paris.)

Binoche's house in **Trois couleurs: Bleu / Three Colors: Blue** also appears to be somewhere in the area, as it looks down on the brasserie Le Mouffetard. But closer inspection reveals that it is actually an amalgam of different angles.

Continue down to the end of rue Mouffetard.

There, in the shadow of the Church of St-Medard, Amélie presents the toy box she has found in her bathroom to its rightful owner in **Le fabuleux destin d'Amélie Poulain / Amélie**. Don't be disappointed, however, when you don't see the phone booth she uses (it was only put up for the movie) or the bar where a totally stunned Monsieur Bredoteau has a drink to calm his nerves. That bar, located at no. 138 rue Mouffetard and originally named Octave's, no. longer exists. It was turned into—yet another—eatery.

Turn left past the church into rue Censier and follow this street up to the corner of rue Monge. Cross rue Monge and stand in front of the restaurant/pizzeria on the corner.

This is the café where Audrey Hepburn "chats up" a goofy German tourist—on one of the outside tables that no longer exist—as a form of cover during her "spying mission" in **Charade** (she is shadowing Cary Grant). She then interrupts her conversation when Grant moves on and, just as suddenly, returns to continue it when Grant looks in her direction, leaving the German tourist by turns impressed by the easygoing charm of "Parisian" women and bemused at their capricious unpredictability.

When Grant boards a bus, Hepburn hails a cab that we see approaching from the small park a little further down rue Censier to the right of the pizzeria, where the street forks. (The entire right half of the street has since been razed and replaced by new apartment buildings.)

Walk a little further down rue Censier to spot two more sites from **Charade**:

- the hotel (called the St-Jacques in the film but actually named Hôtel Maxim), and
- the corner of rue Censier and rue de Mirbel, where we see—in a scene towards the end of the film—Cary Grant chase Audrey Hepburn before she escapes into the Métro station.

That Métro station, also called St-Jacques in the film, would logically have been the station Censier-Daubenton (Line 7), although Grant and Hepburn appear to take a long and rather complex detour to reach it. Thankfully, we don't have to do the same, as our walk ends here.

ARRONDISSEMENT: 8
DURATION: 4 ½ hours (minus 10 minutes if you choose Start #2)

Walk 3

Park Monceau to the Élysée Palace

From the Park Monceau along the Grands Boulevards to the Arc de Triomphe and down the Champs-Élysées to the pont Alexandre-III and the Élysée Palace.

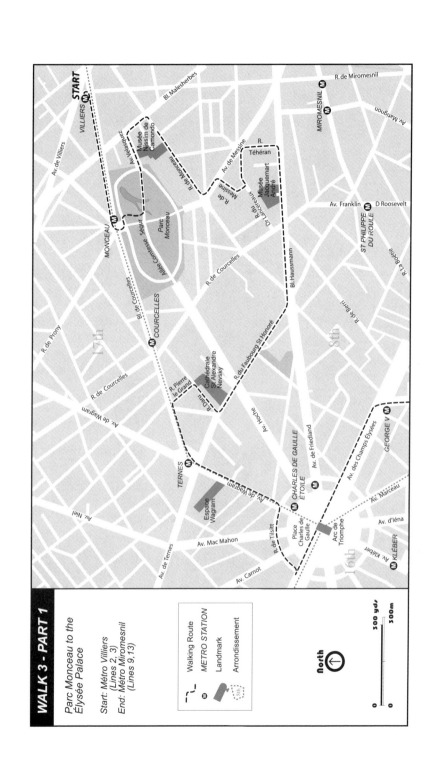

WALK 3 - PART 1

Parc Monceau to the
Élysée Palace

Start: Métro Villiers
(Lines 2, 3)
End: Métro Miromesnil
(Lines 9, 13)

Walking Route

M METRO STATION

Landmark

Arrondissement

north

500 yds
500m

Some movies have alternate endings, this movie walk has an alternate start.

Start #1: This is for fans of Nick Nolte and/or the episode in **Paris, je t'aime** where Nolte and Ludivine Sagnier take a walk together.

Take the Métro to station Villiers (Lines 2, 3). Leave through exit no. 1 and veer left as you come out, walking to the left side of the bank office at the corner into boulevard de Courcelles. Stay on the right side of the street.

You are retracing, in reverse, the steps of Nolte and Sagnier (Is she his lover? Is she his daughter? And who is the mysterious Gaspard?) in **Paris, je t'aime**, shot in a single take by director Hector Cuaròn, now more famous for his Harry Potter films.

After a block, cross over to the left side of the boulevard to the bus stop in front of the flower shop at no. 31.

You have now arrived at the point where the scene starts, when Nick Nolte gets off the bus.

Now cross the boulevard Malesherbes and continue straight down boulevard de Courcelles to the entrance of Parc Monceau.

Start #2: If you haven't seen the movie and/or you're not a big fan of Nick Nolte, you'll probably want to skip Start #1, because it takes you along a fairly nondescript stretch of a rather nondescript street. So instead of taking the Métro to station Villiers …

… Go straight to the Métro station Monceau (Line 2), which has only one exit. Enter the park, Paris's poshest, through the golden gate right next to the neoclassical pavilion.

In Guillaume Canet's **Ne le dit à personne / Tell No One**, François Cluzet waits on a bench nearby in hopes of clearing up the mystery surrounding his murdered wife. (Or was she?)

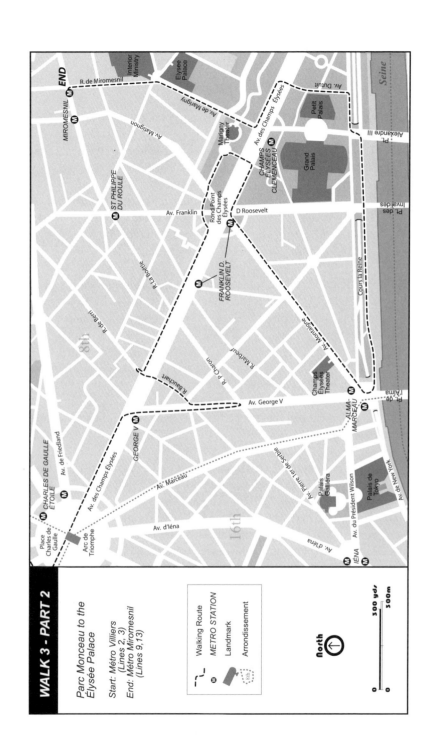

WALK 3 - PART 2

Parc Monceau to the Élysée Palace

Start: Métro Villiers
(Lines 2, 3)
End: Métro Miromesnil
(Lines 9,13)

Walking Route
METRO STATION
Landmark
Arrondissement

north

300 yds
500m

Seine

END

R. de Miromesnil

Interior Ministry

Élysée Palace

MIROMESNIL

Av. Matignon

Av. de Marigny

Av. des Champs Élysées

Av. Dutuit

Petit Palais

ST PHILIPPE DU ROULE

Marigny Theater

CHAMPS ÉLYSÉES CLEMENCEAU

Grand Palais

Pt. Alexandre III

Pt. des Invalides

Av. Franklin

Rond Point des Champs Élysées

D Roosevelt

FRANKLIN D. ROOSEVELT

R. la Boétie

Cours la Reine

R. de Berri

8th

Av. Montaigne

R. Marbeuf

R. P. Charon

R. Bayard

Champs Élysées Theater

Av. George V

ALMA-MARCEAU

Pt. de l'Alma

CHARLES DE GAULLE ÉTOILE

Av. de Friedland

GEORGE V

Av. des Champs Élysées

Av. Pierre 1er de Serbie

Av. Marceau

16th

Palais Galliéra

Palais de Tokyo

Av. du Président Wilson

Av. de New York

Place Charles de Gaulle

Arc de Triomphe

Av. d'Iéna

Av. d'Iéna

IÉNA

Take the second path to the left, right before the kiosk. When the path forks, keep left, leaving the poet, a statue of the author Guy de Maupassant, and his muse to your right.

The little lake in front of you with the sweeping row of slender classical columns (below) is the most famous feature of the park—and the one that has attracted the most attention from moviemakers. For example, after being expelled from Gigi's home in **Gigi**, Louis Jourdain takes a musical journey through Paris and drums up his resolve to return while sitting under the park's colonnades, while in the 1995 **Sabrina**, the columns provide the setting for a fashion shoot.

Walk behind the colonnade and underneath the classical arch and keep going until you meet the park's central thoroughfare—called the allée Comtesse-de-Ségur (you will have to take my word for it; there is no street sign). Turn left into the allée and take it all the way out of the park.

The lane between the low iron gates and the higher gold-trimmed gates (above) one block down is called avenue Velasquez. No. 5 on your right (actually the Musée Cernuschi) is the house where Audrey Hepburn has her flat in **Charade**—the one she finds completely empty after she gets the news of her husband's death.

Pass through the gates into boulevard Malesherbes and turn right.

Those of you of a more literary bent may care to know that the boulevard Malesherbes—no number—is given as Chad's address in Henry James's *The Ambassadors*. It would have been a house very much like no. 84 just across the street.

And Marcel Proust, author of *À la recherche du temps perdu (Remembrance of Things Past)*, one of the seminal novels of the 20th century, spent 30 years of his life in a house at 9 boulevard Malesherbes, where Oscar Wilde once paid him a visit and afterwards made some bitchy remarks about the stodgy décor. That building, however, is quite a long way to your right almost at the end of the boulevard near the Church of the Madeleine.

Turn right again at the next corner into rue de Monceau and walk up to the Musée Nissim de Camondo at no. 63.

This is where interior shots were made for Milos Forman's **Valmont**. You can walk into the forecourt without charge and take a peek inside.

Continue down rue de Monceau until you reach the next big intersection, the place de Rio de Janeiro. Make a 90-degree turn to your left into avenue de Messine.

You may recognize this street. In Bernardo Bertolucci's **The Dreamers**, the cops have a street fight with the revolutionary students here.

Pause on the left side of the street to look at the wonderfully grand building across the street at no. 23.

This is the house where Catherine Deneuve leads her life as the rich bourgeoise between shifts at the local brothel in Luis Bunuel's **Belle de jour**.

*Cross avenue de Messine and take the first right into rue de Messine (the street between no. 23 and no. 23bis) to explore the side streets where the final chase of **Belle de jour** was shot. Follow rue de Messine to the end, then turn left into rue du Docteur-Lancereaux to rejoin avenue de Messine. Turn immediately right into rue de Téhéran. At the end of the street, turn right again into boulevard Haussmann.*

This road was one of the first to be cleared in the mid 19th century when Napoleon III and his right-hand man, Alfred (later Baron) Haussmann, embarked on one of the greatest feats of urban renewal of its and indeed any time. In a project that was partly political, partly hygienic, and partly for the glory of it all, they ploughed the narrow maze of residential streets that had made central Paris such a hotbed for revolution, crime, and pestilence from medieval times on and created modern Paris. Ancient wooden-framed hovels on narrow lanes made way for modern stone buildings on broad tree-lined boulevards. In the process, the "revolutionary rabble" was displaced from central Paris to what were then the outskirts of town, now mainly the

10th, 11th, and 12th arrondissements. Thanks to strict building regulations, the four- and five-story buildings that displaced the hovels are identical in principle—with a rather grand and high-ceilinged "piano nobile" on the first floor and maids' chambers under the receding aluminium roof—yet subtly different in decor. The iron railings, for example, are approximately, but never exactly, at the same level on the facades, jumping up and down the vista of any Hausmannien boulevard like notes on a sheet of music paper, creating visual interest without disrupting the overall symmetry.

It is Baron Haussmann's Paris that set the scene for the Belle Époque, the period between the Franco-Prussian war of 1870-71 and the outbreak of World War I in 1914. This was the greatest period in the history of the French capital in many ways, and "Les Grands Boulevards" always feature prominently in Belle Époque movies, such as **Gigi**.

Walk a few steps down the boulevard Haussmann.

No. 158, the Musée Jacquemart-André, is Louis Jourdain's home in **Gigi**. They shot some interiors here, too, including the boudoir and the lobby with its grand *escalier d'honneur* (main stairway). However, you have to pay to look inside; all you can see for free is the beginning of the driveway into the front courtyard. (By the way, the musée was also used for the exterior shots of the fictitious Musée Kléber-Lafayette in William Wyler's 1966 film, **How to Steal a Million**.)

One of the problems of shooting Belle Époque street scenes on location is that while the buildings may not have changed much since the late 19th century, the shops at street level certainly have. One suspects that upmarket Italian designer shops, travel agencies, and luxury car showrooms—common sights in today's posh 8th arrondissement—were much thinner on the ground in the 1890s. In **Gigi**, one of the first movies set in that period to be shot on location, they solved this problem by shooting the Grands Boulevards scenes—where Maurice Chevalier and Louis Jourdain drive their horse-drawn carriages through Paris—straight from the street level as semi close-ups, in effect showing the buildings only from the second story up. This works rather well on the whole, but less well when a side street comes into view. Then you can get a deep look into those receding side streets, complete with rows and rows of TV antennas planted on the roofs.

On a literary note: if we were walking in the opposite direction, we would pass the place in which Marcel Proust wrote his masterpiece *À la récherche du temps perdu*, a second-floor apartment at 102 boulevard Haussmann. Make a detour if you like, but don't worry if you don't. You won't miss much in terms of aesthetic delight: Proust called the building "one of the ugliest things I ever saw."

Once you have reached the traffic lights a few steps further down the boulevard Haussmann, pause to take a look at the building just off the corner in the street to your left, 29 rue de Courcelles.

This is the office building where Maurice Ronet kills his boss in 24-year-old Louis Malle's celebrated debut feature from 1958, **Ascenseur pour l'échafaud / Elevator to the Gallows**, one of the key movies of the Nouvelle Vague, stylishly scored with the cool jazz of Miles Davis. After the murder, Maurice, who is having an affair with the boss's wife, daringly descends by rope from the top floor to a lower level, only to be trapped overnight in the elevator on his way down. That's why he has no alibi for a crime committed by a young man (the boyfriend of the flower shop girl next door) who has stolen his car. The structure is still used as an office building by the Caisse Centrale de Réassurance.

Now continue down boulevard Haussmann on the office-building side of the street past the corner location of the movie's flower shop (now a car showroom), and on to the next corner. Turn right to cross boulevard Haussmann and rue de Monceau. Then turn left and pass by the bar-brasserie Le Bouquet Haussmann, called "Royal Camée" in the same movie.

This is where Jeanne Moreau waits (in vain) for her lover after he has killed her husband.

Now look ahead to spot an important site from **Ascenseur pour l'échafaud / Elevator to the Gallows**, the large street sign HÔTEL FRIEDLAND. You see the sign several times in the movie when, first, Maurice Ronet and then, later, the car thief (accompanied by the shop girl) are shown driving towards the Arc de Triomphe.

Glance back to the other side of the boulevard just before you bear slightly right into the rue du Faubourg-St-Honoré.

On the corner of rue Washington and avenue de Friedland—next to the branch of the Société Générale—is the place where Lino Ventura's girlfriend has her restaurant in Jean-Pierre Melville's laconic gangster flick **Le deuxième souffle / Second Breath**.

Continue down the rue du Faubourg-St-Honoré, past the Rothschild Foundation on your left at the junction with rue Berryer, and up to the corner of avenue Hoche. Turn left, crossing avenue Bertie Albrecht, until you reach the Hôtel Royal Monceau at no. 35 - 39.

This is where the American opera singer resides in the French cult film **Diva**. And also where the young mailman who has made an illicit recording of the diva's concerts eventually goes to meet her in person—and then strikes up a somewhat unlikely romance.

Retrace your steps to the corner of rue du Faubourg-St-Honoré, but before you cross avenue Hoche at the traffic lights to continue down the rue du Faubourg-St-Honoré, look right towards the golden gate of the parc Monceau.

On the sidewalk between this street corner and the entrance to the park, Simone Signoret is shot from a car by her erstwhile Resistance colleagues in Jean-Pierre Melville's **L'armée des ombres / Army of Shadows**. The killers, including Lino Ventura, then continue to drive down avenue Hoche before they are stopped by a patrol of German soldiers right in front of the Arc de Triomphe.

Turn left down rue du Faubourg-St-Honoré, past the Salle Pleyel on your right …

… one of the most famous concert halls in the world and the arena where Charles Aznavour's sweet-natured pianist plays in the flashback sequence of François Truffaut's **Tirez sur le pianiste / Shoot the Piano Player**.

At the next corner, turn right into rue Daru. About half way down to your right ...

... you will see the Cathedral of St-Alexander Nevsky, one of the truly hidden gems of the French capital, so well hidden, in fact, that you only see it when you stand more or less right in front of it. This is where the Russian Orthodox Easter celebrations are taking place in the movie **Anastasia**, with Ingrid Bergman as the "lost" daughter of the last Czar.

Turn left into rue Pierre-le-Grand opposite the church and left again into the boulevard de Courcelles, which you follow up to the place des Ternes. Turn left into avenue de Wagram.

The distant high-rise buildings on your right when you cross, for the 137th time, the rue du Faubourg-St-Honoré, form the skyline of the La Défense business district, of which you will find more in the chapter *Further Afield*.

Continue down the left-hand side of avenue de Wagram.

Just beyond no. 39 you can spot the building that houses Salle Wagram, without a doubt the most beautiful and distinguished banquet hall in Paris. It's used in **L'amante / The Lover** as the restaurant where Tony Leung seduces Jane March and where, in **Le dernier tango à Paris / Last Tango in Paris**, Marlon Brando and Maria Schneider disrupt the tango competition.

You used to be able to enter Salle Wagram through a side door in a cinema located at no. 39/41. But the cinema has since burned down. So if you want to see the hall, you should turn right on rue de l'Étoile, the next street to your right, and take another right at the next corner: it's the classical building at 5bis rue de Montenotte. Alternatively, if you want to take a close look at the hall's sumptuous interiors, you can get a good panoramic view at www.sallewagram.com.

Continue to the end of avenue de Wagram, marching towards the Arc de Triomphe, easily recognizable even in rarely seen profile. You're confronting the "Big Beast" head-on after having circled it for so long.

The Métro entrance "Wagram" (just across the avenue to your right) at the corner of place Charles-de-Gaulle—formerly named "Étoile" (the star), which is how everybody in Paris still refers to it—is the station featured in Eric Rohmer's Episode 4 **Paris vu par... / Paris Seen By...**. This is the station where the man steps off the bus and completes a near-360-degree turn around the Étoile rather than get his feet dirty by walking in the opposite direction through a building site. The same exit is used by James Fox in **The Day of the Jackal**. He leaves the station, and the camera zooms out to illustrate—with a panoramic sweep over the Étoile and the Arc—that he has arrived in Paris.

> *Now cross avenue de Wagram, walk a short distance, and turn right into avenue Mac-Mahon and then left into rue de Tilsitt, staying on the left side of the street.*

The building facing you is the Hôtel Splendide Étoile, where some of the key members of the fashion pack are staying in Robert Altman's **Prêt-à-Porter**.

> *Continue straight down rue de Tilsitt past the hotel to reach avenue de la Grande-Armée. Cross the street to the small traffic island with the underpass.*

This underpass, which connects avenue de la Grande-Armée to the Champs-Élysées on the other side of the Étoile, is used in the introductory scene of John Schlesinger's **Marathon Man**. Schlesinger contrasts shots of the busy underground traffic with the image of the Arc de Triomphe (opposite). The shot illustrates the similarity of Paris to American cities, one of the visual leitmotifs of the movie. Schlesinger will show us a busy underpass or a high-rise building that implies "America," only to cut away to a typical Parisian monument or building, catching us by surprise.

Now you decide: either you continue almost full circle around the Étoile—in honor of the man in **Paris vu par... / Paris Seen By...**, passing the tie shop where he works on avenue Victor-Hugo—or you take a shortcut to the Champs-Élysées through the underpasses.

To take the shortcut, turn towards the Arc de Triomphe, and walk to the stairway next to the building at no. 2; it will take you down to a pedestrian underpass. Follow the directions to exits "Hoche" and "Friedland" and then later to the "Champs-Élysées." Take the escalator to the exit "Champs-Élysées."

If you want to take a close look at the Arc de Triomphe …

… instead of taking the shortcut, walk straight ahead to the stairway labelled "Arc de Triomphe" and follow the signs. Do not even think of trying to reach the Arc overground by dodging the traffic. Not even Parisians are crazy enough to do that.

Any excess energy you may still have would be much better employed by greeting the Arc de Triomphe in the spirit of Fred Astaire in **Funny Face**, performing a shimmy on the other side of the Champs-Élysées, more or less in front of the building on the corner (no. 133), which is today a Publicis Drugstore.

Walk down the Champs-Élysées on the left side of the street.

If you feel peckish, you may be interested in the building at no. 122. Sadly, the Burger King restaurant where William Hurt and Geena Davis dine in **The Accidental Tourist** (on the second floor, overlooking the Arc de Triomphe) no longer exists. But the premises are occupied by another inexpensive restaurant, part of the French chain Bistro Romain. Eating out on a movie theme doesn't come any cheaper than this.

A few steps further down, at no. 116 Champs-Élysées …

… is the Cinéma Normandie. This is where Jean-Paul Belmondo—in **À bout de souffle / Breathless**—strikes his famous Bogey pose. The jump cuts and handheld camera style director Jean-Luc Godard used in this 1960 movie, along with its casual eruptions of extreme violence and dialogue mixing the conversational with direct quotations from Faulkner, Dylan Thomas, and Nietzsche, have influenced countless Hollywood directors since, none more so than Quentin Tarantino. Tarantino even named his production company A Band Apart in honor of *Bande à part*, one of Godard's later movies.

Next door to the cinema …

… is the entrance to the Lido cabaret where another French movie icon, Alain Delon, "disappears" in another totemic French movie of the 1960s, Jean-Pierre Melville's gangster flick **Le samouraï / The Godson** (1967).

Delon's melancholic hit man resurfaces through a cabaret service door that's located right next to the stage entrance at 1 rue Lord-Byron. You could get to it by taking a left into rue Washington at the next corner and then taking the first left into rue Chateaubriand and looking for the building behind the corner where rue Lord-Byron branches off from rue Chateaubriand. But it would be somewhat pointless to make the detour. The stage doors, which had remained unchanged for decades, fell victim to a large redevelopment project recently.

Time to move on. Cross the Champs-Élysées and take avenue George-V, the street that veers off between the large Louis Vuitton shop on the right and Fouquet's, an old showbiz hangout, on the left.

Fouquet's (photo page 262) is the place where the *César* film awards are traditionally celebrated. The tradition goes back to February 28, 1980 and the fifth annual presentations of the Césars, the Oscars of the French film industry.

All those attending the ceremony were afterwards invited to a gala dinner at le Fouquet's, and they've been heading there ever since.

The entranceway to the restaurant is decorated with both plaques engraved with the names of those who've won Cesars as well as iron plates bearing the handprints of French movie personalities, much in the style of the cement squares in front of Grauman's Chinese Theatre in Los Angeles. But in Paris, the handprints (though not the names) are normally covered by a red carpet between grand celebrations.

Stroll down avenue George-V to the Hôtel George-V, one of the city's most luxurious lodgings.

You'll pass a number of posh shops on the way, including Morabito, where Roy Scheider has apparently been doing his shopping early on in **Marathon Man**, for we see him with a Morabito shopping bag.

Walk inside the hotel—if you dare—

to check out the place in the lobby where Meg Ryan's wallet is stolen in **French Kiss**. The George-V also appears as the St-James and Albany Hôtel in **Travels with My Aunt**.

Now walk back toward the Champs-Élysées, but before you reach it, turn right in front of the Bulgari and Hermes shops into rue Quentin Bauchart.

Have a look at the building on your right at the next corner: no. 79 Champs-Élysées. This is where the heist is carried out in Luis Bunuel's **Belle de jour**. (It was actually the office of the two guys who produced the movie.) The place has since been gutted and turned into a car showroom.

Cross the Champs-Élysées and continue straight into rue de Berri.

You may recognize the row of shops and restaurants on your right from François Truffaut's **La peau douce / The Soft Skin**, even though the restaurant Le Val d'Isère, the favorite hang-out of the lecherous lecturer played by Jean

Desailly, where he meets a sticky end when his jealous wife guns him down with a hunting rifle, has since been closed and replaced with the Impala Lounge, possibly the capital's swankiest African restaurant.

About half a block or so down, just opposite the Hôtel California (such a lovely place, such a lovely place) at no. 21 …

… you will find the building where the *New York Herald Tribune* once had its offices and where Jean Seberg works in **À bout de souffle / Breathless**. The building has been renovated and now houses a pensions company, but a plaque on the outside commemorates its place in history as the home of the *Herald Tribune*.

Retrace your steps to the Champs-Élysées and continue down the left side of the street, away from the Arc de Triomphe.

The Lido-Musique shop where the protagonist meets the Asian girl in **Diva** was located at no. 68. It has since been converted into a perfume supershop.

If you cross the avenue now, you will enter the stretch of the Champs-Élysées where Marlon Brando chases Maria Schneider in **Le dernier tango à Paris / Last Tango in Paris**. The look of the street may have changed a lot, but in one shot, we can clearly see the building on the right corner, no. 63.

The first street leading right at the next corner, rue Pierre-Charron, is also worth a look.

In the 1930s, the club Gerny's was located about half way down rue Charron, at no. 54 (now a hotel). Singing at Gerny's was Édith Piaf's first step to stardom. At the time, the club was run by a guy named Louis Leplée, the Gérard Dépardieu character in the Piaf biopic **La Môme / La Vie en Rose**. Leplée was shot in an underworld feud the year after he engaged Piaf. It was never reliably established whether she had played any part in his murder or, more likely, whether she knew more than she was willing to tell at the time. What is certain is that after Leplée's death, Piaf left Paris and did not come back for months.

Continue walking down the Champs-Élysées. At no. 39 on the corner of rue Marbeuf (the first street to your right) ...

... we find another upmarket restaurant, L'Alsace. It is one of the places Jean Seberg's spoiled and deeply unhappy teenager frequents in Otto Preminger's **Bonjour tristesse**.

The corner of the Champs-Élysées and rue Marbeuf is also the starting point for the wild car chase in **Rush Hour III**. We see Chris Tucker's and Jackie Chan's car—piloted by their, at this stage, still very reluctant Parisian cab driver—in the Rond-Point, i.e., the large traffic circle and pedestrian ring road a couple of blocks ahead of you. They're being followed as they speed toward the Seine and the Invalides beyond.

Now walk on down to the traffic circle.

For plot reasons, the movie needed a Parisian street with an American name for the scene where the two cops start their inquiries. But after inspecting the real avenue Franklin-D.-Roosevelt (the cross street just a block ahead of you), the crew apparently decided that it did not look "Parisian" enough. So they shot the brief scene of the cops' arrival somewhere on the Left Bank in a narrow side street that they renamed Franklin D. Roosevelt for the movie.

Cross the Champs-Élysées at the traffic lights, casting a glance from the curb back towards the Étoile.

Goldie Hawn and Alan Alda are shown on this section of the street in **Everyone Says I Love You**, with the Arc de Triomphe in the background. In the scene, all the trees are decked in Christmas lights. This is almost the same shot you get in **The Devil Wears Prada** and **The Truth About Charlie**. Could it be that a Hollywood law requires that no night shot of the Champs-Élysées may be released without Christmas lights?

Turn right and on reaching the Rond-Point, which marks the midpoint of the avenue des Champs-Élysées (basically the spot where the part of the street with all the shops and restaurants meets the boring bit), turn left (clockwise) into its sweep. Cross avenue Franklin-D.-Roosevelt and rue Jean-Mermoz then turn left into avenue Matignon.

No. 3 on your left side—the building also marked by a plaque telling us that the German poet Heinrich Heine died here in 1856—is the place where William Holden's screenwriter lives in **Paris When It Sizzles**. Audrey Hepburn is shown crossing the gardens opposite and entering this building on the way to her appointment in the movie's opening scene.

Following so-to-speak in her footsteps, cross avenue Matignon and head straight into the little garden on the other side, to the right of the underpass that leads to a subterranean parking lot.

Immediately on your left, you will find the Guignol puppet theatre where Audrey Hepburn and Cary Grant meet in **Charade**, observed by a French commissaire, who winces every time Punch hits the policeman puppet over the head. We see them in the garden again later when they look for the little boy who appears to have escaped to the stamp market here (photo below) with some very special postage stamps.

Sit down for a moment on one of the benches and imagine that you are overhearing Peter O'Toole and Audrey Hepburn (again!) as they sit on the neighbouring bench plotting their heist in **How to Steal a Million**.

Now leave the garden on the Champs-Élysées side. Cross the Champs-Élysées (at the traffic lights approximately 100 yards to your right) and then avenue Franklin-D.-Roosevelt before heading—past the Gucci shop on the corner—into avenue Montaigne at the next corner.

The palais on the other side of the street, the Hôtel Dassault (photo page 90), may look incredibly posh but it is, in fact, an auction showroom—albeit one where only really expensive stuff is shown and sold. In Brian de Palma's **Femme Fatale**, it is the U.S. Embassy where Antonio Banderas's *paparazzo* "steals" a picture of the ambassador's young wife and sets the film's chain of events into motion.

Continue down avenue Montaigne, the most luxurious thoroughfare in the country, walking down the left side …

… because that's where all the action is. By the 1990s, the title of "top-flight fashion neighborhood" had shifted away from the rue du Faubourg-St-Honoré towards avenue Montaigne. This was due in part to the LVHM group which has invested heavily in the area's real estate, creating a suitably regal environment for its stable of leading labels: Loewe (no. 46), Céline (no. 38), Dior (no. 30), Christian Lacroix (no. 26), and Inès de la Fressange (no. 14). Its prestige has, consequently, attracted other world-class brands to the avenue like Germany's Jil Sander (no. 56) and Escada (no. 53), Chloé (no. 44), Chanel (no. 42), Italy's Dolce & Gabbana (nos. 54 and 2), Salvatore Ferragamo (no. 45), Giorgio Armani (no. 18), and Prada (no. 8), the UK's Joseph (no. 14), and even the American Calvin Klein (no. 53).

Fashion is notoriously fickle, however, and by the time you read this, some of these shops may already have moved elsewhere. The stores where Teri Garr does her shopping (for her big-busted "friend" who turns out to be—careful: spoiler!—her transvestite husband) throughout **Prêt-à-Porter**, at any rate, have mostly disappeared.

One shop that's still here—and unlikely to move any time soon, considering how long it's already been here—is the Dior store at no. 30. I don't know when Christian Dior moved in, but the shop has been here since at least the late 1950s. Jean Seberg (that girl again; she should get around Paris more!) looks into its window in **À bout de souffle / Breathless**, dreaming about expensive frocks, while Jean-Paul Belmondo makes phone calls for free in the same movie from a defective booth a few steps away at the corner of rue François-1er. And in **Paris When It Sizzles**, we are treated to a cameo appearance by Marlene Dietrich who disembarks regally in front of the shop from a white Rolls Royce.

Continue down avenue Montaigne.

A few doors down on the other side of the street, you can spot the five-star Plaza Athenée (at no. 27). This is the mysterious Mrs. Telfer's hotel in Roman Polanski's quasi-remake of *Rosemary's Baby*, **The Ninth Gate**. This is also the place where Chris Tucker and Jackie Chan are staying in **Rush Hour III**. (Just the right address for an LAPD cop on an assignment in Paris!)

We see Chris Tucker, after a quarrel with his Chinese partner, leave the hotel for a Chinese meal and a night cap. While having his drink, he spots the black girl from the gambling den, the mysterious Geneviève, and follows her to the Théâtre des Champs-Élysées (where she has her own one-woman show). The theater actually is located almost next door to the hotel at no. 15 avenue Montaigne (never mind that Tucker appears to pass the Opéra on the way).

Avenue Montaigne is also, as one might expect, the location for much of the action in the French Oscar-nominated film of the same name (**Fauteuils d'orchestre** in the original). You may already have recognized some of the posh shops along the way, starting with Gucci right at the top of the street, that arouse Cecile de France's small-town-girl curiosity (and desires, of course). The Théâtre des Champs-Élysées is the place where Valérie Lemercier's overworked actress appears in a rather shrill Feydeau farce, and right across the street—at no. 6 avenue Montaigne—you'll find the Bar des Théâtres where the different strands of the story are all woven into one.

More fashion finally at the corner of the place de la Reine-Astrid to your left. No. 2 avenue Montaigne—the building that currently houses the offices of designer Emanuel Ungaro—is the location for the first big fashion parade in **Funny Face**. That's the one where Audrey Hepburn is late for designer Paul Duval's show because she has spent too much time chatting with some existentialist loons.

Cross the street on your left at the next traffic lights.

Now look around a bit before continuing. You are on historic ground here. In the underpass beneath your feet, Diana Princess of Wales died in one of the most dramatic real-life soaps of the 20th century. (A little more about this in Walk 5 when we visit the place de l'Alma on your right.)

Cross the busy street above the underpass—at the traffic lights on your right—and continue left alongside the river.

Down by the river is the pleasure boat station where you can board one of the so-called *Bateaux-Mouches* if you fancy a boat trip along the Seine. These shallow-hulled excursion boats ply the Seine daily, and there are actually worse ways of spending an afternoon in Paris. Just be sure you don't catch a boat that will take you round and round in a loop, like the one Audrey Hepburn and Cary Grant obviously boarded in **Charade**, which passed the same buildings over and over again as if on a "Groundhog Boatride."

Glance left to the windowed top of the Théâtre des Champs-Élysées …

… Where Cecile de France spends a chilly night on the roof in **Avenue Montaigne**.

Now continue straight ahead—past the church with the "Gothic" steeple on the other side of the river, the American Church of Paris— until you reach the next bridge, the pont des Invalides. Cross the street and walk down to the riverbank, following the path along the Seine.

Right in front of you is the setting for the big gun battle between Robert De Niro's gang of mercenaries and the crooked arms dealers in **Ronin**. The battle is ignited by De Niro when he spots a sniper in the bridge's ironwork, thanks to the spotlight cast on him by a passing pleasure boat.

It is at the foot of the steps below the bridge that Ingrid Bergman contemplates suicide in **Anastasia**.

Now walk up the stairs to the bridge itself ...

... echoing, so to speak, the movements of Fred Astaire who walks down the stairway on the other side in **Funny Face**. We also see the bridge when he takes Audrey Hepburn for a fishing trip on the Seine in the same movie. A fishing trip! You've got to leave it to old Fred: he really knows what girls fancy. Maybe he even let her squeeze the wiggly worms onto his fishing hooks.

The bridge you are standing on is the pont Alexandre-III (photo page 68). It's all decked out in typical Belle Époque style, which served as the "negative blueprint" for the "ornament is crime / less is more" austerity of much of modernist architecture. Joseph Cassien-Bernard and Gaston Cousin, the bridge's architects, in contrast, appear to have belonged to the "more is not nearly enough" school. We who have grown rather tired of seeing houses as "machines for living," and bridges as machines for driving over, can look at the bridge with something resembling pleasure, and Hollywood movies have certainly shown us the way. American moviemakers have used the pont Alexandre-III almost to excess: whenever something must look unmistakably, but not too obviously, Parisian, it seems they send their cameras here. Consequently, we encounter the bridge in such "early" Parisian Hollywood movies as **Funny Face** (see above) and **Gigi** (when Louis Jourdain passes it on his musical journey through Paris), as well as in films of more recent vintage such as **Forget Paris** (when Debra Winger and Billy Crystal choose the bridge for a romantic on-screen kiss). In John Huston's **Moulin Rouge**, Jose Ferrer as Toulouse-Lautrec quarrels with his girlfriend in this spot after she has stormed out of a restaurant. Later, he returns to save the woman who, possibly overwhelmed by the bridge's rich decorative features, decides she can't take any more and is about to throw herself into the Seine. In **The Man Who Cried**, Cate Blanchett and Christina Ricci discuss future assignments here, and James Bond a.k.a. Roger Moore—or his stuntman, to be more precise—jumps off the bridge into a pleasure boat in **A View to a Kill**. The bridge undoubtedly gets its best outing in Robert Altman's **Prêt-à-Porter** when Jean-Pierre Cassel chokes on his ham sandwich in a traffic jam, prompting Marcello Mastroianni to panic and jump out of the car and straight into the river.

French director Gérard Oury used the bridge in **Les aventures de Rabbi Jacob / The Mad Adventures of Rabbi Jacob**. The popular French comedian Louis de Funès, playing the title character, follows a military parade across the bridge in his car and ends up steering it straight into the court of the Invalides (on the far side of the river to your right), where his daughter is about to get married.

Incidentally, the pont Alexandre-III is one of only three Parisian landmarks faithfully recreated for the brilliant **Ratatouille**. The other two are Notre-Dame Cathedral and, inevitably, the Eiffel Tower.

Be careful here. There seems to be something about this bridge that makes people want to throw themselves off it. Resist the urge and instead …

… walk back to the Cours la Reine, the promenade between the river and the two huge steel-framed buildings on your left, the Grand Palais and the Petit Palais, 19th century exhibition halls and fine art museums. Cross to the left side of the street and turn right, leaving the Petit Palais, the smaller of the two, to your left before turning left into avenue Dutuit. Continue past …

... the Restaurant Le Doyen at 1 avenue Dutuit, where the big celebratory dinner is held in **Prêt-à-Porter**. Kim Basinger delivers some more malapropisms into her mike here, in front of its entrance door.

Walk the fairly short way to the end of avenue Dutuit, where you will rejoin the Champs-Élysées. Turn left and cross to the far side of the Champs-Élysées at the traffic lights.

Remember, I warned you about this section of the street. I can well believe that it had its charms for 19th century Parisians on their Sunday afternoon strolls, but they didn't have scooters, trucks, and buses vrooming past them at 80 miles an hour. Pause however, if you dare, for a second or two at the traffic island in the middle for a last majestic view down the Champs-Élysées.

Walk toward the Arc de Triomphe (detail, opposite) and turn right at the next corner into avenue de Marigny, crossing over to the left side of the street.

You'll see the Théâtre Marigny on your left at the corner of avenue Gabriel and avenue de Marigny. In **How to Steal a Million**, however, that corner is home to the fictional Musée Kléber-Lafayette, which looks suspiciously like the Musée Jacquemart-André on boulevard Haussmann—where, indeed, the fictional museum's exteriors were shot. We passed it earlier in our walk. One might well ask: why on earth did the filmmakers find it necessary to invent a museum when Paris has over 100 of them, more than enough, one would think, for all the movies you would ever want to make—or see—that require a Paris museum location?

The answer is actually quite simple: It is vital to the plot of **How to Steal a Million** that the museum be located next door to the residence of someone powerful enough to tell the museum guards, after the umpteenth false burglar alarm, to turn off their alarm system for the night so he can get some sleep. Here we are approaching the home of someone who fits this bill exactly. Everything you see—or don't see—beyond the walls on your right belongs to the compound of the Palais de Élysée, the seat of the French President. And the building you'd be walking straight into at the end of the street—if the armed policemen in front were to let you—is another seat of state power, the French Ministry of the Interior on place Beauvau. You saw it—yes, this was the real thing—in **The Day of the Jackal** as the destination of a rather important letter from the Prime Minister, delivered by a policeman.

So it is in the company of the high and mighty that we conclude this walk. Instead of trying to walk into the Ministry of the Interior at the end of avenue de Marigny ...

... cross the rue du Faubourg-St-Honoré and walk to the left of the building into rue de Miromesnil. The nearest Métro station, also called Miromesnil (Lines 9, 13), is a couple of blocks ahead.

ARRONDISSEMENT: 18
DURATION: 3 to 3½ hours

Walk 4

Around Montmartre

From the Moulin Rouge up and down the narrow lanes and staircases of Montmartre, past Sacré-Coeur Basilica and the artists' square, with some breathtaking views over Paris.

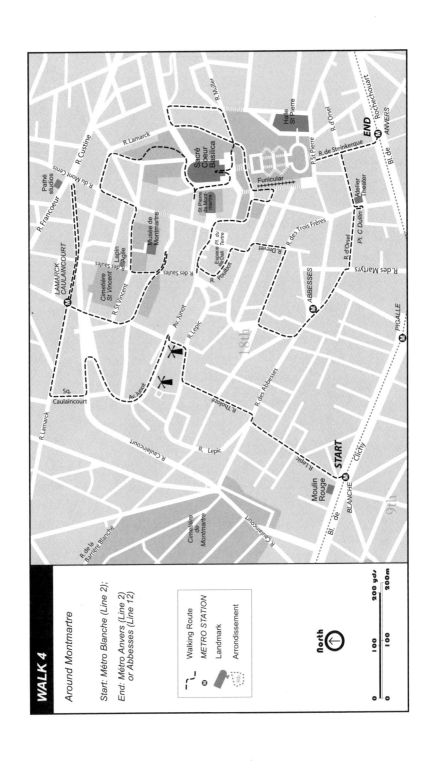

WALK 4

Around Montmartre

Start: Métro Blanche (Line 2);

End: Métro Anvers (Line 2)
or Abbesses (Line 12)

⌐┘ Walking Route

Ⓜ METRO STATION

▰ Landmark

⬚ Arrondissement

north
⊕

0 ————— 100 ————— 200 yds
0 ————— 100 ————— 200m

R. Mûller

Halle
St Pierre

R. d'Orsel

R. Custine

END
Ⓜ Rochechouart
ANVERS

R. Lamarck

Bl. de

P. St Pierre
R. de Steinkerque

R. Francoeur

R. du Mont Cenis

Pathé
studios

Sacré
Coeur
Basilica

St Pierre
de Mont-
martre

Funicular

R. des Trois Frères

R. Drevet

R. d'Orsel

Atelier
Theater

Pl. C Dullin

LAMARCK
CAULAINCOURT
Ⓜ

Musée de
Montmartre

Lapin
Agile

R. des Saules

Cimetière
St Vincent

R. St Vincent

R. des Saules

Espace Pl. du
Dali Tertre

R.
Poulbot

ABBESSES
Ⓜ

R. d'Orsel

R. des Martyrs

Sq.
Caulaincourt

Av. Junot

Av. Junot

R. Lepic

18th

R. Tholozé

R. des Abbesses

R. Lepic

PIGALLE
Ⓜ

R. Lamarck

R. Caulaincourt

R. Lepic

START
Ⓜ
BLANCHE

Clichy

R. de la
Barrière Blanche

Cimetière
de
Montmartre

R. Caulaincourt

Moulin
Rouge

Bl. de

9th

Take the Métro to station Blanche (Line 2). Right ahead of you, as you exit (the station has only one exit), you will see one of Paris nightlife's most famous landmarks …

… the Moulin Rouge, a byword for saucy pleasures and frilly excess ever since it opened in the late 19th century. It has given its name to two movies, the 1952 **Moulin Rouge** directed by John Huston and Baz Luhrmann's 2001 musical extravaganza. The former is a biopic of Toulouse-Lautrec in which Jose Ferrer somewhat misleadingly portrays the famous painter as a kind-hearted if slightly grumpy elderly uncle. The real Toulouse died at not quite 37, of alcoholism and syphilis, having toured from brothel to brothel for the last five years of his short life. Jean Renoir's **French Cancan** also pays homage to the place.

In fact, none of these three films was shot here—partly because the nightclub's historic *salle de danse* was destroyed in a 1910 fire. Luhrmann didn't even travel to France while making his **Moulin Rouge**: it was shot entirely on a sound stage in Australia. The jewel-encrusted elephant which features so prominently in his take on the place, however, was a real feature of the Moulin Rouge in its heyday. But don't bother to look for it in an area of the city that has lost none of its seediness but quite a lot of its charm.

Things brighten up almost immediately, however, when you …

… turn right into rue Lepic.

There is a daily street market here, picturesque even by Parisian standards and stretching all the way to the rue des Abbesses. This street market provides the setting for several moments in **Le fabuleux destin d'Amélie Poulain / Amélie**, most memorably the scene where she leads the blind beggar on a whirlwind tour of her neighborhood, or *quartier*, explaining all the sights in loving if slightly breathless detail. About halfway up the street, at no.15, you'll find the coffee shop where Amélie works as a waitress, the Café des Deux Moulins (photo page 280). Yes, this café really exists and yes, the scenes set in the film were actually shot here. The "Deux Moulins" (Two Windmills) was director Jean-Pierre Jeunet's "local" for years before he decided to give it a starring role in

Amélie. It got the part when he returned to his beloved Montmartre after shooting *Alien 4* in Hollywood. Sadly, the cigarette counter is gone—ripped out after the old owner cashed in and sold out, but the café preserves most of its other fixtures and all of its picturesque appeal.

If you look closely enough, you may recognize other establishments that appear in the movie, mainly in the tour Amélie gives the blind beggar:

- Right across the street at no. 18 you'll find the Boucherie des Gourmets, the place where the roast chicken, the baby, and the dog eye each other.
- The shop window of the bakery at no. 26 (Les Petits Mitrons) still displays the "Pierrot Gourmand" figurine that you see in the movie.
- The comics shop, Le Temps Libre, at no. 28, also puts in a cameo: the blind beggar stands in front it when Amélie approaches him.

Only the horse butcher's at no. 30, with the wooden, one-eared horse's head over the door, is gone. It's now home to a mobile phone shop.

Continue to the end of the street. Cross rue des Abbesses, turn right and then immediately left into rue Tholozé.

The small art-house cinema on your right (Studio 28 at no. 10) was at the heart of one of the most famous scandals in 20th century art when it hosted the premier of Salvador Dali's and Luis Buñuel's *L'âge d'or* in 1930. As word of the content got around, members of a right-wing league of Catholic students decided to protest, shouting, among other things, "kill the Jew"— rather incongruously, it appears, since both Dali and Buñuel were Catholic gentiles. The French Government, ever willing to stand up courageously for what is good and right in the face of determined opposition, reacted by banning the film—a decision it only rescinded in 1981.

The event is featured in the Henry Miller biopic *Henry and June*, but the scene was shot elsewhere. If you want to see the real interiors of Studio 28—which were designed by Jean Cocteau, whose color scheme has survived to this very day—watch the scene in **Amélie** (near the beginning) where she confides to us that she sometimes, during climactic movie sequences, turns around to look at the enraptured faces of the audience rather than at the screen. Studio 28 is also the place where **Amélie**'s director, Jean-Pierre Jeunet, held a gala-performance-cum-grand-reception for all the shopkeepers of the area who had helped him in the making of his film.

Continue up rue Tholozé.

Just ahead, you will see one of the two remaining windmills of Montmartre (those *deux moulins* Amélie's café is named after). The grounds around this windmill, the "Moulin de la Galette," were a famous meeting place for late-19th century working-class Parisians—just two blocks and a million miles away from the sophisticated blend of rich bourgeoisie, decadent aristocracy, and criminal low-life that patronized the Moulin Rouge. The entertainment on offer at the Moulin de la Galette was also far less sophisticated: no cancan dancers or cabaret acts, only a band that played simple dance hall tunes.

Nowadays, the Moulin de la Galette is mainly famous as the backdrop for some of the greatest ever impressionist paintings, with Renoir's *Bal au Moulin de la Galette* probably the best known of the bunch. You can see the painting in the Musée d'Orsay, which we'll pass in Walk 6.

At the end of rue Tholozé, walk up the stairs and rejoin rue Lepic, turning right to wind up the hill.

The only scene shot on-location for the Édith Piaf biopic **La Môme / La Vie en Rose** was filmed here. We see the young Piaf "bribe" a policeman (by singing his favorite tune) to let her ply her trade as a street singer, and she sings so well that the passersby literally shower her with coins. In the scene, Piaf—brilliantly played by Marion Cotillard, who won the Oscar for Best Actress for her performance, a rare accomplishment for a foreign actress in a foreign-language film—stands in front of house no. 77 on your left, and the camera pans down rue Lepic.

At the next corner, turn left into rue Girardon.

To your left, you see the other surviving windmill of Montmartre, Moulin Radet, which now houses a fairly posh restaurant.

Walk up rue Girardon to the next corner and cross the street into place Marcel-Aymé, on your right. Look for the statue that adorns the wall on the far side.

Whoever said that "monument" and "wit" are two mutually exclusive concepts—much like, to paraphrase Groucho Marx, "military intelligence"—obviously hasn't seen this piece. Commissioned by the city of Paris to commemorate the writer Marcel Aymé, who spent most of his creative life in the house to your left (no. 26), the sculpture portrays Aymé as his most famous creation, a man named Dutilleul who is the title character of *The Man Who Could Walk Through Walls*. The sculptor and famous movie actor, Jean Marais, another lifelong *Montmartrois*, captures the moment near the end of the short story when Dutilleul suddenly becomes the man who can no longer walk through walls and finds himself imprisoned in a garden wall on the rue Norvins forever. The story, by the way, was turned into a movie twice, in France in 1951 and in Germany in 1959.

Retrace your steps to the corner of rue Girardon and place Marcel-Aymé, the windmill and Cine 13 to your left.

Cine 13 is a small art house cinema run as a hobby by the French director Claude Lelouch (most famous for *Un homme et une femme / A Man and a Woman* more of which later). Lelouch used it as the meeting place ("Studio 5") for Édith Piaf and her lover, the boxer Marcel Carpentier, in his own Piaf biopic, the 1983 **Édith et Marcel / Edith and Marcel**.

Continue straight into avenue Junot (and don't let the "Impasse Girardon" street sign confuse you).

Behind the wall on your left, some of the once-loved and now-forgotten movie and stage actors of the *grande nation* live out their remaining days in an Old People's Home run by an actors' charity. You won't find any Delons or Belmondos of the French cinema here, but some of the building's inhabitants are still famous enough that no actors' names appear on the doorbells, only the names of their individual apartments.

What is now avenue Junot was, until the 1920s, Paris's largest and most notoriously lawless squatter area, the so-called *maquis* or "bush." You can get an idea of what the place once looked like by checking out the nostalgic postcards that the local newsagents often carry. Proving that they have a keen sense of humor, property developers have since turned this street into Montmartre's most expensive and exclusive neighborhood— the perfect environment, in other words, for the wealthy gambler in Jean-Pierre Melville's **Bob le flambeur.** (Check the prices in the window of the estate agent *Junot Investissements*, a little further down the road, if you don't believe me.) "Bob" (played by Roger Duchesne) lives in the curved section of the street, on the right-hand side at no. 24. On your way, keep an eye out for the house at no. 15, which was built by the famous modernist architect Adolf "ornament is crime" Loos.

On the other side of the street (no. 39), at the corner where the avenue meets rue Juste-Métivier), you can see the entrance to the (fictional) Hôtel Alsina, where Francois Truffaut's alter ego Antoine Doinel works as a very incompetent night porter in **Baisers volés / Stolen Kisses.** The building actually houses some fairly luxurious flats.

At the end of avenue Junot, continue straight ahead down the tree-lined path past the statue, and cross rue Caulaincourt (the street on your left) at the traffic lights right next to the cast-iron advertising column. A few steps on your right ...

... you can see the famous restaurant Chez Ginette, for many years run by a rather resolute lady "with a past" and a penchant for handsome young men; she was known to pinch male customers' behinds if she fancied them. Chez Ginette (called "La Pergola" in the movie) is the epicenter of the very successful 1996 French movie, **L'appartement** from the moment when Vincent Cassel thinks he recognizes the voice of a former mistress coming from another room. The mistress, incidentally, is played by Monica Bellucci, Cassel's wife in real life. The film was remade by Hollywood as *Wicker Park* in 2004.

Walk down the stairway to your left, cross the street (rue Lamarck), and turn around ...

... to have a better view of the Lamarck-Caulaincourt Métro station (photo next page) now in front of you. This station, arguably the most picturesque in the whole of Paris, has been used in many French movies including **Amélie.** This is where she eventually leads the blind beggar at the end of the

whirlwind tour through her *quartier*, leaving the beggar rightfully confused. How did I get here, his bewildered expression seems to ask, all the way from the rue Lepic street market—in the space of a single shot?

Two blocks to your left, by the way, where rue Caulaincourt meets rue Francoeur at 6 rue Francoeur, …

… you'll find Pathé Cinema's famous rue Francoeur studios, nowadays a film school. Most of the French movie classics of the 1930s and '40s were edited and prepared for release here, among them Marcel Carné's films, *Les enfants du paradis / Children of Paradise* (1945) and *Hôtel du Nord* (1938).

If you fancy a short break before moving on, have a quick coffee at the bar of Le Refuge behind you. It's a wonderful little place.

Retrace your steps now up the stairs of Métro Lamarck to rejoin rue Caulaincourt. Cross the street at the traffic lights in front of you and walk up the left side of the place Constantin-Pecqueur, leaving the little garden and the war monument at its end to your right and passing rue St-Vincent on your left. Climb the stairway ahead of you (stay on the right side), and once you have reached the top—and taken a break on the park bench should you feel the need …

… you may catch your breath while marvelling at one of the city's—and the world's—great picture postcard views, complete with winding village streets, ivy-covered house fronts, and the onion-shaped towers of Sacré-Coeur in the distance. You'll see this view, used more or less as a beauty shot, at the beginning of **Paris, je t'aime** where Bruno Podalydès's grumpy driver is looking for love and a parking place, not necessarily in that order, and eventually finds both a little bit further down the hill.

Turn left into rue de l'Abreuvoir (2) and follow it through to the end.

The house on the corner to your left, Le Maison Rose, once inhabited by the painter Maurice Utrillo, is the building where the cartoon existentialist Flauster holds his party in **Funny Face** (attempting to seduce Audrey Hepburn until Fred Astaire tells him where he can stick his beret). If you cross the street and stand on the other side of rue des Saules, you are in the position of the camera for the scene when Astaire and Kay Thompson arrive in their three-wheeled car, in essence a small motorcycle with a roof, which was very popular in post-war Europe. The contemporary American audience, on the other hand, must have thought it was hallucinating.

Walk into rue Cortot, which is the extension of rue de l'Abreuvoir across rue des Saules, and go as far as the museum of Montmartre, which was once the home of the painter Auguste Renoir. Now stop and turn around.

This is the exterior view you get of the place Woody Allen's narrator-daughter refers to as his "James Bond fantasy of a Parisian apartment" in **Everyone Says I Love You.** But closer analysis reveals that the interior scenes could not possibly have been shot here or in any apartment in this street. The houses with a view of Sacré-Coeur are not high enough to allow their occupants to see over the roofs on the other side, and the angles don't match. More of that later. First …

... retrace your steps down rue Cortot and turn right at the corner into rue des Saules As you approach the next corner ...

... you will, on your right-hand side, see the last remaining vineyard of Paris. The grapes are harvested on the second weekend of October, amid some great media brouhaha. The wine is auctioned off for charity and reputed to be undrinkable. The saying goes that it is so sour that you—pardon my French—"drink a quart and piss a gallon."

When you reach the corner ...

... look briefly left into rue St-Vincent. This view is the opening shot of **Le fabuleux destin d'Amélie Poulain / Amélie**.

Now cross rue des Saules ...

... and take a closer look at the Lapin Agile, in front of you, one of Montmartre's oldest cabarets. This quaint little 19th century building—as seen from the other side of rue des Saules—has been used by Jean-Pierre Jeunet in his follow-up to *Amélie*, **Un long dimanche de fiançailles / A Very Long Engagement**, where it provides the setting for the Jodie Foster flashback sequence. It is to the Lapin Agile, patronized and painted by such artists as, among others, Picasso and Utrillo, that we owe the old chestnut of "artists covering their bill with their paintings." This actually seems to have happened once or twice in the Lapin's heyday.

Continue into rue St-Vincent, leaving the vineyard to your right and eventually behind.

No. 12, the last house on the left before the stairway, is where Debra Winger lives in **Forget Paris**. We see her enter the door.

Now take a closer look at the stairway to your left before moving on.

If you have seen the movie **Head in the Clouds**, this vista—with the view over (northern) Paris framed between the redbrick house on the left and the whitewashed school building on the right—may look strangely familiar to you. That is because it is used, thanks to back-projection, to provide the neighborhood for Charlize Theron's "Montmartresque" Parisian flat. All the scenes around her home were actually shot on a set, but director John Duigan used the view you see before you to instill a bit of Parisian street cred. You get a good look at it in the scene where Stuart Townsend comes back from Spain and meets Charlize Theron in the street, and she just looks at her former lover and walks away without giving him as much as a smile.

Now walk down the stairway and follow the street (rue du Mont-Cenis) past the school building on your right.

The schoolyard—which you can't see from the outside—was used for the black-and-white flashback sequence in **Amélie** where little Dominique Bredoteau, the boy whose box of toys Amélie discovers behind her bathroom tiles, quite literally "loses his marbles."

Walk to the end of the street where it meets rue Lamarck.

The small court straight ahead of you, on the other side of rue Lamarck, is the place where the bench was put up for Martine Dugowson's **Mina Tannenbaum**, a French "chick flick" about the friendship between two women. Much of post-war French history provides the background for this 1994 film.

Turn to your right into rue Lamarck and continue along until you reach the Italian restaurant on the next corner. Now turn right towards the curved house on the corner of rue Becquerel and rue de la Bonne.

This is the place where the homicidal albino monk stays in **The Da Vinci Code**. Director Ron Howard gives us a view of his second-floor window with Sacré-Coeur in the back.

Walk over and stand right in front of the ground-floor corner window of the building …

… and then look across the street for more **Mina Tannenbaum**. The top of the stairway on the other side of the street is the place where the two friends first meet as young girls, on May 2, 1968, pulling their mothers away in opposite directions. A famous date in contemporary French history, May 2 was the start of the 1968 rebellion, which we talk about in Walk 2 (see page 60).

You can cross to the other side of the street to enjoy the view over the rooftops of Paris, but don't expect to see any famous sights. You'll be looking at the unfashionable working-class north of Paris and some of its notoriously ugly suburbs.

Turn right now into rue de la Bonne …

… from which you have a magnificent view of Sacré-Coeur.

Just before you reach the stairway at the bottom …

… look for the *pétanque* playing ground on your right and a little bit of local color. If you are lucky, a game will be going on and you will be able to watch the French "national sport" in action. Although, truth be told, Parisians are normally far too busy to play and leave the game to the lazy Southerners. The rules of pétanque are easy to follow and very similar to those of English lawn bowling and Italian *bocce*.

The Story Behind Sacré-Coeur

I will make it brief: For much of the 19th century, something like a Cold Civil War was fought in France between progressives (post-revolutionary, republican) and conservatives (monarchist and Catholic). When Paris was under siege by the Prussians in 1871, the progressives took their chance and established the Commune de Paris. The rule of this Commune—short, ferocious, and bloody—culminated in the lynching of a couple of old generals in the progressive stronghold of Montmartre. The exact spot is marked by a signpost across the street (at the blank wall), which provides some information about the event.

Once the old order had been (inevitably) re-established, many people on the right felt that a symbolic act of penitence would be in order. Eventually, the Basilica of the Sacré-Coeur, visible from almost anywhere in the

Walk up the stairs, staying on the left side. Once you have reached the top, turn immediately to your left into the Parc de la Tourlure (which is well-equipped with park benches should you like to take a rest while admiring the scenery).

This park, with its "hanging gardens" arbor, appears in both **Forget Paris** (twice) and Sydney Pollack's 1995 **Sabrina**. In **Forget Paris**, Billy Crystal and Debra Winger are first shown together, walking under the hanging gardens you see ahead of you and enjoying the view of Sacré-Coeur in the background. Later, after their separation, Debra Winger is shown alone here in a rather more downbeat mood. In **Sabrina**, Fanny Bryant and Julia Ormond can be seen at the end of the hanging gardens with Sacré-Coeur providing a majestic backdrop.

Walk through the arbor past the green roundhouse (public toilet) and leave the Parc through the exit immediately on your right.

You are now standing right behind Sacré-Coeur, one of the "troika" (with the Eiffel Tower and the Arc de Triomphe) of famous Parisian landmarks and used as such in countless "establishing shots." In fact, you are standing on the very spot where the events unfolded that led to Sacré-Coeur's construction (see below).The building itself is generally disliked by people who pride themselves on their architectural taste. Adolf Hitler, for instance.

Île-de-France, was planted in the middle of Communard Montmartre, a powerful symbol of the triumph of the establishment over the defeated upstarts on the left. Which is all a little bit, if you want a modern-day equivalent, as if the state government of Alabama had reacted to the Birmingham race riots back in the Sixties by planting a grandiose Confederate Hall of Fame right in the middle of a black neighborhood.

There was nothing the "Reds" in the Montmartre town hall could do—or make that *almost* nothing. They decided to thumb their noses at the forces of the restoration by naming the street right in front of the church after a notorious freethinker and atheist, the Chevalier de la Barre, who was executed in 1766 for blasphemy—for shouting obscenities at a Catholic procession among other things. Which is a little bit akin to giving our hypothetical Confederate Hall of Fame the address, no. 1 Tupac Shakur Street.

Hitler invaded Sacré-Coeur on the one and only afternoon he ever spent in Paris—no doubt much to the terror of the elderly concierges and chambermaids who tend to populate the church at those hours. He is said to have disliked it intensely. A kind of miracle, then, that it is still standing.

Now walk around Sacré-Coeur, keeping the church building to your left, until rue du Chevalier-de-la-Barre veers sharply off to the right, immediately in front of Montmartre's other church, the Église Saint-Pierre. Turn right here and stop just before you reach the corner with rue du Mont-Cenis.

This is the exact spot where Tyrone Power dissuades his friend from drinking goat's milk straight off the goat in **The Sun Also Rises**, a small homage to Montmartre's rural past, one assumes. The commercial fortunes of the itinerant goat milk vendors have since taken a sharp turn for the worse.

Retrace your steps back to the corner and continue on your way around Sacré-Coeur, first turning right into rue du Cardinal-Guibert, as it is called from here on, and then left to reach the main portal, with its magnificent view of Paris spreading out below you.

On the stairs leading up to the main entrance, Jet Li lights the candles and says the nocturnal Kaddish for his dead mentor in **Kiss of the Dragon**. This is also a good moment to step in if you want to take a look at the church from the inside.

Coming out of the main entrance, turn sharply to your left and look for the staircase (between the kiosk and the stand for the floodlights) that leads down to the street in front of the church. Walk down the stairs and cross rue Lamarck …

… and you will find yourself standing in the very spot where Bridget Fonda hands the tapes to Jet Li in **Kiss of the Dragon**. In truth, the scene is a bit of a disaster, and you can see exactly how it came about. Having just finished the take in front of the Basilica, they must have thought: now that we're here, let's make more use of this picturesque Montmartre setting. For instance, wouldn't it look really dandy to have Bridget hand Jet Li the tapes on this beautiful staircase, with nocturnal Paris at the lovers' feet and street lamps engulfing them in a warm glimmer like distant stars? On screen, however, nocturnal Paris is invisible due to darkness, the street lamps are blurry and out of focus, and the only background you really see is the blank wall of the apartment building to your left. They could just as well have shot the scene in a dimly lit housing project in East L.A.

Walk down rue Maurice-Utrillo (the stairway) which heads downhill right in front of you and pause when you are about halfway down.

This is the camera position for the scene in the 1995 **Sabrina** where Sabrina is shown writing her last letter home before her return. The café where she sits is the *Au Soleil de la Butte* at the bottom of the stairs (photo page 6), and the camera slowly zooms in on her table. It is an important shot in the movie's narrative: this is last view of Paris we'll see for a while, and the image is meant to reverberate for the rest of the movie whenever Paris is referred to in the dialogue or otherwise. So the producers must have taken great care to come up with an image of Paris that combined all of the city's unique beauty and charm. This is what they came up with, and I think it is perfect—from the garden on your right and the stairway under your feet, to the lampposts and the street behind them that veers off into the distance.

Continue down rue Utrillo. When you reach the picturesque little area right at the bottom …

… turn around to have another look. From about where you are standing, the camera catches Fred Astaire very briefly walking down this stairway in **Funny Face** and, further up the stairs, Mathieu Kassovitz having a conversation with **Amélie**'s helpful colleague from the Deux Moulins.

Take a few steps forward and look into rue Paul-Albert on your left.

The pickpocket in **French Kiss**, who steals Meg Ryan's purse in the hotel and who is then visited by her and Kevin Kline, has an apartment on this street. We see Kline and Ryan walking up rue Paul-Albert from about halfway down the street all the way to the triangular corner of rue Muller, across from you. There Ryan angrily throws away the money Kline has just forced upon her—only to retrieve it, on second thought, a few steps later, when Kline has moved away in the other direction.

Turn left and cross rue Paul-Albert, continuing on the right side of Paul-Albert until you are even with house no. 12.

Now turn around and look back in the direction of the pretty little square you just came from. Take a particularly close look at the bar-restaurant on the corner. This building was transformed into a dance club for **The Truth About Charlie** (interiors were, of course, shot elsewhere), and the scene where the black girl is run over by a car on leaving the "cabaret" was shot on the intersection of rue Paul-Albert and rue Muller. The assassin's car crashes into the shop window of another bar-restaurant underneath the rue Muller street sign.

Follow rue Paul-Albert to rue du Chevalier-de-la-Barre, where the street ends, and cast a brief glimpse to your right at the building at no. 18.

Its ground floor, itself a former restaurant in a perpetual state of redecoration, was used as the home of the (fictitious) Pizzeria 2000 in the movie **Le Nouveau Jean-Claude / The New Jean-Claude**. The movie, written and directed by Didier Tronchet, is based on Tronchet's own comic strip, which regularly appeared in *Fluide Glacial*, a kind of French *MAD* magazine.

Turn left. The street corner ahead of you, where rue du Chevalier-de-la-Barre joins rue Lamarck in front of the stairway ...

... is where the lengthy dream sequence in Claude Lelouch's **Un homme et une femme / A Man and a Woman** was shot. Anouk Aimée has been told by Jean-Louis Trintignant that he has an "unusual" job and "earns a lot of money"—whereupon she imagines him as a pimp who receives the money from his whores right here on this crossing. He is, as we later find out, a race car driver.

Cross rue Lamarck ...

... and take a closer look at the stairway in front of you, which leads up to Sacré-Coeur. Or rather: have a closer look at the stones to either side of the stairway. Little lights have been inserted in between the slabs. They mirror the stars over Paris when they are lit at night. This work of "street art" was conceived by a former assistant to the film director and poet, Jean Cocteau.

Stay on the right side of the street while turning left into rue Lamarck.

No. 14, the second house past the nursery school, is where Anouk Aimée lives in **Un homme et une femme / A Man and a Woman**. We get a good view of the entrance door when Jean-Louis Trintignant drives her home.

Continue along rue Lamarck and follow it through the 90-degree turn it makes in front of the church.

The view over Paris that now opens up in front of you is also the opening shot of Jean-Pierre Melville's **Bob le flambeur**.

Cross the street ...

... so you have a better view of the place where Kevin Kline realizes in **French Kiss** that the necklace he wants is not, after all, in the plant he has just recovered. The scene is set to your left, just off the street in the Parc Willette, under the lamppost—on the left side of the church as you face the view.

This last stretch of rue du Cardinal-Dubois (which is an extension of rue Lamarck) also provides the background for the conversation between Mathieu Kassovitz and Gina, the other waitress at the "Deux Moulins," in **Amélie**. The two of them turn from rue du Cardinal-Dubois into rue Maurice-Utrillo (the stairway you've just left behind) while discussing the shortest route into Audrey Tautou's drawers.

Walk straight on ...

… while admiring the magnificent view over Paris that's also enjoyed by Tyrone Power and his friend in **The Sun Also Rises** (they are walking one level below you, near the balustrade).

Pass the group of Japanese tourists freshly out of the Funiculaire cable railway …

… which has saved them the trouble of walking up all those stairs to the top of the hill for the price of a Métro ticket, plus their wallets, cameras and passports. The Funiculaire is the favorite spot of Parisian pickpockets.

Walk down the stairway immediately past the Funiculaire station— called rue Foyatier—and take the first turn to your right into rue Gabrielle.

The little stairway you are facing provides the setting for the end of the opening sequence of the comedy caper **Les ripoux / My New Partner,** a.k.a. *Le Cop.* Directed by Claude Zidi, it was one of the most successful French films of the 1980s—and one of the few comedies ever to win the *César,* the French Oscar, for best film of the year.

Philippe Noiret plays a middle-aged cop who is "on the take," welcoming graft from petty crooks and thieves all over the immigrant's quarter east of Montmartre. When he and his partner in corruption follow a crooked businessman to his garage, their plan suddenly begins to unravel. Noiret can only save himself by literally shooting himself in the foot and letting his partner take the rap. He is eventually arrested at the place where the little stairway leads up to rue Gabrielle. The garage was located in the building to your right, which is actually a former academy for street sweepers: a worthy subject for a movie in its own right, no doubt. (*Street Sweeper Academy 7,* anyone?)

Walk up the little stairway and, just ahead, take the long stairway to your right up rue Chappe. (Don't you wish you had brought your own private stairlift? But this is the last stairway you have to climb— promise!) Pause at the second landing, across from the park on your left, which is a little open-air theater.

This stairway is used in both **Funny Face**, where we see a very dapper Fred Astaire sprinting up it, and **Forget Paris**, where a more downbeat Debra Winger is shown—after her separation from Billy Crystal—shlepping herself up the last stairs to rue St-Éleuthère.

Before you move on, turn around to enjoy the view over the rooftops of Montmartre to the city's distant skyline. In addition to being a pretty panorama in its own right, this is exactly the view we get in the final scene of **An American in Paris**, both when Gene Kelly's eyes follow Leslie Caron for what seems to be a good-bye for good (only to see her return a few moments later) and when the two lovers celebrate their reunion with a passionate embrace before they walk hand in hand into the night.

The shot looks so real that I begin to doubt what I've always read about the making of the film (and repeated for your benefit in Walk 2). All the books on the subject say that the entire movie was shot on a Hollywood sound stage, where the original settings were more or less faithfully re-created. But if you compare the view you're seeing with the film's final tableau, the similarities seem too striking to believe that we're merely seeing a re-creation in the film. Take the arch-shaped windows of the building on your left, for instance. Why would anybody have gone to the trouble of re-creating *those*? And if they had re-created the view in the studio, would they have been able to resist the temptation of putting in an Eiffel Tower?

I, for one, suspect that this scene wasn't shot in Hollywood at all but on location in Paris—probably by a second unit using body doubles—and that the material was later intercut with close-ups of the stars. Take a close look the next time you watch the movie and see if you agree.

Now continue up the stairs and turn left at the top.

On your left, another spectacular view is slowly opening up, this time featuring the Eiffel Tower. This view, too, has been used in countless postcards (often with a pair of smoochy cats in the foreground) and quite a few movies as well. In **The Bourne Identity**, for example, you see Paris at night, with the Eiffel Tower shimmering in the distance and two windows lit in one of the houses nearby, before the filmmakers cut to Treadstone's offices. The other exterior Treadstone shots, however, were shot in the Marais, which we visit in Walk 2.

*Follow the bend in the street, leaving Treadstone and the smoochy
cats safely behind you, and then cross the street …*

… to have a closer look at the iron railings just past the next crossing.
Early on in **An American in Paris**, Gene Kelly is shown selling his
paintings to a rich American lady, but the place de Tertre, where most
of the street painters actually ply their trade, is only "hinted at" in the
background. Now this is a scene that was definitely and undeniably shot
on that MGM sound stage in Hollywood, which is why this is as close as
you get to actually standing in Gene Kelly's outdoor atélier.

> *Continue on the right side of the street until you reach St-Pierre
> de Montmartre, Montmartre's old parish church, and turn left
> into the place de Tertre, also known the world over as the "artists'
> square."*

If, however, you are looking for artists of the "young and budding" variety whose works will one day be worth millions of dollars (keep on dreaming), you should avoid the painters who are exhibiting their works in the stalls here. They tend to be well-established, middle-aged French commercial artists, licensed by the Mairie de Paris (City Hall). Patronize instead one of the portrait painters you see walking around the side streets with a sketchpad and a set of crayons. They're younger and cheaper, too, although they are more likely to come from the Ukraine these days than from the U.S. of A.

Continue straight, with the place de Tertre on your left side, into rue Norvins …

… following in the footsteps of Audrey Hepburn and Fred Astaire on their nightly stroll in **Funny Face**. The restaurant La Mère Catherine, on your right, served as the blueprint for **Ninotchka**'s Chez le Père Mathieu. You may remember the scene: Melvyn Douglas falls off his chair to make Greta Garbo laugh. Director Ernst Lubitsch had pictures of the Mère Catherine sent to Hollywood, where the interiors were painstakingly reproduced.

Walk to the end of the street (the junction with rue des Saules, on your right) past the bakery on your left, and then turn around.

You are now looking at the restaurant Le Consulat, one of the landmarks of Montmartre (photo page 95). It was used in both **Everyone Says I Love You** and **Forget Paris** (Debra Winger dines here alone after her separation from Billy Crystal). It was also reconstructed for Doris Day in **April in Paris**. (April on the Warner Bros. sound stage, actually.) One word of advice, however: You may find Doris Day's experience of a rather raw April in Paris confirmed—April in Winnipeg, more like—but do not expect the April breeze to blow autumn leaves into your *café au lait* as it did into hers. For that, you will have to spend your April in Capetown or Brisbane.

The street to the left of Le Consulat is the rue St-Rustique (opposite above) where Audrey Hepburn sings her part of the "Bonjour Paris" number in **Funny Face**. You may remember that each of the three American tourists in that film is associated with a certain area of Paris, Kay Thompson with the posh shops of the rue de la Paix, Astaire with the classy and stylish Champs-Élysées, and Audrey Hepburn, the kookie librarian, with Montmartre—which happens to rhyme with Jean-Paul Sartre, fortunately (for the purpose of the song), because she is about to meet his alter ego a few yards down the road. In real life, however, the leading French intellectuals would never reside in Montmartre. They are, after all, French, therefore more practical than romantic, and they prefer to live on the Left Bank, within walking distance of the universities where they teach.

Retrace your steps back down rue Norvins, and take the first street to the right, rue Poulbot.

The second house on the right side (no. 4) is the building where Woody Allen's "Bond's fantasy of a Parisian apartment" in **Everyone Says I Love You** (mentioned on page 103) is actually located, directly under the roof.

Follow the street past the Dali museum to the place du Calvaire.

The view on your right, onto rue Gabrielle below, is admired by Natalie Portman and Lukas Haas in **Everyone Says I Love You**. It also provides the opening shot in **Paris vu par… / Paris Seen By…**, a 1960s' collection of Paris-based vignettes by six different directors.

The place du Calvaire and the restaurant to your left provide the backdrop for the big World War II (WWII) victory party thrown by James Caan and his jazz band in Claude Lelouch's ambitious epic **Les Uns et les Autres / Bolero**.

More famously, the house on your right, 1 place du Calvaire, may be said to have "inspired" the final scene in **An American in Paris**. During the New Year's Eve party, Gene Kelly stands forlornly on the balcony, gazing at the rooftops of Paris. There can't be many balconies in the city of lights that would give you a better view—or would have a room behind them big enough to host a ball with a cast of thousands.

The scene in **An American in Paris** continues on the stairway of rue Chappe, which we have just visited. But before we move on, take another look at that house on the right. Constructed by an artist at the turn of the 20th century, the house is now owned by a Swiss pharma zillionaire. Its garden statues, which you can glimpse through the hedge from the street level downstairs, are original works by Niki de Saint-Phalle, who created the statues for the fountain next to the Centre Pompidou.

Now walk down the stairway (called rue du Calvaire) to the left of the house, turn left at the bottom into rue Gabrielle, and take the next street on your right (rue Drevet). Cross rue Berthe and walk to the top of the stairway.

You are now in the exact place where Robert De Niro stands at the beginning of **Ronin**. Although you can't see it from here, the crane shot takes in Sacré-Coeur in one sweeping movement and then follows De Niro down the stairs to the Irish pub (which is actually, as I write this, a restaurant with specialties from Madagascar). There he encounters the other "drifting and masterless samurais," or "ronin." (The term "ronin" for the film's highly skilled, but apparently unprincipled mercenaries derives from feudal Japan). De Niro and Jean Reno meet again in the final scene of the film, this time in broad daylight, and Jean Reno speaks the film's final lines as he walks up these stairs and away from the camera.

The same stairway is used to introduce the rue Lepic street scene in the Édith Piaf biopic **La Môme / La Vie en Rose** (see above). A title over a shot down rue Drevet, the place where the adolescent Piaf makes her entrance into the French capital, identifies the time and place as "Paris Montmartre, October 1935."

Walk to the bottom of the stairs. Turn right and walk down rue des Trois-Frères to the next corner, the junction with rue Androuet.

The grocery shop in front of you on your right (photo next page), actually named Chez Ali, has become world-famous under its assumed name, Maison Collignon—for the simple reason that this is where **Amélie** does her shopping. The shopkeeper has actually preserved the look given to his premises by *Amélie*'s art directors and has even kept the Collignon sign over his entrance door. Take a look at the international press clippings in his window, and you'll learn that Monsieur Ali has also used the movie as a springboard for a showbiz career of his own: he's released a record with old-style French songs. Do not hesitate to inquire within.

The next door down, no. 56 rue des Trois-Frères, by the way, is the place where Monsieur Collignon lives. We see **Amélie** open the door on her way to his flat, where she tries to drive him insane by exchanging the door handles, etc. However, all of the interior scenes were actually shot in a studio in Germany.

> *Walk on to the next corner and turn left into rue Ravignan, pausing first …*

… to take a quick glimpse to the right into the leafy and romantic place Émile-Goudeau and, to the left, at the Bateau-Lavoir, the place many art historians consider the cradle of cubism. The Bateau-Lavoir was an abandoned piano factory that was converted at the end of the 19th century into cheap lodgings and studios for artists. Many famous painters lived and worked there, none more famous than Pablo Picasso. In the summer of 1907, Picasso locked himself away from the world for several weeks in the Bateau Lavoir to complete his first true masterpiece *Les Desmoiselles d'Avignon*.

While you can't visit the Bateau-Lavoir because it still serves as a hostel for artists, you'll find copies of a few of the "locally produced" paintings—including Picasso's *Desmoiselles*—along with photographs from the period in a display window, giving you the opportunity to sample the atmosphere, so to speak.

If you'd like to rest for a few minutes before the final stage of this walk, the place Goudeau is a lovely spot to take a breather.

When you're rested, walk down rue Ravignan and turn left into rue des Abbesses at the end of the street. After about 50 yards, you'll reach the place des Abbesses, the picturesque focus of this lively area at the foot of the hill.

Immediately to your left on entering the square, you may see the spot where **Amélie** buys her newspapers—but don't look for the kiosk. It was only set up for the film.

Stay on the right side of the square, passing the beautiful Abbesses Métro station entrance.

One of only two Métro entrances that have been preserved in their totality, canopy and all, the Métro Abbesses entrance provides the backdrop for one of Kevin Kline's and Meg Ryan's witty exchanges in **French Kiss**. This time, it is all about virility in general and Kline's in particular, which Ryan is questioning while they are on the way to challenge the pickpocket who has stolen her passport.

Continue along rue des Abbesses until you reach rue des Martyrs. Cross it and head straight into rue d'Orsel (pharmacy to the left, bakery to the right). Follow this street for a block—past the school building on your left —toward the place Charles-Dullin.

The main building on the square, the Théâtre de l'Atelier, which you can see from the far end of rue d'Orsel, provided the blueprint for the Théâtre de Montmartre in François Truffaut's most successful film ever, **Le dernier métro / The Last Metro**, winner of a record 13 *Césars*. The film's story was inspired by events that actually took place at this theater during WWII. Most of the exteriors, however, were shot at the Théâtre St-Georges in the 9th arrondissement, half a mile or so to the south.

Turn right into rue Dancourt before you reach the square. After a few steps, when you're roughly even with the restaurant on the corner of rue Dancourt and the place Charles-Dullin, you will find a fenced-in compound on your right called villa Dancourt.

This is the place where the music publisher in **Trois couleurs: Bleu / Three Colors: Blue** has his office. Juliette Binoche visits it to recover her dead husband's composition, only to throw it into a passing garbage truck as she leaves the office. When Binoche leaves the office, we get a nice view of the square.

Go back past the theater and continue down rue d'Orsel. Turn left at the next corner into rue de Steinkerque.

The building on your left at the end of the street is where young Antoine Doinel lives in **Baisers volés / Stolen Kisses** and where he gets a visit from the owner of the shoe shop (Delphine Seyrig), on whom he has such a terrible crush. The camera pans to the window on the top floor, so we are to assume his flat is there. Later on, we see one of his fellow private detectives shadowing the shoe shop owner outside the building, on the other side of the street just under the carousel in place St-Pierre.

Oh, yes, and that church on top of the hill is Sacré-Coeur again—nice view, isn't it, and used for establishing shots of Montmartre and Paris itself in countless movies.

This is also the place where one of the key scenes in **Amélie** is set, i.e. Amélie's rendezvous with the hapless Mathieu Kassovitz. It starts at the foot of the carousel, where she phones him to send him all the way up to the church. The pay phone she uses was set up just for the movie.

If you have any energy left, you may take the path on your right, following in Kassovitz's footsteps, but don't expect any arrows, pigeons, and "living statues" to show you the way. From here on, you are on your own because this is where the walk ends. The nearest Métro station is Anvers (Line 2), about two blocks away. Walk back down rue Steinkerque to the boulevard de Rochechouart. The station entrance is to your left in the median.

Alternatively, if you have the energy, you may want to trace your steps back to the station Abbesses (Line 12) …

… whose platform puts in a performance in **Amélie.** Here Amélie drops a few coins into the hat of the blind beggar with the gramophone. She also sees Kassovitz for the first time here. He's busy digging discarded passport pictures out from under the floor of a photo booth, which, needless to say, was only placed here for the shoot.

Two final notes: Every year, about fifty feature films are shot in Paris, and most of them have at least one street scene set in Montmartre. Add to that the large number of TV series (mainly French), commercials (mainly Japanese—they seem to love the place), and countless fashion shoots that are shot here, and you can be assured that there is always a good chance that, on any day in Montmartre, you may walk into something big and glamorous. Be on the lookout for the tell-tale signs: not just cameras, but also cables, lights, large catering vehicles, and yet larger trailers—or even the little notes that producers stick to the doors of apartment houses, warning the inhabitants that a shoot is scheduled.

You should also keep your eyes open for celebrities. Two of the country's most famous movie directors, Claude Lelouch and Jean-Pierre Jeunet, live in Montmartre (no, I will not tell you exactly where, but you passed their homes on this walk). Both are well-known for their chummy relationships with their leading actors and frequently invite them to their homes, for social occasions as well as informal rehearsals and readings. And you just might come across a beautiful young woman, possibly carrying a garden gnome in her arms. If so, tackle her. It could be the beginning of a beautiful friendship. It worked for Mathieu Kassovitz, after all.

ARRONDISSEMENTS: 8, 7, 16, 15
DURATION: 3 hours and 15 minutes without an extended stay at either the Eiffel Tower or its gardens. Subtract 20 to 25 minutes if you don't take the suggested detours.
Note: Don't take this walk on a wet day. It would be muddy in spots.

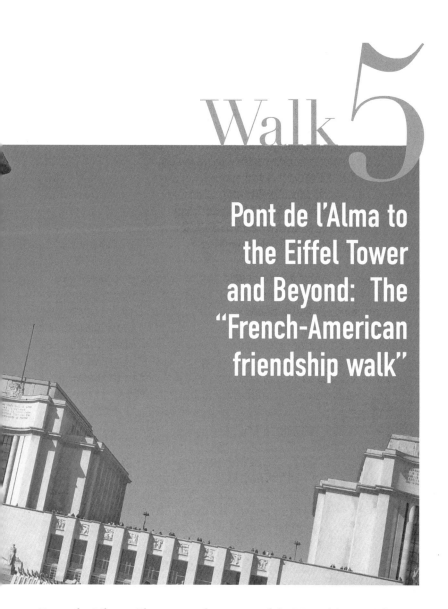

Walk 5

Pont de l'Alma to the Eiffel Tower and Beyond: The "French-American friendship walk"

From the Liberty Flame past the square of the United States, Thomas Jefferson square, and the George Washington Memorial to the Eiffel Tower and the Statue of Liberty itself.

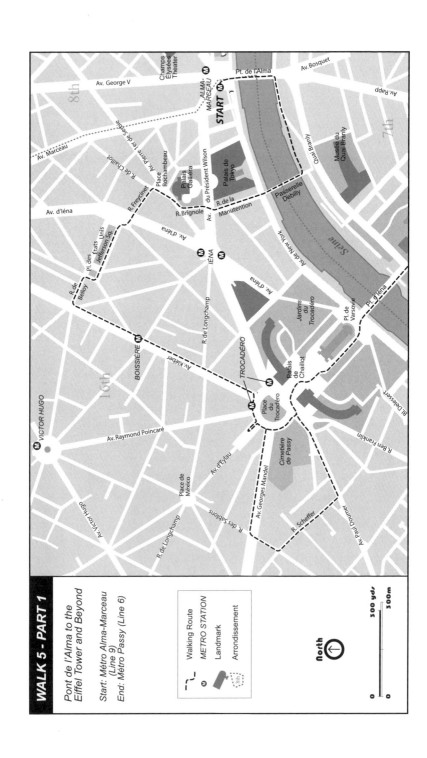

WALK 5 - PART 1

Pont de l'Alma to the
Eiffel Tower and Beyond

Start: Métro Alma-Marceau
(Line 9)
End: Métro Passy (Line 6)

Walking Route
METRO STATION
Landmark
Arrondissement

north

500 yds
500 m

0
0

Map labels

Av. George V
Champs Elysées Theater
Pt. de l'Alma
Av. Bosquet
8th
ALMA-MARCEAU
START
Av. Rapp
Av. Marceau
R. de Chaillot
R. Pierre 1er de Serbie
Place Rochambeau
Palais Galliéra
Av. du Président Wilson
Palais de Tokyo
Quai Branly
Musée du Quai Branly
7th
R. Freycinet
R. Brignole
Av. de la Manutention
Passerelle Debilly
Av. d'Iéna
États Unis
Pl. des
Jefferson Sq.
Av. d'Iéna
IÉNA
Seine
R. de Belloy
Av. de New York
R. de Longchamp
Av. d'Iéna
Jardins du Trocadéro
Pl. de Varsovie
Pt. d'Iéna
BOISSIÈRE
Av. Kléber
TROCADÉRO
Palais de Chaillot
16th
Bl. Delessert
VICTOR HUGO
Av. Raymond Poincaré
Place du Trocadéro
Cimetière de Passy
R. Ben Franklin
Av. Victor Hugo
Place de Mexico
Av. d'Eylau
Av. Georges Mandel
R. Scheffer
Av. Paul Doumer
R. de Longchamp
R. des Sablons

Take the Métro to station Alma-Marceau (Line 9) on the Right Bank of the Seine and take the exit pont de l'Alma. Walk straight to the flame ...

Some people will tell you this is the original flame from the Statue of Liberty. Well, not quite. The "Flame of Liberty" you see before you (photo page 127) is one of two copies that were made in the 1980s by French artisans working under contract in New Jersey. One copy was used to replace the original flame as part of a 100th anniversary spa treatment for Lady Liberty. The one you are looking at was shipped to France as a thank you gift from the American people. Both are closer to sculptor Frédéric Auguste Bartholdi's original design than the flame Lady Liberty's torch actually held for nearly a century.

That original *original* flame was redesigned (badly) in 1916, resulting in the deterioration that required its replacement. It is now in a museum at the base of the statue on Liberty Island in New York harbor.

Ironically, this symbol of Franco-American friendship has become the focus of collective world-wide grief for Princess Diana following her death in the underpass practically beneath your feet. Her car, driven by a security manager of the Ritz hotel, actually entered the tunnel on the other side of the underpass, about 100 yards to your left. It crashed against a pillar before it could reach the exit a few feet to your right. Many conspiracy theories have been cooked up since, some of them clever enough to earn their chief propagators a Hollywood contract (such as Tom Cain's apparently quite excellent thriller, *The Accident Man*, coming soon to a multiplex near you). Others implicate almost everybody from the Egyptian Secret Service to Prince Philip (yes, *that* Prince Philip), but your best bet at an answer to the question of what happened still involves a lot of alcohol, a lot of bravado, and a good portion of sheer bad luck. The torch became an unofficial Diana shrine when mourners from all over the world laid down their flowers here and stuck little poems to its shiny golden surface.

Walk straight past the torch and cross the bridge. Turn right on the other bank in front of the RER city rail station, and continue down the riverpath. Turn right on to the next footbridge, ignoring for the time being the strangely familiar structure to your left.

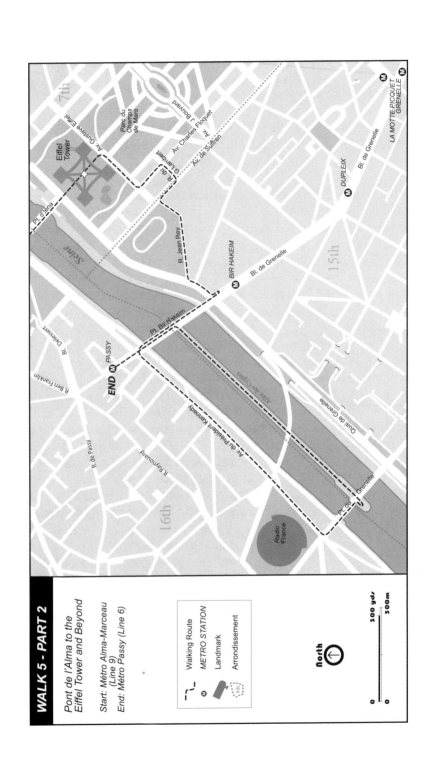

WALK 5 - PART 2

Pont de l'Alma to the
Eiffel Tower and Beyond

Start: Métro Alma-Marceau
(Line 9)
End: Métro Passy (Line 6)

Walking Route
METRO STATION
Landmark
Arrondissement

north

0   300 yds
0   300m

This bridge, called the passerelle Debilly, is the location for one of the key scenes in Brian DePalma's **Femme Fatale**. It is here that the money exchange takes place after the presumed kidnapping and where Rebecca Romijn-Stamos, the former jewel-thief turned wife of the U.S. ambassador, is—apparently—thrown into the Seine. Not much in this movie is as it appears.

> *Once back on the Right Bank, use the passage souterrain (underpass) to cross the busy avenue de New-York. Walk through the underpass—keeping to the speed limit and carefully avoiding pillars and other obstacles of all sorts—and, having safely arrived on the other side, turn right into rue de la Manutention. Walk to the end of the street and climb up the stairs to avenue du Président-Wilson. Cross avenue Wilson and continue straight into rue Brignole.*

The building on your right is the Palais Galliera, built to house the art collection of the Duchess of Galliera who, on her death-bed, decided to leave all her paintings to her beloved hometown of Genoa instead. The building, which nowadays houses the city's Fashion Museum, was used for the press conference in **The Devil Wears Prada** where Meryl Streep announces who is to take over as creative director of an up-and-coming fashion house. Only exterior shots were made in front of the palais' main entrance, which you can see after turning right into avenue Pierre-1er-de-Serbie and walking half a block to the corner with rue de Galliera, which is also on your right.

Cross avenue Pierre-1er-de-Serbie to the left side and walk into place Rochambeau.

Here we see Anne Hathaway on her way to Streep's press conference. The camera follows her as she hurries across the avenue and enters the Palais Galliera.

Cross the square, which is dedicated to a French hero of the American War of Independence, the Count of Rochambeau, whose statue in the middle of the square (opposite) bears a "thank-you note" from George Washington. Then continue ahead into rue Freycinet.

The French-American Friendship

The truth is that, as love affairs between countries go, this was never the stormiest of passions, but something much more cerebral and platonic. Some well-educated people on either side of the Atlantic in the late 18th century more or less simultaneously observed that the U.S. and France found themselves on the same side of the divide that appeared to separate the past—the monarchies of the "old Europe"—from the future. France and the U.S. thought of themselves as the first modern nations, founded on reason rather than ancient customs and superstitions, shining lights of hope for the oppressed peoples of the world.

Whereas this still holds true in many ways for today's U.S., France has had to scale down her ambitions quite considerably over the past 200 years. That's what the loss of a few major wars, of a colonial empire, and of global power do to you. There was a time when France was not only the largest and most powerful country in Europe (and therefore the world), but also the most elegant and sophisticated: the belle of the ball. Nowadays, she is little more than the bitter old lady of international politics, raising her voice only to bicker about the disrespectful youngsters of today.

It is tempting to see the recent fissures in the once so solid Franco-American alliance solely as a result of this "continental drift." But that would be at best a gross over-simplification, and at worst simply wrong.

Let us take an example. Quite easily the most common complaint of Americans who have been on a visit to France is that the people in France are incredibly rude. But what is this observation actually based on? Very few of these American visitors will have spent any meaningful time in the company of "ordinary" people such as office workers, businessmen or (unless they have been very unlucky)

doctors and nurses. Instead, their contacts with "the French" will have been restricted to the kind of people you usually meet on a holiday: hotel staff, taxi drivers, and—particularly—waiters. The rather sweeping accusation that all people in France are rude can therefore be boiled down to a much more specific observation: that the quality of service in France, and particularly in French restaurants, is not nearly so friendly (the French would probably say "overly familiar") as you would expect to find in the U.S.

But you don't need to search for a "rude gene" or develop complex socio-psychological theories to explain this. The fact is

Cross avenue d'Iéna and carry on—slightly to your right—along the left side of the place des États-Unis, the "square of the United States," passing the World War I (WWI) memorial on your right.

The memorial honors the American soldiers who aided France—another reminder of times past when the two nations still seemed to love each other dearly rather than just staying together for the sake of the kids.

Walk past leafy Thomas Jefferson square …

… and a bust of Myron T. Herrick, a former American ambassador to France—one who was not married to a six-foot-tall jewel thief à la *Femme Fatale*. Take a break here, sit down on one of the park benches in the shadow of a beautiful tree—it says a lot about the glorious history of the French-American relationship that Paris named one of her prettiest places in honor of her trans-Atlantic friend and ally—and consider the question: Where did our love go? (See "The French-American Friendship," page 128.)

---

simply that U.S. waiters rely exclusively on tips whereas French waiters automatically get a fixed cut of every bill. Come to think of it, maybe the U.S. should extend this "tips only" approach to other service industries—banking, for instance, or municipal administration. Never again would you have to complain about a grumpy public official.

So: instead of a profound underlying cultural difference, all we have is a different way of doing things. That's really all there is to it.

Quite easily the most frequent complaint raised by the French against Americans is that they are "loud." When American visitors discuss their itinerary in the Parisian subway, massacring the names of all the Métro stations in their way, all the passengers on the train are forced to listen in, and when Americans run into other Americans in a Parisian restaurant, they happily exchange experiences across aisles, tables, and (French) heads. That, as a whole, does not go down too well with the locals who feel that American tourists behave in much the same way as an occupying foreign army.

But this is just another cultural misunderstanding. America is, in all possible ways, a country of wide open spaces—and that includes personal spaces. Americans like to

At the end of the square, just behind the Lafayette-Washington-statue on the right (the George Washington) side, continue straight into rue de Belloy. Follow this street until it joins the busy boulevard at the end, avenue Kléber.

Right there, on the corner to your left at 39 avenue Kléber, you can see the Café Fleurus which, under its former name, the Heliopolis Bar, provides the backdrop for the opening sequence of Michael Winner's 1973 cold-war thriller **Scorpio**. A bit further to your right on avenue Kléber, Burt Lancaster's renegade secret agent buys himself a copy of *Le Monde* with a gun wrapped inside (it must be the weekend edition) before he disappears into rue de Belloy.

Turn left into avenue Kléber. After a couple of blocks, …

… we meet another renegade CIA agent: no. 104 avenue Kléber, on your right, is the address of Matt Damon's Parisian flat in **The Bourne Identity**. It's where he shows Franka Potente he knows how to handle a kitchen knife.

---

stay clear of one another: at anything less than a yard, they feel decidedly queasy, so if you have a group of five or six Americans standing around, they cover quite a lot of ground. No wonder they all have to SHOUT. In contrast, the French (and more generally all Latin people) seek a conversational climate of close intimacy, preferring to come so close that they don't have to raise their voices much above a whisper. This rarely fails to make Americans squirm in embarrassment.

Ultimately, it is this different sense of space that is responsible for some of the key differences between the two cultures. Americans are descendants of people who came to the New World to find space (in all possible senses of the word). The French and particularly the Parisians are descendants of people who had to accommodate themselves to the lack of it. The city of Paris crams more than 2 million people together on a surface area of 35 square miles. That gives Paris six times the population density of Chicago and almost ten times that of Los Angeles. It is also more than twice as densely populated as New York City. Spare a thought: New Yorkers find it difficult enough to get on with one another as it is. Imagine if there were twice as many of them to every crowded subway train, sidewalk, and street in the city. *(cont'd. on next page)*

Cross to the far side of avenue Kléber …

… for a closer view of the building. The little grocery shop next door also puts in an appearance in the film.

Walk on for another block or so. When the avenue meets the place du Trocadéro, turn right, rounding the place counterclockwise on your way, ultimately, to the Eiffel Tower. Begin by crossing avenue Raymond-Poincaré (the first avenue to the right of avenue Kléber).

We'll visit the grounds of the Palais de Chaillot, on the other side of the *place*, shortly. But first, be aware that each of the next streets on our journey around the place du Trocadéro has a little something up its sleeve that some of you may find worth a little detour. To accommodate those of you who want to visit all three, I'll give directions to each from both place du Trocadéro and directly from one to another.

- First up is avenue d'Eylau. In the James Bond movie **Thunderball**, we see Adolfo Celi pull his car up opposite the sinisterly named "Interna-

---

Social codes are in many ways like traffic rules: the denser the traffic, the more of them are required—written and unwritten. What the Parisians see as their respect for other people's privacy can easily be mistaken for reserve or even aloofness in the eyes of an outside observer. The American habit of generating social warmth by sharing details from their private lives with total strangers, on the other hand, is—in the eyes of the Parisians—better suited to the wide open spaces of the prairies. If you live as densely packed as they do, the last thing you need is more warmth.

So finally to the biggest jibe of all, known—in its shorthand form—as

the "cheese-eating-surrender-monkey-argument" which more or less accuses the French of opting to live the sweet life while letting other countries pick up the tab. The truth is that the U.S. and France have drawn different lessons from the wars they fought side by side in the 20th century. The Americans have learned that, if you courageously confront evil wherever and whenever you find it, you will eventually triumph—a proudly Churchillian, grand and noble position, befitting a country that strives for moral leadership as much as it strives for military superiority. The French, however, have acquired a different, more close-up perspective of war. In World War

tional Brotherhood for the Assistance of Stateless Persons" at no. 35 avenue d'Eylau, on the left side near the end of the street. To nobody's great surprise, the Brotherhood office turns out to be nothing of the sort but the HQ of the secretive SPECTRE organization.

Attentive observers may already have suspected that not everything was quite what it seemed the moment they caught sight of Adolfo Celi's Captain-Hook-like eyepatch.

• The second optional stop is the former home of Maria Callas, one of the greatest opera singers of the modern era and "the jilted woman" in one of the 20th century's most famous love triangles. Callas became a virtual recluse in her apartment at 36 avenue Georges-Mandel, a couple of blocks from the place du Trocadéro, after her long-term lover, the Greek shipping magnate Aristotle Onassis, left her to marry the widow of an assassinated American President. Callas died there in 1977. You couldn't make that story up; no Hollywood screenwriter would be that bold. So it's no surprise that when Hollywood did pick up the story—in *The Greek Tycoon* in 1978, with Anthony Quinn in the title role—the scriptwriters weren't bold enough to tell it straight, preferring to change it just enough

---

One, France lost nearly 2 million lives (out of a population of less than 40 million), the highest toll of any major combatant country. The French army had a casualty rate of 67% (vs. the U.S. of 7%), and one in six soldiers died on the battlefield (U.S.: one in 40), surrendering too late, presumably, never to eat cheese again. That, lest we forget, was a war where France was on the winning side, and the experience taught the French that there aren't any winners in war, only survivors. Now: who's to say which of these two is right—and which wrong?

That's perhaps the most difficult, but certainly the most important of all insights: that there is often more than one truth and more than one way of doing things. Once you understand this, you will be well on your way to having a wonderful vacation. Because the French, of course, do not really dislike the Americans. They actually quite admire their energy, optimism, and coltish enthusiasm—although they may quietly think that they will grow out of it soon enough. They only dislike being shouted at, bullied, or condescended to.

Much like Americans, in fact. Which only goes to show that you may have more in common with the French than you originally thought. Maybe this is the beginning—or more to the point: the continuation—of a beautiful friendship. ⟨

to avoid lawsuits. It certainly helped that, by then, Jacqueline Kennedy Onassis was the only survivor of the three protagonists.

> *To get to the Callas house from place du Trocadéro, take a right into avenue Georges-Mandel/allée-Maria-Callas, the next spoke in the wheel after avenue d'Eylau, and look for the corner of avenue Mandel and rue des Sablons. The Callas house is across rue des Sablons on the northwest corner.*
>
> *If you're coming from our **Thunderball** stop, take a left into rue des Sablons at the end of avenue d'Eylau. No. 36 will be on your right at the corner of rue des Sablons and allée-Maria-Callas.*

Avenue Mandel is the street that divides the ordinary rich of the southern part of the 16th arrondissement (you'll even find a few lawyers and dentists several blocks to the south) from the real plutocrats in the north. But both sides of the avenue Georges-Mandel, in case you haven't noticed, are firmly in the latter camp. (See page 244 for two movie sites to visit in the southern part of the 16th.)

The Eiffel Tower

Easily the most famous structure in the world, the tower has become so familiar that we tend to overlook how magnificent and graceful it actually is. When it was built for the World Exhibition in 1887, it was not only the tallest building in the world—toppling Cheops Pyramid in Egypt from the spot that it had occupied for a piffling 3,000 years or so—but also one of the most controversial: For Parisians, it was hardly a case of *coup de foudre* or love at first sight. Many people detested the new structure in their midst, not least because they felt that it challenged their own standards of aesthetic classification and judgment, being neither a real building nor a real statue but a somewhat unclean mix.

But once it had survived all the early attempts to tear it down, *la tour Eiffel* became an icon. Its "paperclip" shape must rival the head of Mickey Mouse as the most easily recognizable nonreligious symbol anywhere in the world. More than 200 million people have visited it over the years, and 20-odd replicas have been built in various places around the world, from Brisbane to Siberia. Las Vegas, of course, houses the largest one, a model built in a scale of 1:2.

- The third and final optional detour takes us into avenue Paul-Doumer where, at no. 19—the entrance immediately in front of the Franprix supermarket—jewel thief Alain Delon has his apartment Jean-Pierre Melville's **Le cercle rouge**.

If you are coming from the Callas house, turn left, cross avenue Georges-Mandel, and walk into rue du Pasteur-Marc-Boegner (the continuation of rue des Sablons south of avenue Mandel). Take the first street to your left, rue Scheffer, which leads straight to avenue Paul-Doumer in about three blocks. Turn left, and you will find no. 19 on the right side of the street.

If you are coming from the place du Trocadéro, avenue Paul-Doumer is the next street after avenue Georges-Mandel, and no. 19 will be on your left.

Now walk down (or back up) avenue Paul-Doumer in the direction of the place du Trocadéro. Stay on the right side of the avenue when you reach the large building complex, the Palais de Chaillot, and walk directly into the spacious area between the two wings.

Overused and overly familiar it might be, nevertheless the Tower still had power enough to enrich two of the most famous French New Wave movies, Louis Malle's **Zazie dans le métro / Zazie in the Metro** and François Truffaut's **Les 400 coups / The 400 Blows**. Both feature scenes in which the camera happily swirls around the Eiffel Tower, almost oblivious to the films' characters and detached from everything that happens to them. It seems that, after having been studio-bound for so long, French cinema celebrated its newfound freedom with an unselfconscious dance in the fresh air—not once, but twice.

In Hollywood movies, the Eiffel Tower is the classic establishing shot for Paris—used again and again to the point that it's become the most tired of clichés. In Billy Wilder's 1954 **Sabrina**, for example, the only bit of Paris we get to see is the Eiffel Tower, through the window of the cooking academy, once in summer and once through the snow. They say that in Hollywood movies, every Paris flat has a view of the Eiffel Tower. And if you think that's a thing of the past, think again. The location of both the Parisian scenes in **De-Lovely**—shot in 2006—is identified by the Eiffel Tower: You can see it from the window of the ballroom where Kevin

And, well: enjoy the view. Because it is one of the best in Paris or in any city in the world. Even Adolf Hitler (not one of Paris's greatest fans) enjoyed it, if the newsreel footage of a beaming Führer, surrounded by his generals and various sycophants, on the one day he came here to inspect his latest and greatest conquest is anything to go by.

Walk past the wonderfully restored 1930s' statues that line the parvis (square) towards the balustrade to get a better view of la tour Eiffel.

Turn right and walk down the stairway of the Palais ...

... which was more or less faithfully reconstructed for the Doris Day vehicle **April in Paris**. Much of that movie's final segment is set in and around a building that's obviously been modelled after the Palais de Chaillot, including—of course—its view of you know what.

You may feel a little peckish after all the walking, but don't make the mistake of looking for the café bar at the bottom of the stairs that you may have seen in the French comedy **La doublure / The Valet**; it doesn't exist.

Kline is introduced to Ashley Judd and from the back of the public garden where they take a walk a couple of scenes later. And in **Ratatouille**, even the kitchen boy's shabby little attic room looks out on the tour Eiffel. At some stage, Hollywood itself seemed to acknowledge the cheesiness of this world view. Perhaps that's why in **French Kiss**, the lights of the Tower go black whenever Meg Ryan looks in its direction during her nightly walks, leading us to believe that she never actually gets to see it. Who says Americans don't do irony?

But for every "ironic" take on the Eiffel Tower, contemporary Hollywood still shoots about ten "straight" scenes in its light or in its shadow, at its top or at its feet. Possibly the most famous of all Eiffel Tower scenes is the one in the James Bond adventure **A View to a Kill** where Grace Jones sky-dives from the top. In **Funny Face**, the Eiffel Tower—of course—is the place where Fred Astaire, Audrey Hepburn, and Kay Thompson meet for the finale of their musical number, "Bonjour Paris," after singing and dancing their separate ways through the city. The three friends in **An American Werewolf in Paris** spend the night on an Eiffel Tower observation deck, one of the few scenes in the movie that were actually shot in Paris. And in James Ivory's **Le divorce**, a movie that—by and

The "valet" of the film title, played by France's top stand-up comedian Gad Elmaleh, parks cars for the café. At one point, we see him parade down that curb at the bottom of the stairway (background in photo page 123) with his new supermodel girlfriend. This is also where we see Naomi Watts's French husband and his Russian mistress roller skate in **Le divorce**, time and again teasing her jealous husband, who is watching from the balustrade above—once too often, as it turns out. The fountain a little bit further down is the place Audrey Hepburn and William Holden seal with a kiss a happier end to their affair in **Paris When It Sizzles**—and where, in **Rush Hour III**, Chris Tucker and Jackie Chan land from their aerial escape off the Eiffel Tower using the French flag as an improvised hang-glider.

Continue toward the Seine, walking on the right side of the fountain. Cross the place de Varsovie on your way to, and eventually across, the bridge (the pont d'Iéna), heading towards the Eiffel Tower itself.

Closer inspection will reveal some surprises. The more detailed your view of the Tower's fine 19th century ironworks, for instance, the more you will

large successfully—strains hard to avoid both visual and literary clichés about Paris and the French, Matthew Modine's crazed lawyer chooses the Eiffel Tower as the place to take Kate Hudson and her sister-in-law hostage. Following which Hudson throws her expensive handbag to the wind, quite literally, paying a nice homage to Albert Lamorisse's classic *Le ballon rouge / The Red Balloon*, released in France in 1956.

As a matter of fact almost every movie set in Paris has its own "Eiffel Tower moment." **Ocean's Twelve** director Steven Soderbergh may lay claim to the coolest way ever to shoot the Tower—as a mirror image in a pair of sunglasses. The shot is all the more cool because those sunglasses are worn by Brad Pitt, in the scene where Pitt and George Clooney visit Albert Finney's "king of thieves" in his Parisian flat. Actually, you could fill an entire book with scenes where people glimpse at, point to, pass by, or wave at the Eiffel Tower.

On which note we ourselves will wave farewell—not to the Eiffel Tower itself (we'll inspect it from much closer range in a sec), but to the spectacular view of it that we get from the courtyard of the Palais de Chaillot. This is the same view, incidentally, that we get in the fashion shoot in the 1995 **Sabrina**, the one with the artificial rain. ⌡

realize how delicate the structure actually is. And only by standing right underneath it will you get an impression of how much ground the Eiffel Tower actually covers. You could play a game of football under it! It is here at the Tower's ground level that the final showdown of **Rush Hour III**, with the exchange of hostages, starts before moving on to higher ground, mainly Platform 2 in the Jules Verne restaurant. If you want to follow: you'll find the elevators in the eastern pillar at the top left-hand corner of the square as you face away from the Seine and toward the park.

On the way down, however, you may want to use the stairs in the opposite pillar—in the spirit of **Zazie dans le métro / Zazie in the Metro** and the excellent 1950s' Ealing comedy **The Lavender Hill Mob**. In the latter, bullion thieves and gold smugglers Alec Guinness and Stanley Holloway rush down the spiral staircase to catch up with an elevator full of English schoolgirls who have just acquired half a dozen of their "special edition" souvenir Eiffel Towers—only to see the girls drive off in a taxicab just as they reach the ground floor.

The slapstick scene where they keep on spinning long after they have reached "terra firma" again, propelled by the momentum of their run down the spiral staircase, is echoed in **Zazie dans le métro / Zazie in the Metro**—a film that did a fair amount of such "echoing," quoting a whole library of slapstick classics, while it also foreshadowed and influenced much that was to come comedy-wise in the swinging Sixties. Richard Lester's Beatles movie *A Hard Day's Night* certainly owes a lot to *Zazie*, as does—such is the trickle-down nature of artistic inspiration—the TV comedy series "The Monkees." So if you ever laughed at the antics of the "prefab four," as they were unkindly labelled, you have enjoyed a recipe cooked up by some egghead cinéastes over their red wine on the Parisian Left Bank. Amazing, if you think about it, but true.

> *Leave the Tower area between the eastern and southern pillars (they're marked "est" and "sud"). Then, after perhaps a brief stroll through the gardens and a short break on one of the benches …*

… much like Debra Winger and Billy Crystal in **Forget Paris** in the scene where Winger tells him thanks for the offer but no thanks because she already has a husband …

... turn right and then left into avenue Charles-Floquet. It's the asphalt street just past the footpath.

We are now walking through one of the most expensive areas in the French capital, albeit one where nobody in his right mind would want to live (no shops, no bars, no restaurants)—the perfect place, in other words, for people with more money than sense, people like Daniel Auteuil's adulterous industry magnate in **La Doublure / The Valet**, for example. And even he does not live here fulltime; he only uses his apartment at no. 11—on the corner of rue du Général-Lambert—to stash away his mistress. This is where the paparazzo takes the photo of him, his mistress, and the innocent bystander Gad Elmaleh that is at the heart of the movie's plot.

Turn right into rue du Général-Lambert and right again into avenue de Suffren. Cross the avenue and cut left into place de Sydney which changes its name into rue Jean-Rey after a few steps.
Note: If you've wandered through the park, you may have passed rue du Général-Lambert. Not to worry. Wherever you find yourself along avenue Charles-Floquet, face away from the Eiffel Tower, turn right, and walk one block to avenue de Suffren. Once there, head back toward the river to reach place de Sydney and walk down rue Jean-Rey.

The curved concrete building at the end of rue Jean-Rey is the Australian Embassy. It was here, on the roof gardens at the very top of the building, that the wonderful scene with Brad Pitt, his sunglasses, and the Eiffel Tower was shot for **Ocean's Twelve**.

At the end of the street, turn left and then immediately right onto the bridge, pont de Bir-Hakeim, with the railway viaduct above the roadway. Walk down the middle, underneath the viaduct, ...

... following the route of the great gypsy horseback race (featuring Johnny Depp) in **The Man Who Cried**. This bridge (photo next page) is also one of the stages in the slapstick chase sequence of **Zazie dans le métro / Zazie in the Metro**, where Zazie catches her companion with a magnet.

A bit further down, where the bridge almost joins the right bank …

… is the location of the street market where Eric Bana meets his contact in Steven Spielberg's **Munich**. This meeting was the only "Parisian" scene in the film that was actually shot on location. The assassination of the Palestinian representative—a complex scene that would have ground Paris traffic to a halt for at least a week—was shot in Budapest, where the municipal authorities were apparently more willing to accommodate the moviemakers.

But, of course, this bridge and this part of Paris will forever be associated with another movie, one of the most famous and notorious films of all time. The bridge where we are walking now is the bridge where we first meet a desperate Marlon Brando in Bernardo Bertolucci's **Le dernier tango à Paris / Last Tango in Paris**. The scene is echoed in Julie Delpy's **2 Days in Paris**: Delpy, who wrote, directed, and acts in the film, has to imitate Brando—screaming in pain, hands on her ears—for a photo taken by her American boyfriend, who has seen *Tango* "more often than anyone else." No wonder he is always so grumpy!

On approaching avenue du Président-Kennedy, which runs by the river …

… you can spot the Kennedy Eiffel Bar on the right side of the stairway. This is the bar from which Maria Schneider—early on in **Le dernier tango à Paris / Last Tango in Paris**—makes a phone call.

We'll come back here later. For the moment, walk down to street level—use the stairs to the left of the wooden bridge—and turn left into avenue du Président-Kennedy, the Seine on your left and some gloomy apartment blocks on your right.

The buildings look alarmingly like New York's Dakota multiplied several times over. One of those buildings is scary enough—the Dakota, after all, was where Roman Polanski shot *Rosemary's Baby* and where John Lennon was gunned down by a crazed fan. Collectively, they make the area look like Count Dracula's housing estate.

To your left, on the far side of the Seine, you can see the complex of modern high-rises, mostly Japanese-owned hotels, where Bruno Ganz is staying in Wim Wenders's version of Patricia Highsmith's *Ripley's Game*, called **The American Friend** (which features Dennis Hopper as Tom Ripley, the eponymous "friend").

A little closer on your left, down by the riverside, you can see the *quais*, one of the true disasters of contemporary urban planning. They come to us straight from the Seventies, of course, when converting the ancient streets and highways of historic European cities into six-lane racetracks seemed a splendid idea. The quais were designed to speed incoming cars straight into town by eliminating traffic lights, pedestrians, or any other feature of urban street life that might slow them down. As a consequence, some of the most scenic promenades in Paris are off-limits to pedestrians. In fairness, one must hasten to add, the city administration has begun to recognize the lunacy of it all, and on weekends throughout the summer, the quais are reserved for cyclists and pedestrians.

Pass beneath the railway bridge …

... the shots in **French Kiss** when Meg Ryan leaves Paris for the south—finally seeing the Eiffel Tower for the first time—were taken from here ...

... and walk on past the Maison de Radio-France, home of national French radio, on your right at no. 116. Before you turn left onto the next bridge, the pont de Grenelle, ...

... take a look at the building right in front of you, the one with the bluish panes in front of the balconies, which faces the river on one side and the bridge on the other. Jonathan's client in **The American Friend** lives on its eighth floor. It's from here that he gives his instructions by phone as to how exactly he would like the killing executed.

Now start across the bridge—and, no, just in case you are wondering, you are not hallucinating. When you reach the stairs about halfway across the bridge, walk down the stairway to your left and then turn left again through the unkempt little garden to the tip of the island in the middle of the river.

If—as is normally the case unless you have come here on a weekend—nobody is around, you may make this your very own Charlton Heston (*Planet of the Apes*) moment. Fall on your knees and confess that you have suspected it all along, that deep down you knew you had never really left the U.S. and that this is all some dirty "Operation Capricorn"-like trick.

In reality, of course, it is nothing of the sort. Neither are you hallucinating. The replica of the Statue of Liberty (opposite), built roughly on a scale of 1:4, was a gift by the French community in the U.S.A. to the old homeland. She was built in 1889, only three years after her big sister, and is one of about half a dozen replicas in France alone. In fact, there is another, smaller one right here in Paris, in the jardin du Luxembourg.

The statue and the tip of this man-made isle, known as the Île-des-Cygnes, feature prominently in Roman Polanski's **Frantic** in the movie's somewhat, well, frantic climax with the handover of the trigger device in exchange for Harrison Ford's wife and a hail of bullets. The device itself is a classic example of what Hitchcock would have called a "McGuffin"—an object that isn't important in itself but is used to move the plot along.

Before you turn back, take a good look downstream.

Twenty or thirty years ago, this was the part of the Seine where Paris spat in her hands and got down to serious, dirty work. The Citroën motor factory operated on the site now occupied by the park on your left, fittingly called the Parc André-Citroën, and a bit further downstream you would have found the Renault car plant. Luc Besson's 1990 release, **Nikita**, was largely shot in abandoned factory buildings at the old Citroën site. And much of the surrounding area was still derelict in the late 1990s when John Frankenheimer used some of the deserted streets as a set for **Ronin**. For instance, the scene where De Niro and Reno are waiting in the car for Jonathan Bryce to come out of the safe house was shot there.

Nowadays, the main industry of this part of Paris is media. You have already passed the Maison de Radio-France offices on avenue du Président-Kennedy. In the distance on your right, you may see the round tower that is home to the country's largest and most popular free channel, TF1, which is the equivalent of CBS, ABC, and NBC all rolled into one. Look for its red-and-blue logo. The headquarters of Canal+, the French equivalent of HBO, is a bit closer, on your left.

Turn around now, and walk up the first flight of stairs. Then continue straight on along the tree-lined walkway, the allée des Cygnes (the swans' path).

Take a peek at the houseboats moored in front of the quai de Grenelles on your right behind the railway bridge. Harrison Ford is imprisoned on one of these boats in **Frantic**—one with a view of the quarter-scale Statue of Liberty we've just visited. The view in front of you is even more picturesque, a classic postcard motif actually: bridge with trains atop it and the Eiffel Tower providing a perfect backdrop.

Once you reach pont de Bir-Hakeim, walk up the stairs and turn left. But this time walk straight ahead to the end of the bridge, climb the wooden stairs, and cross avenue du Président-Kennedy on the wooden bridge.

The first building immediately on your left on the far side of the avenue, no. 1 rue de l'Alboni (opposite above), is the house where Marlon Brando lives in **Le dernier tango à Paris / Last Tango in Paris**. This is where he does all those unspeakable things to Maria Schneider. The scene—you know which one I'm talking about—still has the power to shock, but more shocking to a "modern" audience is the sheer level of Brando's emotional exhibitionism. For better or for worse: they don't shoot them like that anymore.

Walk past the entrance to 1 rue de l'Alboni and straight ahead to the corner where the street meets the square Alboni.

You are now standing in the exact spot where, in **Trois couleurs: Bleu / Three Colors: Blue**, Juliette Binoche searches out Olivier, her late husband's former assistant, to confront and challenge him about the right to finish her husband's composition.

Now walk up to the Métro station Passy (Line 6).

The most dramatically located station in the whole of Paris, Passy is where our walk ends. Or I should say, it is where the "walky" part of our walk ends. You have two further options:

- You can take Métro line 6 to Bir-Hakeim (Direction Nation) across the river for a look at the Île-des-Cygnes (Island of the Swans) and the Eiffel Tower from a more elevated position, or ...

- You can follow Bruno Ganz on his deadly mission in **The American Friend**. It is here, at station Passy, that Ganz begins to follow his victim, boarding the train in the direction of Étoile and changing there to Line 1 to La Défense. There, on the escalator of the La Défense station, he pulls the trigger. But that, as they say, is another story—and another walk.

If you decide to follow Ganz, be sure you choose the platform for the train to Étoile; once inside, you cannot change platforms. For more details on La Défense, see the chapter, *Further Afield.*

ARRONDISSEMENTS: 7, 6, 14
DURATION: 2 ½ to 3 hours

From the Assemblée Nationale past the Musée d'Orsay and along the boulevard St-Germain into the Montparnasse quarter, passing a number of art galleries and antiques shops in the course of your walk.

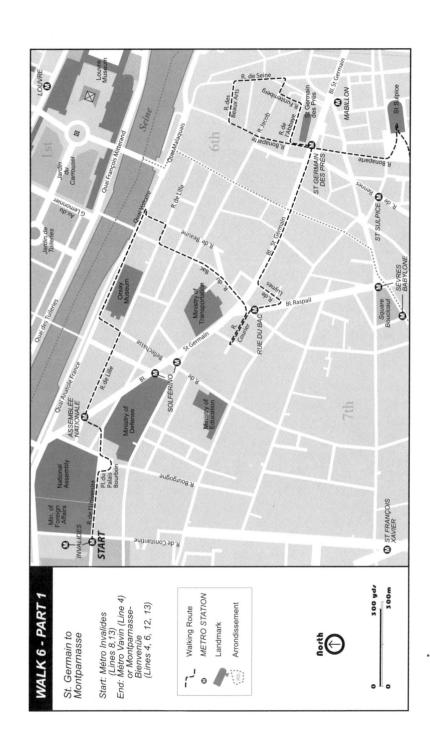

WALK 6 - PART 1

St. Germain to
Montparnasse

*Start: Métro Invalides
(Lines 8,13)
End: Métro Vavin (Line 4)
or Montparnasse-
Bienvenüe
(Lines 4, 6, 12, 13)*

Walking Route
MÉTRO STATION
Landmark
Arrondissement

north

0 ——— 300 yds
0 ——— 500m

Go to the Métro station Invalides (Lines 8, 13). Leave through exit Université and make a 180-degree turn.

Les Invalides itself with its shiny golden cupola is now to your right, hidden—in summer at least—behind the trees. You may want to keep it that way. A frank piece of advice: if you were to miss one of the major landmarks of Paris, make it this one. Les Invalides, formally known as the Hôtel des Invalides, is one large complex of military buildings—a hospital, a chapel, a parade ground—turned into a military museum and mainly used these days by sadistic provincial teachers of French history to torture their students. Once the kids have observed the building's main exhibit, Napoleon's coffin (housed under the cupola) to their hearts' content, they can go next door to count the buttons on the uniforms worn by various Napoleonic regiments from 1792 to 1815. As they say: a great time was had by all.

Continue down rue de l'Université, passing on your left ...

... first, the Foreign Office—where, on the other side of the building, the one facing the Seine, Chris Tucker and Jackie Chan pay a surprise visit to Max von Sydow's villainous diplomat in **Rush Hour III**.

... and then the French Parliament (Assemblée Nationale).

Turn right into place du Palais-Bourbon opposite the main entrance to the Assemblée National.

No. 4, the second building from the corner on your right (left background in photo page 151), houses the Parisian offices of *Vogue* ("Condé Nast" it says on the doorplate). Both exteriors and interiors were filmed here for the 1995 version of **Sabrina**.

Walk back to rue de l'Université and continue straight ahead for a block before turning left into rue de Courty. Cross boulevard St-Germain and turn right into rue de Lille. Walk one block and cross rue de Solférino.

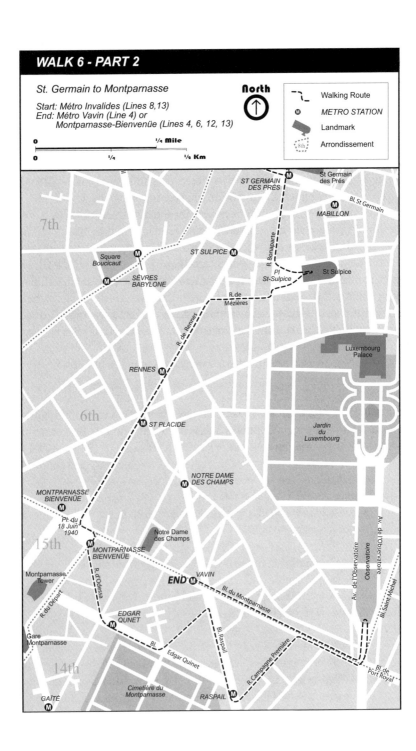

WALK 6 - PART 2

St. Germain to Montparnasse

Start: Métro Invalides (Lines 8,13)
End: Métro Vavin (Line 4) or
Montparnasse-Bienvenüe (Lines 4, 6, 12, 13)

North ↑

- - Walking Route
Ⓜ METRO STATION
Landmark
Arrondissement

0 ¼ Mile
0 ¼ ½ Km

ST GERMAIN DES PRÉS Ⓜ
St Germain des Prés

Ⓜ Bl. St Germain
MABILLON

7th

Square Boucicaut Ⓜ
Ⓜ SÈVRES BABYLONE

ST SULPICE Ⓜ

R. Bonaparte

Pl St-Sulpice
St Sulpice

R. de Mézières

Luxembourg Palace

R. de Rennes

RENNES Ⓜ

6th

Ⓜ ST PLACIDE

Jardin du Luxembourg

NOTRE DAME DES CHAMPS Ⓜ

MONTPARNASSE BIENVENÜE Ⓜ

Pl. du 18 Juin 1940

15th

Ⓜ MONTPARNASSE BIENVENÜE

Notre Dame des Champs

Montparnasse Tower

R. d'Odessa

VAVIN
END Ⓜ
Bl. du Montparnasse

Av. de l'Observatoire

Av. de l'Observatoire

Bl. Saint Michel

EDGAR QUINET Ⓜ

R. du Départ

Gare Montparnasse

Bl. Edgar Quinet

Bl. Raspail

R. Campagne Première

Bl. de Port Royal

14th

GAÎTÉ Ⓜ

Cimetière du Montparnasse

RASPAIL Ⓜ

The second house on your right, no. 10 rue de Solférino, is the HQ of the French Socialist party. You may have seen it on TV, as it is a French custom for leading politicians and their sympathizers to gather at their party HQ after every major election to celebrate or, as has been the case for the Socialists depressingly often of late, to comfort each other. The HQ of their main rival, the centre-right UMP, used to be at 123 rue de Lille, just a few hundred yards away. But it was recently relocated to the other side of the Invalides.

Continue down rue de Lille past the main office of the French Legion of Honor, and turn left at the next corner, into rue de la Légion d'Honneur.

The large building on your right is the world-famous Musée d'Orsay, home of modern French art, as opposed to the Louvre which is mainly a collection of international and classical art. If the d'Orsay looks like a railway station, it is no coincidence, because that's exactly what the building was for much of its life—from 1900 until WWII. It lay unused for decades thereafter before being turned into a museum in the 1980s.

"Unused" the building may have been as far as the general public was concerned, but moviemakers loved its charming exterior and cavernous interior spaces. Orson Welles came here in the 1960s to film his version of Franz Kafka's novel, **The Trial**. Exteriors for the movie had already been shot in Zagreb when the producers ran out of money and told Welles that the original plans for an intricate set had to be cancelled. But fortunately, Welles fell in love with the Gare d'Orsay—as it was then called—and used its labyrinthine interiors to good purpose in many scenes, including the one where the mysterious official leads Anthony Perkins to the Trial Office, only to realize that he is not in possession of the key—all very, well, Kafkaesque.

The Gare appears as the hotel in Bernardo Bertolucci's celebrated 1970 film **The Conformist** where Jean-Louis Trintignant's secret agent spends his honeymoon awaiting instructions from his fascist bosses as to when and where to kill his former teacher, an anti-Nazi professor. The Gare also lends its period charm to **Paris brûle-t-il? / Is Paris Burning?**: the delegation of the French Resistance, sent to negotiate a ceasefire with the Nazis, is arrested by an over-eager officer right at the corner of rue de Bellechasse and the quai Anatole-France.

Turn right behind the Musée into the quais (or the place Henry-de-Montherlant as the quais are called here) and walk past the original Belle Époque ironworks ...

... which provide the backdrop for the final quarrel between Brando and Schneider in **Le dernier tango à Paris / Last Tango in Paris**.

... to the next bridge, the pont Royal.

In **Surviving Picasso**, we see Anthony Hopkins (as Picasso) and Natasha McElhone (as the woman who does the surviving) return via the bridge (photo opposite) from a nightly excursion to the Right Bank of the Seine. They quarrel before reconciling with a passionate kiss. The large building you see in the background is the Louvre.

While you are here, look toward the next bridge to your right, the pont du Carrousel.

In Philip Kaufman's 1990 **Henry & June**, we see the eponymous protagonists—Henry Miller, a famous American ex-pat, and his wife, played by Uma Thurman—watch the sunrise from beneath the pont du Carrousel. What follows is one of the scenes that earned **Henry & June** an NC-17 rating, the first U.S. film ever to be honored in this way.

Continue along quai Voltaire for a few steps before crossing over to the right side of the street opposite no. 27 ...

... where Voltaire, the greatest French philosopher ever, died in 1778. The French movie star Jean-Paul Belmondo lives one block further down, in the rue des Sts-Pères.

Now walk into the narrow lane next to the Voltaire building, rue de Beaune, and turn right at the next corner into rue de Lille and then left at the following corner into rue du Bac, a street mainly known for its pricey antiques shops.

Alain Delon's wealthy but somewhat crooked antiques dealer lives on rue du Bac in Joseph Losey's multi-award winning **Monsieur Klein / Mr. Klein.** His place, at no. 136, is much further down, near the end of the street close to the Bon Marché department store. We, however, aren't going that far.

At the next major intersection, cross both sections of the boulevard St-Germain (there is a traffic island in the middle) before turning sharply to your right into rue Paul-Louis-Courier. Walk straight ahead, crossing rue de St-Simon, to steal a view into the private little compound (no. 11b) behind the wall at the bottom of the passage de la Visitation.

The beautifully maintained white house and its courtyard provide a suitably aristocratic ambience for Michel Piccoli's Russian spy in Alfred Hitchcock's 1969 **Topaz.** We watch as a fellow traitor, played by Philippe Noiret, first approaches and enters and then leaves the apartment, running into Piccoli's next visitor, an old flame, in front of the entrance door. Okay, admittedly, if the front gate happens to be closed, there is not much to see, but there is a little bit of movie history involved here: Except for a few exterior shots of a restaurant and a scene that was cut from the film before its release (see the chapter, *Further Afield*), this is the only Paris location ever used by the master of suspense.

Retrace your steps now to the intersection of rue du Bac and boulevard St-Germain, turning right into boulevard Raspail.

The Hôtel Cayré on your right at no. 4 is the place where another antiques dealer, Johnny Depp's character in Roman Polanski's **The Ninth Gate**, lives during his stay in Paris. You can look into the reception area from the street.

At the next corner, turn left into rue de Luynes and walk a block to rejoin boulevard St-Germain. Turn right into the boulevard.

We are approaching the heart of the St-Germain district. At no. 151 on the right side of the street, you'll find the famous Brasserie Lipp where Anthony Hopkins takes his two wives, past and present, Julianne Moore and Natasha McElhone, for a surprisingly relaxed dinner à trois in **Surviving Picasso.**

Next door, at no. 149, is the place where Belmondo orders a breakfast he can't afford in **À bout de souffle / Breathless.** At the time, the place was called Le Royale St-Germain. It is now the Emporio Armani and, as though that weren't bad enough, for a while all the windows were pasted over with sticky Armani-branded wallpaper to make the place look like some sort of sensory-deprivation shopping prison. Now—wallpaper gone—it looks like a normal shopping prison again.

Cross boulevard St-Germain to the left side …

… to take a look at the two most famous coffee houses in Paris, coexisting peacefully side by side. To your left, the Café de Flore appears in **Le divorce** when Kate Hudson and Naomi Watts go to meet Watts's increasingly estranged husband and wind up drinking anisette with Glenn Close. It is also the café where a tearful Julianne Moore tells Natasha McElhone towards the end of **Surviving Picasso**—in a somewhat less relaxed encounter than their first one across the road—what a huge void the endlessly fascinating Picasso has left in her life. (Having watched Anthony Hopkins portray Picasso as a balding woodworks teacher with a smutty sense of humor, the audience is left somewhat baffled by this confession.)

Les Deux Magots ("The Two Mandarins"), located right next door to the Flore, holds an even more secure place in Parisian lore and literary history. This is, after all, the place where Hemingway met James Joyce and where Jean-Paul Sartre did much of his writing.

After my associating the Deux Magots with three of the greatest writers of the 20th century, anything I say next is bound to be a bit of a letdown. But here you go: In **Everyone Says I Love You**, Reece Witherspoon and Ed Norton pass by Les Deux Magots on their tour of Paris. In **Les aventures de Rabbi Jacob / The Mad Adventures of Rabbi Jacob**, Claude Giraud's Arab revolutionary is being paged and kidnapped here. (When Giraud goes out to confront the kidnappers who he knows are waiting for him, we can briefly see the place where Belmondo has his breakfast in **À bout de souffle / Breathless** on the other side of the street, called the Drugstore Publicis at the time the Rabbi Jacob movie was filmed.) The Deux Magots is also the place where Klaus-Maria Brandauer encounters his first wife (Krysztyna Janda) in István Szabó's 1981 **Mephisto** (exterior shots only). And in **What's New**

Pussycat?, it is here that Peter O'Toole meets Woody Allen, while Allen is playing chess with a stripper on one of the tables outside. Oh, the sixties!

Walk past the Deux Magots, keeping the Église de St-Germain-des-Prés, one of the oldest churches in Paris, on your right. The original structure was built in the sixth century and then destroyed and rebuilt several times over the ensuing centuries. Behind the church, turn right into rue de l'Abbaye and then left at the next corner into rue de Furstemberg. (Or if you're in need of a rest, sit down for a bit on a bench in the church garden before continuing on into rue de Furstemberg.)

The square in front of you—Henry Miller's favorite place in the whole of Paris—provides the backdrop for the heart-breaking final scene in Martin Scorsese's **The Age of Innocence**: Daniel Day-Lewis stands for a long time outside the flat of the woman he once loved (Michelle Pfeiffer) and then quietly walks away. If you are looking for the exact window that reflects the sunlight into Day-Lewis's eyes, taking him back momentarily to a similarly bedazzling day with his beloved many, many years before: stand where Day-Lewis stands in the scene, i.e. at the southern tip of the square (south is where you entered the square), facing the side of the building at no. 4 (right next to the entrance of the Delacroix Museum at no. 6). Look for the window in the top left-hand corner: it's the one immediately underneath. The square also features in **Gigi**: After being expelled from Gigi's home, Louis Jourdain completes a musical journey through Paris in the space of a single song, passing, among other sites, the rue de Furstemberg. Beat that!

Cross the square, staying on rue de Furstemberg for about a block until it ends at rue Jacob. Turn right into rue Jacob and then left into rue de Seine at the second corner. After walking a long block, pass the sinister rue Visconti on your left and turn left at the next corner into rue des Beaux-Arts.

Julia Ormond in **Sabrina** (1995) escapes to the hotel at no. 13—called, with a somewhat aloof austerity, simply L'Hôtel—only for Harrison Ford's not-as-arid-as-he-looks industrialist to pursue her and ensure a happy end.

The hotel itself is mainly famous as the place where Oscar Wilde died in 1900, just after coining his last ever bon mot, "This room is dreadful: either the wallpaper goes or I," feeling obliged, it appears, to keep on wisecracking until, literally, the very end.

At the École des Beaux Arts …

… which we can spot from afar during the nocturnal street scene in the 1995 version of **Sabrina** …

> *… turn left into rue Bonaparte and walk back to the church. Cross boulevard St-Germain and continue on rue Bonaparte (the left street at the fork). Follow it to rue du Vieux-Colombier (crossing rue du Four on your way), and turn left into place St-Sulpice. Walk past the Fontaine des Quatre Evèques on your right …*

… where, in **Paris nous appartient / Paris Belongs to Us**, Philip tells Anne that her boyfriend is in great danger.

> *Enter the Église St-Sulpice through its main entrance immediately behind the fountain.*

This church is the second largest in Paris. It contains two major works by Eugène Delacroix, a pair of beautiful holy water fonts by the rococo sculptor Jean-Baptiste Pigalle, and a 100-stop pipe organ. But the only thing anybody wants to see nowadays is the place where a homicidal albino monk dug up the floor. Which is all the more mysterious because the scene in **The Da Vinci Code** where Paul Bettany looks for a key to the location of the Holy Grail wasn't even shot here. The parish priest rather liked the floor the way it was, thank you very much for inquiring. So director Ron Howard had the whole thing faithfully reconstructed with the aid of computer graphics. The result, it must be said, looks pretty much like the real thing; I'll bet you couldn't tell the difference.

What's more, that's all we have come in for, too, of course: to look at the original of Paul Bettany's reconstruction work. If you absolutely must know: The two Delacroix paintings are located on your right, just behind the entrance. And if you are interested in the sundial that features in the book, you will find the white obelisk (the gnomon that casts the shadow) halfway up the nave on the left side and the "meridian" leading away from it to the plate on the other side of the altar. (The meridian, by the way, is not part of the Paris meridian; that passes about 100 yards further east. The sundial itself was actually made by an English astronomer in the 18th century with the church's full knowledge and consent.)

> *Leave St-Sulpice through the main entrance, and then stay on the left side of courtyard and square (place St-Sulpice) to walk past the ancient seminary …*

… which was, according to **The Da Vinci Code**, a "hotbed of unorthodoxy" throughout the 19th century and the reason why St-Sulpice could become the virtual HQ for the Priory of Sion. Whatever its real and fictional history, the seminary is now part of the French Finance Ministry.

> *At the front of the square, turn left to rejoin rue Bonaparte and then immediately right into rue de Mézières. Follow this street three blocks to its end and turn left into rue de Rennes.*

Across this busy shopping street, in front of no. 108, you'll see the bus stop where Peter Coyote gets off the bus after having gallantly passed his ticket to the fare-dodging Emmanuelle Seigner in Roman Polanski's **Bitter Moon**.

> *Follow rue de Rennes until it joins place du 18-juin-1940 …*

… whose name commemorates the beginning of the French Resistance movement in WWII. On the top floor of the house at the corner, 150 rue de Rennes, whose windows look out on the *place*, Edward Fox's hitman takes aim at General de Gaulle in Fred Zinnemann's excellent **The Day of the Jackal**. The first impression for someone who remembers the movie is that the station forecourt on the other side of the road has changed beyond recognition since the film was made in 1972. In truth, however, the old Montparnasse station was demolished in 1969. But that's what clever editing can do. The side with Edward Fox's hotel room, at any rate, is virtually unchanged.

If you want to see what the Gare Montparnasse looked like before the whole area was given the radical urban renewal treatment in the Seventies, watch the Nouvelle Vague classic **Cléo de 5 à 7 / Cleo from 5 to 7** of which more later.

Cross over to the other side of rue de Rennes for a better view of the house at no. 150. Then cross boulevard du Montparnasse at the traffic lights and walk left at the fork directly into rue d'Odessa. Follow this street to its end at place Fernand-Mourlot, the heart of the Montparnasse quarter.

Straight in front of you, across the street, you can see the famous rue de la Gaité with its bars and theatres, including—the now refurbished—Bobino's, where Josephine Baker appeared for the first time and, fifty years later, for the last time ever on a French stage. We, however, …

… turn left into boulevard Edgar-Quinet, with the Cimetière Montparnasse behind the wall on our right.

One of the three large Parisian cemeteries, it features the graves of, among others, Serge Gainsbourg, Susan Sontag, Jean Seberg, Samuel Beckett, and the odd couple of Jean-Paul Sartre and Simone de Beauvoir, side by side and facing the windows of their old flat.

Turn left into rue Huyghens.

The eponymous heroine of Agnès Varda's "existentialist-light" **Cléo de 5 à 7 / Cleo from 5 to 7** lives in 4-6 rue Huyghens. One of the key movies of the New Wave, the film is famous for its near-absolute unity of time and space. It covers two hours in the life of a young woman who does all types of ordinary things—like going shopping or visiting friends—while she is waiting for the result of a medical examination.

A few houses further down, on the corner of rue Huyghens and boulevard Raspail …

… immediately to your left, we see—again in **Cléo de 5 à 7 / Cleo from 5 to 7**—a French street performer swallowing a frog. (I know what you're thinking: a Frog swallowing a frog. Let it go.)

Turn right into boulevard Raspail and walk one long block until you are even with the Métro station Raspail. There is a crosswalk just past the station. Use it to cross the boulevard and continue on east into rue Campagne-Première.

Those of you who have seen and remember **À bout de souffle / Breathless** may already have recognized the distinctive house on boulevard Raspail that faces rue Campagne-Première (opposite). In the climactic scene of the movie, Jean-Paul Belmondo's nihilistic punk of a gangster gets shot in the back by the cops (to whom Jean Seberg has betrayed him) as he is running down rue Campagne-Première towards boulevard Raspail. He stumbles on for what seems a very long time before he finally falls down near the corner of boulevard Raspail, telling Jean Seberg that she is *"vraiment dégueulasse"* (really disgusting) with his last words—which she then, famously, fails to understand (*"qu'est-ce que c'est, dégueulasse?"*). We are actually reversing the scene's chronology in our walk—in our own little homage to the movie's director, the forever iconoclastic Jean-Luc Godard. We are entering the scene near the spot where Belmondo stumbles, falls, and dies and then walking down the street in the opposite direction—past the spot from which the cops take aim about two thirds down—and finally reaching the place where he has spent the night with Jean Seberg and where his last escape begins: no. 11.

At the end of the street, turn right into boulevard du Montparnasse. At the next main junction, take the left crosswalk over to the city rail (RER) station of Port-Royal.

The station (entrance pictured on page 162) features in the French crime classic **Du rififi chez les hommes / Rififi**. Tony, the movie's main protagonist, gives an errand to the drug peddler who works in the dyer's shop at 45 avenue Georges-Bernanos (the little lane on the right side of the station) so he can shadow him on his way (taking the train from the Port-Royal station) to the baddies' hide-out.

Continue by walking into avenue de l'Observatoire which runs parallel to the much smaller avenue Georges-Bernanos on the other side of the station, and cross the street to take a closer look at the Fountain of the Observatoire (photo page 147).

The garden around the Observatoire fountain represents the very tip of the tail end of the jardin du Luxembourg. This is one of the main stops in Louis Jourdain's musical journey through Paris in **Gigi**. Remember? We met the guy earlier on the rue de Furstemberg.

Cross over to the avenue's other side and walk back to the boulevard du Montparnasse.

Right at the corner at no. 171, hidden for the most part behind a high hedge, lies another one of Hem's old hangouts and the most famous one at that, the Closerie des Lilas. A decade before Hem began hanging out there, the Closerie had been heavily frequented by the city's Russian émigrés such as

Lenin and Trotsky. But by the time Hemingway met F. Scott Fitzgerald here, it was the unofficial HQ of the Parisian left-wing journalists—who were forever feuding with the "righties" at the Café de Flore barely a mile further to the west. On a completely different note, Woody Allen in **What's New Pussycat?** makes a spectacular entrance into the Closerie, taking half of the tables from the terrace on the top of his convertible with him.

If the walk has made you feel peckish, but you want some simpler fare than what's on offer at the upmarket Closerie, or you'd just like a drink, bear with me just a little longer. I am sure you will find something on the final stretch of this walk down the boulevard du Montparnasse. We'll be passing some of the most famous restaurants and bars of the city.

Stay on the north side of the street (odd numbers), as you walk back towards the Montparnasse Tower (whose top you can glimpse over the rooftops on your left).

The first of the joints that comes into view—on the other side of the street at 108 boulevard du Montparnasse—is Le Dome, where Roy Scheider meets

William Devane in **Marathon Man**. Observing the two, while seemingly playing on the pinball machine, is the Chinese hitman across the street at no. 105, La Rotonde. During her long wait in **Cléo de 5 à 7 / Cleo from 5 to 7**, Cleo also visits Le Dome.

> *A couple of buildings further down on the same side, at no. 101 and no. 99 boulevard du Montparnasse respectively, …*

… you will pass the two bars where Jean Seberg and Belmondo have drinks on their way to the photographer's flat where they will spend their last night together. In **À bout de souffle / Breathless**, they are called Kosmos and Le Select, and while Le Select still exists, Kosmos has morphed into the Lotus Café. Of the two, Le Select is the one with the much better pedigree anyway, having been one of the favorite hang-outs of Lost Generation Yanks in the 1920s. In **The Sun Also Rises**, it appears to be the center of the ex-pats' social life in the city—this is where Tyrone Power takes Ava Gardner from the *bal musette* for a quiet chat, only to run into practically every "American in Paris" he knows.

> *And finally, on the opposite side of boulevard du Montparnasse at no. 102 …*

… you'll find La Coupole, the most famous of all Parisian brasseries. In Joseph Losey's Kafkaesque war-time thriller **Monsieur Klein / Mr. Klein**, Alain Delon almost meets his alter ego face-to-face here. A "Monsieur Klein" is paged, and when Delon goes to receive the call, he is told that someone who resembles him has already been there and left a few moments before.

> *This is where our walk ends. You can retrace your steps down boulevard du Montparnasse to the Métro station Vavin (Line 4) or continue to the station Montparnasse-Bienvenüe (Lines 4, 6, 12, 13). It's about the same distance either way. Alternatively, if you still have the energy, turn left on rue du Montparnasse, which will lead you to place Fernand-Mourlot, the perfect starting point if you want to explore the Montparnasse quarter in greater depth.*

ARRONDISSEMENTS: 9, 2,1
DURATION: 3 to 4 hours

Walk 7

The Opéra to Sentier

Through the city's main shopping district behind the Opéra into place Vendôme, then on through mysterious "passages" past the Forum les Halles and into the R-rated rue St-Denis.

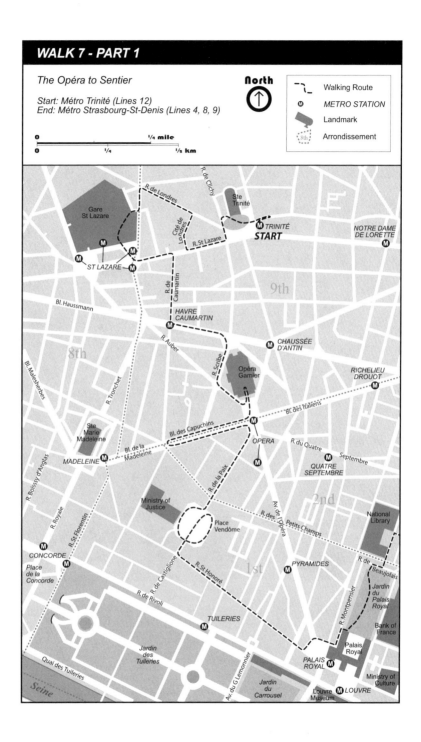

WALK 7 - PART 1

The Opéra to Sentier

Start: Métro Trinité (Lines 12)
End: Métro Strasbourg-St-Denis (Lines 4, 8, 9)

North

	Walking Route
Ⓜ	METRO STATION
	Landmark
8th	Arrondissement

0 — ¼ mile
0 — ¼ — ½ km

R. de Clichy
R. de Londres
Ste Trinité
Gare St Lazare
Cité de Londres
R. St Lazare
Ⓜ TRINITÉ START
NOTRE DAME DE LORETTE Ⓜ
Ⓜ
Ⓜ
Ⓜ ST LAZARE
Ⓜ
9th
Bl. Haussmann
R. de Caumartin
HAVRE CAUMARTIN
CHAUSSÉE D'ANTIN Ⓜ
8th
R. Auber
R. Scribe
Opéra Garnier
RICHELIEU DROUOT
Bl. Malesherbes
R. Tronchet
Bl. des Capuchins
Bl. dès Italiens
Ⓜ
Ⓜ
R. du Quatre Septembre
Ste Marie Madeleine
Bl. de la Madeleine
OPERA
MADELEINE Ⓜ
R. de la Paix
Ⓜ OPERA
QUATRE SEPTEMBRE Ⓜ
R. Boissy d'Anglas
Ministry of Justice
2nd
National Library
R. Royale
R. St Florentin
Place Vendôme
Av. de l'Opéra
R. des Petits Champs
Ⓜ CONCORDE
Place de la Concorde
R. St Honoré
1st
PYRAMIDES Ⓜ
R. de Beaujolais
R. de Castiglione
R. Montpensier
Jardin du Palais Royal
R. de Rivoli
TUILERIES Ⓜ
Bank of France
Jardin des Tuileries
Av. du G Lemonnier
PALAIS ROYAL
Palais Royal
Ministry of Culture
Quai des Tuileries
Jardin du Carrousel
Louvre Museum Ⓜ LOUVRE
Seine

Go to Métro station Trinité (Line 12) and take the exit rue St-Lazare. Walk right out of the exit into rue St-Lazare and up to the Hôtel Langlois at no. 63.

This is the hotel where Mark Wahlberg is staying in Jonathan Demme's 2002 film, **The Truth About Charlie**.

Walk over to the other side of the street to get a better view of the hotel …

… and while you are there, look into the passage at no. 56, into which we see Wahlberg disappear as he chases after Thandie Newton.

Retrace your steps to the Métro station and cross rue Blanche on your way to the Church of Sainte-Trinité, which gives the Métro station its name.

In the large fountain at the foot of the stairway in front of the church, little Antoine Doinel breaks the ice to wash his face after he has run away from home in **Les 400 coups / The 400 Blows**.

Walk past the front of the church and cross rue de Clichy at the traffic lights before continuing into rue St-Lazare.

Admittedly, this is not the most charming shopping street in Paris, so we'll take the first opportunity to leave it.

Just past the splendidly named avenue du Coq and the similarly eye-catching Pharmacie du Coq on your left (isn't it great to be puerile?), pass through the iron gates on the right-hand side of the street (open Monday to Friday from 8:00 a.m. to 7:30 p.m.) into the passageway (called the cité de Londres). Follow this passage until you reach another set of iron gates on the other end and turn left into rue de Londres. Follow it to the place de Budapest on the next corner and turn left into the square.
Alternative: If you're taking this walk on the weekend, stay on rue

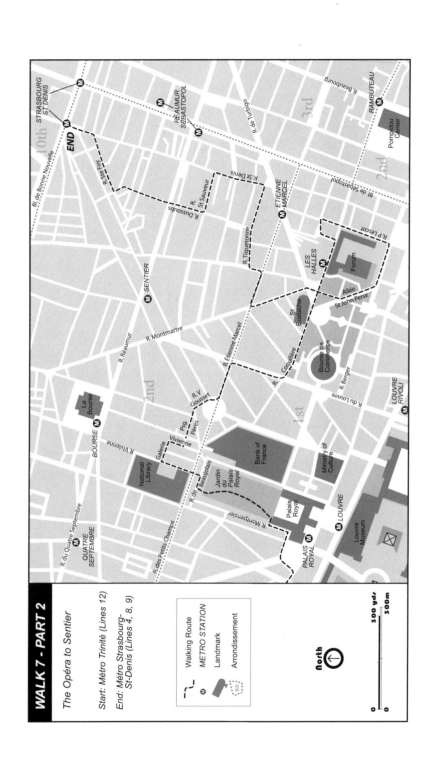

WALK 7 - PART 2

The Opéra to Sentier

Start: Métro Trinité (Lines 12)

End: Métro Strasbourg-
St-Denis (Lines 4, 8, 9)

Walking Route
METRO STATION
Landmark
Arrondissement

north

300 yds
300m

STRASBOURG
ST DENIS

END

REAUMUR
SEBASTOPOL

R. Beaubourg

RAMBUTEAU

Pompidou
Center

3rd

R. de Turbigo

Bl. de Bonne Nouvelle

R. Ste-Foy

R. St Denis

R. Dussoubs

R. St Sauveur

R. de Sébastopol

2nd

ETIENNE
MARCEL

10th

SENTIER

R. Reaumur

R. Montmartre

R. Tiquetonne

R. Etienne Marcel

LES
HALLES

St
Eustache

Forum

R.P. Lescot

Allée
St John Perse

R. Coquillère

R. Berger

R. du Louvre

LOUVRE
RIVOLI

Bourse de
Commerce

1st

La
Bourse

BOURSE

2nd

R.V.
Gousset

Psg.
Pérs

R. Vivienne

Galerie

Vivienne

National
Library

R. de Beaujolais

Jardin
du
Palais
Royal

Bank of
France

Ministry of
Culture

Palais
Royal

PALAIS
ROYAL

R. Montpensier

LOUVRE

Louvre
Museum

R. du Quatre Septembre

QUATRE
SEPTEMBRE

R. des Petits Champs

St-Lazare for another block. Turn right into rue de Budapest and continue into place de Budapest.

At the far end of the square, on the corner with rue d'Amsterdam, there is a bar (L'Atlantique), which is called the Fox Bar in **Diva**. This is where the policewoman and the witness are sitting when they observe their target come out of the train station, slip something (an audio tape as it turns out) into the mailman's bag, and get knifed in the back—all before the two of them can finish their coffees and stub out their cigarettes.

From the bar, cross rue d'Amsterdam—using the pedestrian crossing immediately on your right—and walk straight through the glass door into the Gare St-Lazare.

Platforms 20 to 27 on your right serve the Grandes Lignes, the intercity rail services that include the trains arriving from the Normandy seaside resorts. Jean-Louis Trintignant was waiting here for Anouk Aimée on her return from Deauville in Claude Lalouche's 1966 **Un homme et une femme / A Man and a Woman**.

When you are opposite platform 26, turn left, leaving the trains behind you, and walk through the archway leading to the SORTIE or exit. Just before you reach the exit in the vestibule …

… look to your left into the Brasserie Alizé. Every major French railway station has a brasserie similar to this, but it is in this one that Irene Jacob meets the mysterious puppeteer in one of the key scenes in Krzysztof Kieslowski's first international film, the Golden Globe-nominated **La double vie de Véronique / The Double Life of Veronique**. Irene Jacob is not at all pleased to hear what this strange man is telling her and leaves the café, in a somewhat sad and depressed state, for a walk to clear her mind.

We follow her out of the St-Lazare station: through the exit, down the escalator, and across the station's forecourt, turning left at the intersection into rue St-Lazare and then right into rue de Caumartin at the next corner.

Follow this pedestrian-only shopping street all the way past Le Printemps department store to the corner of boulevard Haussmann and seek shelter in the department store's entrance, the one facing the boulevard.

This is where we leave Véronique to deal with the complications of her double life all on her own (hoping she has cleared her mind sufficiently).

Turn left into boulevard Haussmann and enjoy some window shopping in Le Printemps—but not in the even more famous Galeries Lafayette right behind it, because just where the shop windows start—on the corner after the Lafayette food hall or "Lafayette Gourmet" as it is called—we turn right, crossing boulevard Haussmann into place Diaghilev and rue Scribe to the right of the Opéra.

Strictly speaking this is the Opéra Garnier, or Palais Garnier, so called to distinguish it from the Opéra Bastille, which was constructed in the 1980s as the new stage for the lyric theatre. The Opéra Garnier is nowadays used only for ballet and concert performances.

Continue down rue Scribe to the next corner and turn left on rue Auber, which will lead you straight to the place de l'Opéra.

The large building to your right that takes up the entire block between rue Scribe and the place de l'Opéra is the hotel Paris-le-Grand, which features prominently in Robert Altman's **Prêt-à-Porter**. The entire press pack stays here, and Lauren Bacall gives an interview in its lobby to the hapless Kim Basinger. The hotel also hosts Harrison Ford and his wife in Roman Polanski's **Frantic**. We can see the Opéra from their hotel window.

Turn left at the square and left again up the stairs. The main entrance to the Opéra is to your right.

Looking inside is free, up to the section that's been cordoned off, and you can catch a glimpse of the magnificent stairway that's featured in **Funny Face** as the setting for yet another fashion shoot.

If, however, you want to see the place where Roy Scheider goes to meet the antiques dealer (only to find him dead) in **Marathon Man**, you will have to buy yourself a ticket to tour the interior. If you do, don't miss the spooky basement, haunt of the original **Phantom of the Opera**. Gaston Leroux's gothic novel was filmed several times, most memorably in 1925 with Lon Chaney, Sr. in the title role that made his career.

> *Leave the Opéra through the main entrance and head for the right side of the place de l'Opéra.*

In **Rush Hour III**, Chris Tucker, on assignment from the LAPD, takes his evening coffee at a table outside the famous Café de la Paix (above left, Palais Garnier in background) while being serenaded by a street musician with an "unplugged," so-bad-it's-nearly-good version of "California Girls."

> *Just past the café, turn right into the boulevard des Capucines.*

The Scribe hotel on the corner of the boulevard and rue Scribe is secret agent Lemmy Caution's hotel in Jean-Luc Godard's **Alphaville**. FBI agent Lemmy Caution was the 1930s' brainchild of British crime writer Peter Cheyney, both of whom would be totally forgotten if it hadn't been for Lemmy Caution's second life as a cult hero in 1950s' French cinema. The series of low-budget Lemmy Caution movies owed much of its success to the slightly detached rough-and-tumble charm of its leading man, the American ex-pat actor and (conservatory-educated) singer Eddie Constantine. The popularity of the series was already very much on the wane when Godard picked up the character—and the man who had portrayed him—for his own purposes in *Alphaville*, giving Eddie Constantine a new, and unlikely, lease of life as an actor in European art-house films for directors such as Fassbinder and Lars von Trier. In his native America, Constantine—who died in 1993, aged 75—is practically unknown. But for French cinema-goers in the 1950s, Constantine impersonated much of what the U.S. appeared to stand for at the time: self-confidence, insouciance, and a somewhat rugged charm.

Incidentally, the first-ever screening of a moving picture took place next door to the Scribe. One reason Godard is so popular among intellectuals is that they can understand his references and in jokes.

A few doors further down, at the corner of rue de Caumartin …

… you can spot the most famous Parisian music hall, the Olympia, scene of many memorable concerts through the years, possibly none more so than Édith Piaf's final appearance. Racked by terminal cancer and barely able to stand due to the pain, the "Little Sparrow" bade farewell to her fans, singing all her famous songs one last time just weeks before her death. On a somewhat different note, the Olympia was also the place Sid Vicious recorded—in one take—his truly inspired version of "My Way," which provides the climax of **The Great Rock 'n' Roll Swindle** (not only has he killed the cat, oh no: "I did it my way"). Director Julien Temple later said that Vicious would not have been capable of holding out for another take.

Cross the boulevard des Capucines at the traffic lights and walk back toward the Opéra …

… past some of the bars and theatres that have flourished in this area since the days of Baron Haussmann's large-scale urban renewal scheme in the 19th century. Apart from many smaller theaters, the boulevard des Capucines housed the Théâtre des Capucines, the Théâtre de Vaudeville, and the Opéra-Comique back then. It was the most brilliant and most fashionable of all of Haussmann's newly developed Grand Boulevards and the "natural" home for the city's great *flaneurs* (dandies) such as Charles Baudelaire, Stéphane Mallarmé, and Edouard Manet.

Look left as you pass rue Scribe again.

From this side of the boulevard, you can catch a good look at the main entrance to the Grand hotel. This is where Harrison Ford's search for his lost wife begins in **Frantic**.

Back on the place de l'Opéra, cross to the center island using the crosswalk on your right and look left for a panoramic view of the Palais Garnier.

This is also more or less the view you get in director Neil Jordan's **Interview with the Vampire**, where the Opéra puts in an appearance as Brad Pitt and Tom Cruise's Paris hotel. **Funny Face**, too, shows us the Opéra from here, with Kay Thompson dancing on the corner, quivering with anticipation as she thinks about all the luxury shops awaiting her on the rue de la Paix.

Before following her into rue de la Paix on your right, cross the street. Continue to the far side of the place de l'Opéra and walk clockwise, pausing at the top of avenue de l'Opéra to look at the building on the corner across the street.

49 avenue de l'Opéra (now occupied by Air France), was for a long time the address of the *Paris Herald* the European edition of the *New York Herald*. The first international newspaper, the English-language *Paris Herald* (or *Paris Herald Tribune* beginning in 1924) was a platform for the Lost Generation of Ernest Hemingway and all the other American ex-pats who came to Paris after The Great War. In **The Sun Also Rises**, Hollywood's take on Heming-

way's debut novel, this is where Tyrone Power's character works, although for the film, they felt—for unfathomable reasons—that they had to move the *Herald*'s offices to the other side of the avenue. We get a view of Power looking down the avenue from his office window with the Opéra to his left.

Cross avenue de l'Opéra and walk into rue de la Paix ...

... Paris's most expensive shopping street. As the English crime writer Andrew Martin has it, here "the cobblestones always seem to have been recently vacuumed". Look to your right for the Hôtel Westminster at 13 rue de la Paix (below). This is where Catherine Deneuve lives in **Le dernier métro / The Last Metro**, although it is called the Hôtel du Pont-Neuf in the movie. (So her scruffy little theater seems to generate a handsome little profit after all!)

A little further down, on the corner of rue de la Paix and rue des Capucines ...

… is the jewelry shop Poiray, which was renamed ("Mappin and Webb") for the movie in which it has a starring role. Jules Dassin, despite his French-sounding name, was born in Connecticut and came to France only in the early 1950s, after having been denounced as a Communist sympathizer by Joe McCarthy's House Un-American Activities Committee (HUAC). But even in Europe, few people wanted to hire him out of fear that Dassin's movies would find no American distributor. Having had no work for five years, Dassin finally agreed to write and direct what seemed at the time a small genre movie called **Du rififi chez les hommes / Rififi**. As cinephiles know, it became a huge popular and critical success, "the best *film noir* I've ever seen" (François Truffaut), winning Dassin the Best Director's Award at the Cannes film festival.

We see the jewelry shop several times in the film, mainly in the first half when the gang members case the joint from the surrounding streets and from a café on the opposite side of rue de la Paix (La Colombe at no. 2—four doors up from the corner). The scene of the actual break-in, a 20-minute tour de force without a line of spoken dialogue, became one of the most famous and frequently imitated scenes in movie history.

Continue now into place Vendôme and walk counterclockwise around this temple of retail opulence.

Start at the right corner next to the Ritz, no. 19 place Vendôme. The facade was used as the front of the Malivert jewelry shop in Nicole Garcia's subtle and classy thriller **Place Vendôme**.

The next building down the place Vendôme is easily its most famous. "The Ritz" has always been the last word in luxurious accommodation, even before Irving Berlin (and later Fred Astaire) immortalized it as a synonym for the last word in luxury and elegance in the song "Puttin' on the Ritz." Gary Cooper puts in a cameo appearance in the song—"dressed up like a million dollar trooper / trying hard to look like Gary Cooper"—and one might call it ironic that, trying hard to look thirty years younger, Cooper seduces Audrey Hepburn in The Ritz itself in Billy Wilder's **Love in the Afternoon**.

The Ritz has also been used, in much the same way as the restaurant Maxim's (see Walk 1), as a shortcut to character description. The icy fashion editor (Meryl Streep) in **The Devil Wears Prada**, Gene Kelly's matronly benefactress in **An American in Paris**, and the gentleman art investigator (Peter O'Toole) in **How to Steal a Million** all reveal something about themselves by having chosen The Ritz as their Paris address. As, of course, does Kay Thompson in **Funny Face**. We see her dancing here, too, only this time she is not dancing alone but with about a dozen Ritz doormen, and God only knows what pleasures she's anticipating this time.

The Ritz is also the place where Catherine Deneuve tries to sell the diamonds she has inherited from her husband in **Place Vendôme**. The scenes set in the Ritz were really shot here, even those inside one of the rooms (it's no. 253). But, of course, the most famous footage ever shot here consists of nothing more than grainy surveillance video of Princess Diana and her lover, the playboy Dodi Al-Fayed (son of the hotel's owner), leaving through the main entrance on a journey from which they were never to return.

Cross the square now to the other side.

In **Place Vendôme**, Catherine Deneuve tries to run her virtually bankrupt jewelry shop from no. 12, where, in reality, the offices of the Joaillerie Chaumet are located today. Over a century ago, however, Polish composer Frédéric Chopin died in no. 12. You may remember some details of Chopin's story from Hugh Grant's portrayal in *Impromptu* or from the 1945 classic, *A Song to Remember*, which was nominated for seven Academy Awards.

A few doors down at no. 20, the Joaillerie Mauboussin is the setting for the heist in Jean-Pierre Melville's masterpiece **Le cercle rouge**.

Place Vendôme also puts in appearances in **Marathon Man**, where Roy Scheider is seen with bags from some seriously expensive Vendôme shops, and in John Huston's **Moulin Rouge**, as the place where Toulouse buys flowers for Myriam. More recently, in James Ivory's **Le divorce**, we see Naomi Watts's moving van being parked at the foot of Napoleon's obscenely shaped victory column here, presumably to show the social strata she is moving in after the sale of her painting.

Let's follow Naomi's departing van out of the place Vendôme heading towards the Tuileries (in the opposite direction from the Opéra). But instead of going directly to rue de Rivoli as Naomi did, we'll turn left at the first corner into rue St-Honoré …

… another street for shoppers with an exceedingly deep wallet, but this time for frocks rather than beads and baubles. (Gentlemen, distract your ladies.)

Continue straight, crossing rue du Marché-St-Honoré and passing the baroque Church of St-Roch. Cross rue des Pyramides and then rue de l'Échelle on your way to place André-Malraux. Walk over to the fountain and walk across avenue de l'Opéra and rue de Richelieu—using the traffic light on your right—to the entrances of the Comédie-Française.

The stage of this theatre, the oldest in Paris (and the only one in France run directly by the state) provides the setting for the final showdown in **Charade** where Cary Grant proves a deft stagehand who is capable of pulling just the right lever at the right time to ensure a happy ending.

Turn left into rue de Richelieu under the colonnades in front of the Comédie-Française then right into rue de Montpensier. Walk straight into the gardens of the Palais Royal. Once inside, turn left.

Under the colonnades in the paved plaza on your left, in the space right behind the first row of columns that cut across at a right angle, Roy Scheider meets "Nicole" in what is indisputably **Marathon Man**'s most puzzling scene: in a surreal moment, a football mysteriously materializes out of the Paris night. Under the same colonnades, Audrey Hepburn is made to choose between Cary Grant and Walter Matthau in **Charade**—who has come here to protect her and who to kill her? It looks like an easy question on paper, but in the film the suspense holds up surprisingly well.

Eventually, of course, Audrey gets it right, but baddies—even in "romcoms" such as this—are rarely gracious losers. Fortunately, they also tend to be poor shots, very poor in this case (size up the distance: Hepburn can only have stood a few feet away), and that gives her the chance of escaping down the shopping arcade along the left side of the gardens.

Pursue her, but take the time to look into the neatly arranged garden to your right. The view back from the central fountain is especially nice, and there are chairs here if you want to take a breather.

Camille Desmoulins, one of the heroes of the French revolution, holds his rabble-rousing speech in this garden in **Jefferson in Paris**—historically correct, as it happens. In the same garden, Christina Ricci, Cate Blanchett, and some other members of their dance troupe chew the fat (or, more likely, the tofu) in **The Man Who Cried**, while in **Head in the Clouds**, Stuart Townsend chooses this shopping arcade as the perfect spot to tell Charlize Theron that he is about to join the International Brigades in the Spanish Civil War.

In the meantime, while we were looking elsewhere, Audrey Hepburn has escaped through one of the doors on our left into the Comédie-Française—which is, of course, about a hundred yards in back of us. But that's Hollywood for you.

> *So we leave the gardens of the Palais Royal through the archway ahead of us, passing by the legendary restaurant Le Grand Véfour as we head into rue de Beaujolais.*

On your left, at the corner of rue de Beaujolais and rue de Montpensier, is a narrow stairway called the passage de Beaujolais (below left). In **Head in the Clouds**, Stuart Townsend steps down this passage into the street-level brasserie on the right—and straight into the trap the German *Abwehroffizier*, incidentally also his rival in love, has laid for him—but not to worry: Charlize Theron will save him right on time.

Turn right down rue de Beaujolais, and then left at the next corner into rue Vivienne. Cross rue des Petits-Champs and continue straight ahead.

In the restaurant Le Grand Colbert at 2-4 rue Vivienne, Jack Nicholson "gate-crashes" Diane Keaton's *diner-à-deux* with Keanu Reeves in one of the key scenes in the Oscar-nominated **Something's Gotta Give**. The restaurant displays the movie poster alongside its menu in the window, and a 2004 newspaper article tells you what life was like for the restaurant's staff during the nine days of shooting and for a time after the movie became such a big success. The table where the couple dined—at the wall opposite the entrance—was apparently booked solid for months. What's more, the clients all ordered the same dish. "We serve nothing but chicken, chicken, chicken," the *maitre d'* complains in the article. He goes on to describe Keanu Reeves as "polite, but distant", while adding rather icily that Diane Keaton "mainly ate in her trailer." Jack Nicholson, on the other hand, apparently ordered copious amounts of brandy and was soon best friends with everyone. We also learn that Le Grand Colbert had to increase its portions for the film. Apparently, they were afraid that the American public would question the main characters' wisdom in travelling halfway around the world for a kid's portion of roast chicken.

Continue a few houses further down rue Vivienne—past the entrance to the Galerie Colbert—and turn right into the Galerie Vivienne.

Galerie Vivienne was the most fashionable of all the indoor shopping centers that were hugely popular in 19th century Paris. In the WWII thriller **Code Name: Emerald**, Ed Harris shakes off his shadow here, while, in **Zazie dans**

le métro / Zazie in the Metro, the film's naughty little protagonist and her dapper companion photograph each other in front of various shop windows during their long slapstick chase.

Continue down Galerie Vivienne almost to the end, following the 90-degree turn to the right.

The large stairway at no. 13 (above)—all shops here have a number, exactly as if this were a real street—once belonged to the flat of Vidocq, the famous ex-con who became the leader of the Paris anti-crime squad in 1811. (You'll find more on the history of this and the other Paris *galeries* in the "Passages" section of the chapter *Further Afield*.)

Retrace your steps and leave the Galerie Vivienne between nos. 24 and 26 on your right and walk straight into rue des Petits-Pères. Cross rue de la Banque and continue down the dark passage with houses on either side (still the rue des Petits-Pères) into the place des Petits-Pères.

This is the route Juliette Binoche follows in director Nobuhiro Suwa's episode of **Paris, je t'aime**. Binoche, a bereaved young mother—basically picking up from where she left off in the greatest role of her stellar career (in *Trois couleurs: Bleu / Three Colors: Blue*)—is searching for her dead son in the place des Petits-Pères when Willem Dafoe's cowboy rides in from rue du Mail, straight ahead to your left. After Binoche has been reconciled to her fate, Dafoe disappears—with the boy—in the direction from which you've just come, the entrance to the Galerie Vivienne in the background (photo page 183).

Before you leave the place des Petits-Pères, you may want to take a closer look at, or even inside, the church to your left, the Notre-Dame-de-Victoire. It is here that Gérard Dépardieu's contact is arrested by the Gestapo in **Le dernier métro / The Last Metro**, François Truffaut's most commercially successful film.

Cross the square diagonally now into rue Vide-Gousset and follow it into the place des Victoires.

Somewhere in the row of houses right opposite you, on the other side of the square, is the flat occupied by Juliette Binoche and her husband in **Paris, je t'aime.**

Cross rue d'Aboukir (in front of you) and take a left into busy rue Étienne-Marcel. At the large intersection, turn right into rue du Louvre and, at the next corner (past the large Post Office), left into rue Coquillière, less a "street" than a leafy square with cafés and restaurants.

Follow this street, which changes its name to rue Rambuteau, past the Church St-Eustache.

The plaza with the distinctive sculpture on your right provides the backdrop for the first fashion shoot in the 1995 **Sabrina**, the shoot where everything goes haywire.

Continue straight ahead.

On your right, the modern shopping centre of Les Halles now comes into view. In its place stood, until 1971, the wholesale food market for all of Paris, a colorful place of relentless hustle and bustle throughout the night, famous as—after Émile Zola's novel of the same name—*Le ventre de Paris*, the stomach of Paris. But there was no room for the market to expand in this densely built urban area. So in the early 1970s, the whole place—including its beautiful 19th century cast-iron market halls—was razed and replaced by a shopping mall, while the wholesale market moved to the northern suburb of Rungis. When **Charade** was made in 1963, however, the stomach of Paris was still where it belonged, in the center of the city, and this is where Walter Matthau takes Audrey Hepburn for a little tour and some straight talk.

About three quarters down the length of the shopping center, turn left into rue Mondétour and follow it to the corner of rue de la Grande-Truanderie. Turn right to find the famous restaurant Le Pharamond—at 24 rue de la Grande-Truanderie—on the left side of the street.

This is where Tyrone Power takes Juliette Greco's working girl in **The Sun Also Rises**. (She empties her drink in a single go.)

Turn right into rue Pierre-Lescot.

On the terrace of Le Bon Pecheur at 12 rue Pierre-Lescot, Denis Lavant and Juliette Binoche steal wallets by spiking the drinks of the clients in **Les amants du Pont-Neuf / The Lovers on the Bridge**.

Look left when you reach the end of the shopping center.

Right in front of the Fontaine des Innocents, Chevy Chase has his camera stolen when he asks a stranger to take a picture of himself with his family in **National Lampoon's European Vacation**.

Turn right now into rue Berger. Just past the Porte Berger on your right (one of the entrances to the shopping center), cut into the garden towards the church.

From here, you get the clearest view of the shopping center. I refrain from calling it the "best view," because the "best view" is undoubtedly one that shows you as little as possible of this eyesore, quite possibly the ugliest building in Paris. The city administration has closely analyzed different plans for transforming the area, ranging in scope from some largely cosmetic changes to virtually razing the whole thing and making a fresh start. But at this writing, it has not yet made up its mind.

As you near the church, several of the garden paths intersect. Take the path called allée André Breton and continue straight past the church into rue Montmartre.

After their walk through the old market of Les Halles, Walter Matthau in **Charade** takes Audrey Hepburn to *Le Cochon à l'Oreille* at 15 rue Montmartre, towards the end of this stretch, near the corner. There he tells her the story of Carson Dyle, giving her a truthful account of what actually happened and leaving out only one tiny little detail. Look inside from the street and you will find this tiny restaurant almost unchanged. Should you feel hunger pangs, this might be a nice place to stop. The prices are quite reasonable.

Turn right into rue Étienne-Marcel, but go only as far as the next corner. Two doors down on your right …

… at 38 rue Montorgueil, is another famous restaurant, the L'Escargot Montorgueil, where famous stars such as Charlie Chaplin and Humphrey Bogart have dined. It was reproduced in a studio for Billy Wilder's **Irma la Douce**, where it became "Chez Moustache." This is where Shirley MacLaine, the eponymous Irma, takes her breaks and where she meets Jack Lemmon's street cop, who, of course, falls in love with her.

Now that we've seen where Irma takes her coffee, let's see where this lady of the night works.

Retrace your steps to rue Étienne-Marcel and cross this busy street into the continuation of rue Montorgueil on the other side. Take the first street to the right which is called rue Tiquetonne (named after a 14th century baker) and follow it through until you reach rue St-Denis, where you turn left and continue walking till you reach rue St-Sauveur on the left.

On our walks through Paris we have come across one or two of the city's smaller red light districts, but this one is the real thing, the mother of all open-air brothels. We are standing now on the sex-shop end of rue St-Denis, the DIY and discount area. If Les Halles is "the stomach of Paris," the St-Denis quarter takes care of the part a few inches further down.

The "rue Casanova" where Shirley MacLaine plies her trade was only a set, as was everything else "Parisian" in **Irma la Douce**. But Alexandre Trauner, the man who built those sets for Billy Wilder, had long experience constructing near-perfect replicas of Paris streets from his working days in the French movie industry in the 1930s, and he modelled rue Casanova very closely on rue St-Denis.

By the time you reach rue St-Sauveur, I think you'll probably have seen enough of rue St-Denis. Turn left into St-Sauveur and then right at the next corner into rue Dussoubs. Cross busy rue Réaumur into the part of Paris called the "Sentier," literally the "narrow lane."

This is the center of the Paris textile industry and many of the houses you see around you have been converted to ateliers (sweatshops might be a more accurate term) in which clothes are made and mended and then often sold just a few meters away. The "rag trade" in Paris has been dominated by the city's Jews for centuries. Even though other Middle Eastern communities and the Chinese in particular have begun to crowd in, non-Jews may still find it tough to operate certain types of business in the Sentier. That's why Richard Anconina pretends to be Jewish in **La vérité si je mens / Would I Lie To You?**, one of the most successful French comedies of the last twenty years, which is largely set in this part of town.

> *Follow rue Dussoubs across rue du Caire straight into the passage du Caire.*

This is where Richard Anconina escapes from his pursuers early in the film, almost literally into the arms of the wealthy textile merchant who—in the mistaken belief that Anconina, like himself, is Jewish—gives him a job and introduces him to his family, including his beautiful daughter. No prizes for guessing what happens next.

> *Follow the passage du Caire and turn right across from no. 131. Walk out into the street and cross rue d'Alexandrie straight into rue Ste-Foy. Follow this street to the corner with rue St-Denis—where you can meet ladies of the night any time of day.*
>
> *Alternative: If the passage du Caire is closed (as it is when the shops are closed), go back to rue du Caire and turn left to return to rue St-Denis, and then left again into St-Denis.*

On your right, at 226 rue St-Denis, is the wealthy cloth trader's shop , where the opening scene of **La vérité si je mens / Would I Lie To You?** is set.

> *If you dare, you may now walk straight into rue Blondel for that authentic **Irma la Douce** feeling. Otherwise, turn left (or continue straight ahead if you took the Alternative route) towards the Arch and then take a right at the boulevard to the Métro station Strasbourg-St-Denis (Lines 4, 8, 9). For a possible add-on for **Before Sunset** fans, see page 242.*

ARRONDISSEMENTS: 9, 10, 18
DURATION: just under 3 hours

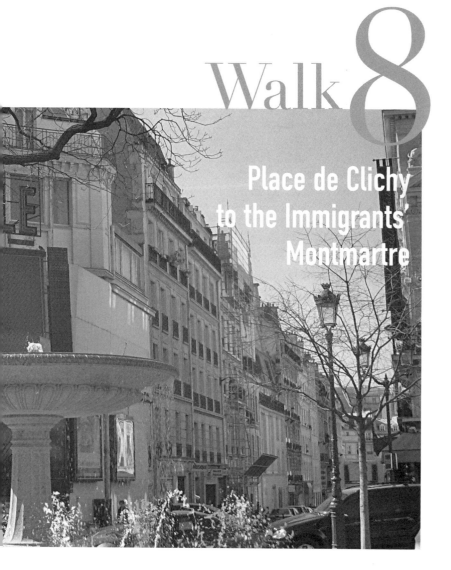

Walk 8

Place de Clichy to the Immigrants' Montmartre

From the place de Clichy at the foot of the Montmartre hill down the legendary streets of the Parisian underworld to the colorful area along the boulevard Barbes, home to many immigrants.

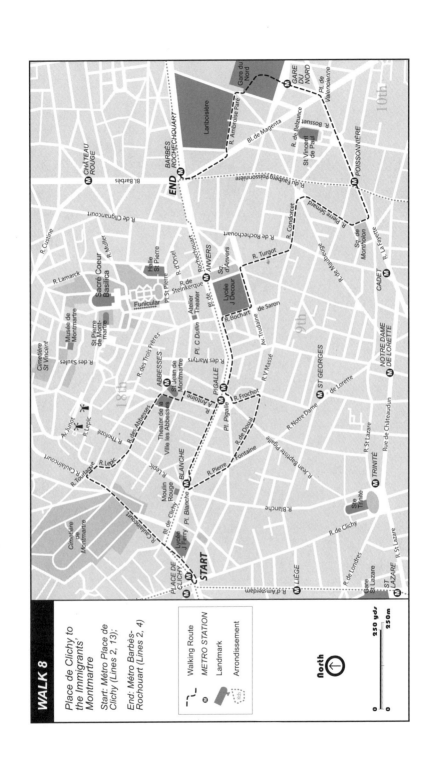

WALK 8

Place de Clichy to
the Immigrants',
Montmartre

Start: Métro Place de
Clichy (Lines 2, 13);

End: Métro Barbès-
Rochouart (Lines 2, 4)

Legend:
- Walking Route
- Ⓜ METRO STATION
- Landmark
- Arrondissement

north

250 yds
250m

0
0

Go to the Métro station Place-de-Clichy (Lines 2, 13), and look around you on your way out ...

... because the station itself has featured in a couple of movies. In **Trois couleurs: Blanc / Three Colors: White**, Julie Delpy's Polish husband meets his morbidly melancholic countryman on one of the platforms of Clichy station; the man offers Delpy's husband money to bump him off in a kind of "assisted suicide." And in **Les 400 coups / The 400 Blows**, the two boys use this station on their way to central Paris.

Leave the station through the exit place de Clichy.

You are looking straight at the Brasserie Wepler, one of the largest restaurants in Paris and the favorite haunt of Henry Miller during his—not all that quiet—*Quiet Days in Clichy*. (Miller actually lived in the suburb of Clichy, on 4 avenue Anatole-France near the Paris city limits just outside the 17th arrondissement, because the rents were cheaper there, but he walked here often—the trip would take about half an hour on foot—and called the Wepler his favorite café in Paris. There is a Danish film based on Miller's Paris memoirs, also called **Quiet Days in Clichy**, which claims to have been "shot on location" but in truth consists of little more than a series of naughty bits. It was banned in the UK for 30 years.)

Before you move on, take a close look at the windows on the second floor just above the restaurant. This is where Julie Delpy lives in **Trois couleurs: Blanc / Three Colors: White**.

Turn right out of the Métro exit into what is in fact a traffic island.

Right next to the exit and the taxi queue is the place where little Antoine sees his mother kiss a man who is definitely not her husband in **Les 400 coups / The 400 Blows**.

The area around the place de Clichy is a lively mix of upmarket restaurants such as the Wepler and the Charlot to your right (the only place in Paris where they serve you the original *Bouillabaisse à la Marseillaise*, the favorite dish of all the home-sick French movie gangsters from the South) with the demi-monde of the rue Amsterdam at your back (where not-so-little-anymore

Antoine goes to search out the prostitutes first thing in the morning after his release from the Army in the Oscar-nominated continuation of *The 400 Blows* called **Baisers volés / Stolen Kisses**) and the mythical Académie des Billards on rue de Clichy, also at your back. (Go there by all means for that *The Hustler / The Color of Money* feeling. It is a members-only club, but if you look respectable, the owner will issue you a free card right on the spot.)

> *Cross over to the right side of the boulevard de Clichy and turn left, crossing rue de Douai. Continue straight ahead, with the beige brick building of the Lycée Jules Ferry on your right and eventually crossing the boulevard de Clichy (which veers sharply to the right at the corner) into rue Caulaincourt straight ahead.*

To your left, on the far side of the street, there is a large DIY store ("Castorama"): this is where the huge Hippodrome once stretched (it also covered the ground of the two hotels behind it), a 19th century "pleasure dome" which in the 1960s was turned into a cinema and later razed to the ground. In François Truffaut's **Les 400 coups / The 400 Blows**, made in 1959, we see Antoine with his mother and step-father come here to watch the impenetrable New Wave classic *Paris nous appartient / Paris Belongs to Us*, a strange choice for a working-class couple with a ten-year old kid maybe, but incidentally the film that Truffaut had cut his teeth on as an Executive Producer a few months before.

> *Continue down rue Caulaincourt onto the bridge across the cemetery.*

This is the bridge across which we see Antoine shlep the typewriter he has stolen from his stepfather's office in **Les 400 coups / The 400 Blows**.

To your left and right, you can see some of the graves of the Cimetière de Montmartre, the last resting place of, among others, Nijinski (the dancer, not the racehorse), the popular 1960s' singer Dalida (whose grave is adorned by a life-size statue of her), as well as both the writer Alexandre Dumas, Jr. and the woman who inspired his most famous creation, Marie Duplessis a.k.a. *The Lady of the Camellias* a.k.a. *La Traviata* a.k.a.

Satine, the Nicole Kidman character in Baz Luhrmann's *Moulin Rouge*. (In **L'Amour en fuite / Love on the Run**, the fifth and final installment of Truffaut's semi-autobiographic Doinel saga, Antoine runs into his mother's former lover who shows him her grave, located right next to Duplessis's in Div. 1 (No. 15). His "mentor" in the detective agency where they both worked in **Baisers volés / Stolen Kisses** is also buried here, in the area near the busy intersection ahead of you—as is, poignantly, Truffaut himself who had a busy, varied, but ultimately short life and died of a brain tumour in 1984, aged only 52. For exact locations of these or other famous graves, inquire at the main entrance—at 20 avenue Rachel, down the stairs before the bridge—or consult one of the many maps in the cemetery itself.

At the busy intersection, just in front of the Hôtel Terrass, Antoine Doinel, forever the schlemihl, has an accident in **Baisers volés / Stolen Kisses**—crashing into, of all the cars in Paris, the one owned by his girlfriend's father.

Continue down rue Caulaincourt, the leafy avenue which marks the northern border of Montmartre.

In the house on the next corner, no. 21 on your left side, you can see the large 3rd floor window (the one facing the intersection with rue Tourlaque) behind which Toulouse-Lautrec painted some of his greatest pictures.

Turn right into rue Tourlaque and right again into rue Lepic. Look for no. 54 on your left side.

This is the house where Vincent van Gogh lived—in the top-floor flat of his brother Theo, a fairly successful Parisian art dealer—for two years in the 1880s. This was not the most fertile period in Vincent's life, but there is one picture—called *View of Paris from Vincent's Room in the Rue Lepic*—which shows us exactly, well, the view he had from his room in the rue Lepic. (It is more or less the same view we get in the van Gogh biopic **Lust for Life** which features Kirk Douglas as the self-destructive artist.)

Follow the street directly into rue des Abbesses, Montmartre's main shopping street, when rue Lepic veers off in a 90-degree right angle into the market. (Note that the part of Montmartre that lies to your left is included in Walk 4.) Cross rue Aristide-Bruant, rue Audran and rue Germain-Pilon, and just before you arrive at the place des Abbesses (with the Métro station Abbesses), turn right opposite the passage des Abbesses—the archway on the left side of the street— into rue André-Antoine.

This is exactly the way José Ferrer's Toulouse-Lautrec is taking in **Moulin Rouge**. Having quarreled with a young *bourgeois* on the rue des Abbesses, opposite the gateway to the passage des Abbesses, he then descends rue André-Antoine to go home, interrupted by a number of flashbacks which is why it takes him half the movie to reach the bottom of the street. Look around you for an impression of the "real" old Montmartre: this is what the entire place would look like without the souvenir shops, the fashion designers and the middle-class tenants who have arrived in successive waves of gentrification.

Follow the sweep of the street to the left and then to the right where rue André-Antoine veers sharply off at a 90-degree angle and continue to walk in the direction of the place Pigalle neon lights, which you can already see at the end of the street.

This area, the streets in back of the Church of St-Jean-de-Montmartre, is the realm of the formidable Martha, a real-life transsexual prostitute and neighborhood watch in one, who looks like a truck driver in high heels (think John Wayne in *Charlie's Aunt* and you're nearly there). Martha is not afraid to mix it up either. Her particular ferocity is reserved for those troublesome kids who dare to come here from other parts of town to intimidate the kids in the 'hood—who, after all, enjoy her special protection. You may catch a glimpse of her or one of her "sisters" plying their trade in these parts.

At the bottom of rue André-Antoine, leave place Pigalle, or "Pig Alley" as it was dubbed by American soldiers after WWII, for the moment and turn right into boulevard de Clichy, past the famous club Les Noctambules at no. 24 …

... where 70-year-old Pierre Carré, hair all revved up like some latter-day Little Richard, has entertained visitors for nearly 40 years, becoming a local legend in the process, and still does so every Thursday, Friday and Saturday night. (He puts in a cameo appearance in **The Truth About Charlie** where you can spot him as a singer in a flea market bistro.)

The area we are about to enter and which is known all over the world as "Montmartre" has, in fact, little in common with the Montmartre of Walk 4. Montmartre, small as it is, actually features three distinct parts: the *chi-chi* Montmartre of Walk 4, the immigrants' Montmartre around the boulevard Barbès (of which more a little later on), and the porn-shop Montmartre—which, in case the three-story SEXODROME on your left has not provided you with sufficient evidence, is where we have now arrived.

Continue down the boulevard ...

... used for the title sequence in the French cop-thriller **La balance**. In Brian DePalma's **Femme Fatale**, we see *paparazzo* Antonio Banderas at work in front of no. 33 b (on the left side of the street). The Palace Video at no. 37 is the sex shop where Mathieu Kassovitz works in **Le fabuleux destin d'Amélie Poulain / Amélie**, although interiors were apparently shot a few yards further down at no. 74 at the Tchiky Boom, now—imaginatively—called Love Shop.

> *Just beyond no. 48, turn into the narrow alleyway on your right, called cité du Midi. A few yards into the alleyway, which becomes a lovely residential mews, …*

… you will see a decrepit-looking grey steel door on your left. This is the door behind which the girl called Lucille works (i.e. strips) in **Trois couleurs: Bleu / Three Colors: Blue**.

> *One building further down on the boulevard de Clichy (no. 50) …*

… is the place where Rebecca Romijn-Stamos goes to purchase a *flingue* (a gun) in **Femme Fatale**. We see her in a window on the 2nd floor, above the night club Le Sydney, now called Glamour, and God knows what by the time you pass by.

Now just when you least expect it, a sudden and total change of key: Peek through the bars of the gates before the Villa des Platanes at no. 58-60 (it's a private residence) into a magnificent Belle Époque courtyard, complete with sweeping stairway and an entrance flanked by life-sized stone statues. This stairway provides the setting for one rather long section of the slapstick chase sequence in **Zazie dans le métro / Zazie in the Metro** (where Zazie first changes into a black cat and then into an old woman.)

> *Cross over to the middle strip of the boulevard now, the "espace civilisée," a pleasant walkway for people who want to escape the attention of the obtrusive guys (and dolls) who try to drag passersby into one of the nightclubs on both sides of the boulevard. At the Métro station Blanche, cross on to the left side of the boulevard and left into rue Pierre-Fontaine.*

The very next corner is the epicenter of the Parisian underworld. It has all the required infrastructure: Le Depanneur, the American-style diner on your right, with its 24/7 service, Le Cloche d'Or across the street—the only place in Paris where they will serve you a three-course warm meal at five o'clock in the morning, not to forget the pool halls and bars with all-night card games where the pimps pass the hours while their loosely dressed girls are smoking cigarettes near the open doors in one of the many nightclubs around, waiting for tourists to step right in for a night they will never forget.

Continue into place André-Breton and veer left into rue de Douai. Walk on past the many shops for musical instruments (the other reason people come to this area) across rue Jean-Baptiste-Pigalle into rue Victor-Massé. When you cross rue Frochot at the next corner, look briefly to your right.

This is rue Henri-Monnier, where director François Truffaut (whom we have met earlier in several of his many Antoine Doinel incarnations) actually grew up. (Now we know why he always returns to this part of town.)

Avenue Frochot follows a few steps beyond. Pause here for a second and look around.

Filmmaker Jean Renoir lived at 7 avenue Frochot from 1937 to 1969.

The stained glass window on your left—behind which you'll find yet another pool room—together with the iron gate in front of the entrance to avenue Frochot (photo next page) provides the backdrop for the quarrel and reconciliation of Bob Hoskins and Fanny Bryant in their episode of **Paris, je t'aime**.

More to the point, two famous underworld bars are located on this corner. First, there is Le Balto (on the corner of rue Victor-Massé and rue Henri-Monnier), seen in, among others, Jean-Pierre Melville's **Bob le flambeur**. Then there is Le Frochot, on the opposite corner of rue Victor-Massé and rue Frochot. In the legendary French gangster caper **Touchez pas au grisbi / Grisbi**, Jean Gabin takes his friend here (later, we see them enter avenue Frochot), and right at the beginning of the *César*-winning **Les ripoux / My New Partner**, the two corrupt cops lie in wait on the street corner for Le Frochot's owner.

Turn into rue Frochot, pool hall to your right, (past such places as the Sully Club with its all-day hostess service) and walk the block to place Pigalle …

… which is actually—considering this is the center of such a seedy district—an amazingly pretty and peaceful little place. (All the dirty business appears to have been crammed into the side streets.) Walk up to the fountain (photo page 187) to have a good look around. In **French Kiss**, this is where Kevin Kline disembarks first on his journey through Paris (and where he does some shady deals with some even shadier characters), underneath the signs for the *Folies Pigalle* and *Le Théâtre*. Much of the demi-monde action in Jean-Pierre Melville's **Bob le flambeur** is set around the surrounding bars and the pharmacy (where the hookers get their morning coffee and headache pills respectively). It may also be worth a thought that it must have been bars like these on and around the place Pigalle, teetering on the brink between respectability and, well, shady deals and shadier characters, where Édith Piaf first plied her trade as a street singer and from where she

was eventually signed to become a nightclub act. On this thought, we'll wave good-bye to the place Pigalle and its seedy back streets.

Walk back to the main street—boulevard de Clichy—and turn right. Take a close look to your left when you cross rue des Martyrs.

The Divan du Monde and Madame Arthur were the two clubs where Serge Gainsbourg had his first assignments as a professional musician, tinkling the ivories for their transvestite revues (before he turned the "Marseillaise" into a reggae song later in his life). Anglo-Saxons mainly know him as the author of the smuttiest song in the history of pop, the much-banned *Je t'aime ... moi non plus,* but in French cultural life, he enjoys a unique rank, Elvis Presley and Norman Mailer rolled into one. (When appearing side by side with Whitney Houston on a French TV chat show a few years ago, he said—in French—that he, well, carnally desired her, although these were not the exact words he chose, which the host then translated to his American guest as "Mr. Gainsbourg says that he likes you a lot". "No, no, no," Mr. Gainsbourg protested, then turned straight to Ms Houston and said: "I want to fuck you.")

Continue down the boulevard, and just before reaching the grey school building in front of the little park, turn right into rue Bochart-de-Saron and, at the next intersection, left into avenue Trudaine.

This is the street—more exactly the far side of the avenue on your right, opposite the school building—where Private Detective Antoine Doinel is learning his trade in **Baisers volés / Stolen Kisses**, shadowing a young woman (very badly).

Continue along avenue Trudaine, and when you reach the quiet and pretty place d'Anvers—with a beautiful view of Sacré-Coeur to your left—turn right into rue Turgot. At the triangle (where rue Turgot joins two other streets), take the first crossing to your right, cross rue Condorcet to the traffic island, and then cross rue de Maubeuge. Turn right into the next street, which is called rue Pierre-Sémard (the street sign "rue Baudin" on the left has been put there for the exclusive purpose of confusing you even further).

This is the street into which Glenn Close a.k.a. Cruella De Vil runs her car in **102 Dalmatians**, underneath the viaduct, before she comes to a crashing halt at the corner of square Montholon (photo page 202). Is it possible that the furrier shop back at no. 26 rue Pierre-Sémard actually belongs to the heinous Le Pelt?

Continue down the left-hand side of the square Montholon and turn left on to busy rue La Fayette.

This is the street taken by Zazie and her poncy uncle (played by Philippe Noiret) in **Zazie dans le métro / Zazie in the Metro** on their way from the station (the Gare de l'Est) to his home.

After you've walked a couple of blocks down rue La Fayette, passing the Métro station Poissoniere on the way, you will pass the Church of St-Vincent-de-Paul on the left-hand side …

… a feat that Zazie's traveling party manages to repeat several times: once they approach the church from the right, once from the left, and once they drive straight towards it (coming out of rue d'Hauteville which leads into the little square on your right), giving different accounts of its name every time (the Panthéon", says Uncle Gabriel, "the Madeleine" contests his friend, the cab driver. Later on in the movie, we see a group of tourists get off their bus in front of the church, announced by the tour guide as "Sainte-Chapelle, the gem in the crown of French Gothic architecture").

Continue along rue La Fayette to place de Valenciennes. Cross the busy boulevard de Magenta at the traffic lights and continue straight into boulevard de Denain and walk to the edge of the sidewalk …

… to get a good view of the grand entrance to the Gare du Nord (above right), Europe's busiest train station, at the end of the street.

From here, you get the best view of the **The Bourne Identity** scene where Franka Potente waits for Matt Damon—in front of the Bar La Consigne—while he puts stuff into a locker inside the station. (When he comes back, she is gone and he experiences a brief a brief moment of panic before she returns.

Damon then gives her one last chance to leave him alone, but she declines. In the meantime, the French police have arrived, and a furious chase all across Paris ensues.) Strangely enough, in **Ocean's Twelve**, it is Damon again whom we see enter the Gare du Nord—albeit from the other side of the boulevard de Denain—on his way to stealing the "real" egg. And believe it or not, in **The Bourne Ultimatum**, the only Parisian scene in the film—maybe this is some kind of running joke?—again shows Damon entering the Gare du Nord, this time on his way to London to meet the investigative journalist.

Enter the station through the main entrance in front of you …

… which is also used by Alec Guinness and Stanley Holloway in the chase for their "souvenir" Eiffel Towers in the classic Ealing comedy **The Lavender Hill Mob**, one of only two original locations for the movie.

(One of the fashion shoots in **Funny Face** uses the facade and the interiors of the Gare du Nord as a backdrop—as a rather sweet reminder of a bygone age when train stations were considered to be sexy and glamorous.)

Once inside the station, we are facing platform no. 10, where **Amélie** arrives with the garden gnome she's just liberated from her father's garden. (The rest of the scene develops in the Gare de l'Est, see Walk 9). Matt Damon in **The Bourne Identity** puts his stuff in a locker opposite platform no. 12. Jane Fonda in **Julia** also departs from the Gare du Nord, and in Sergio Leone's **Once Upon a Time in America**, the Gare du Nord, somewhat bizarrely, stands in for New York's Penn Station.

Train stations may no longer be the last word in glamour (see above), but ever since regular train service shortened the travel time between Paris and London to little more than two hours, the Eurostar terminal in the Gare du Nord—where these trains depart—has attracted attention from moviemakers. In Alain Resnais's **On connaît la chanson / Same Old Song**, Jane Birkin quarrels with her husband in the departure area. In **The Truth About Charlie**, Thandie Newton departs from here on her way to the UK, and Mr. Bean's troublesome journey to the Cannes film festival, a.k.a. **Mr. Bean's Holiday**, starts for real at the Gare du Nord when he arrives here from London. If you want to take a look: the stairs and escalators on both your left and right lead straight up to the departure area on the mezzanine.

Incidentally, it is Birkin who moans and groans the song *Je t'aime ... moi non plus* on the famous 1969 recording with composer Serge Gainsbourg. Gainsbourg had recorded a version of the song the previous year with Brigitte Bardot when the two were an item, but BB withdrew her consent at the very last moment. So Gainsbourg, not wanting to take any more risks, re-recorded the song with Birkin, his then-girlfriend who was to become his muse and long-time companion.

Leave the station through the side entrance labelled "18 rue de Dunkerque / rue de Maubeuge" (standing inside the station with your back to the main entrance, it is on your left-hand side). Turn right past the taxi queue and left at the next crossing into rue Ambroise-Paré. Walk past the hospital on your right to the end of the street and turn right into the busy, tree-lined boulevard de Magenta.

We're now approaching the immigrants' Montmartre I was telling you about a little earlier. This section of the boulevard de Magenta is a sort of border zone between the predominantly white and middle-class area around the place de la République (behind you) and the so-called Goutte d'Or district east of the Montmartre hill. In the distance you can see the TATI department store on the corner of boulevards Barbès and de Rochechouart, the busy intersection which marks the entrance to this district.

There is normally a lively trade going on under the bridges of the overhead railway—counterfeit designer bags and perfumes in the daytime, more sinister things at night, which is one reason why you should stay clear of the entire area after sunset. But during daylight hours, the hustle and bustle is great fun to watch. (In **Les ripoux / My New Partner**, we see Philippe Noiret and his young sidekick Thierry Lhermitte squeeze the lowlife under the bridge of Barbès-Rochechouart.) It's even more fun to watch the African women in their colorful dresses do their shopping on boulevard Barbès or at the Château-Rouge street market, particularly on a bright summer's day.

Have a look around before you finish the walk by taking your train from Métro Barbès-Rochechouart (Lines 2, 4). Once inside the station, explore the iron stairway that leads up to the no. 2 line trains.

This is where **Amélie** puts up her "I have something to return to you" notices and where she receives the "where and when" reply from Kassovitz.

The Paris of Classic French Cinema

An Introduction to Walks 9 and 10

The first eight walks of this book have featured locations from all sorts of movies, which meant that we have, by and large, looked at Paris through the lens of Hollywood directors. For the last two walks, we will assume a different perspective, discovering the mythical Paris of classic French cinema which is often little known to the foreign viewer.

American and French movies have two entirely different ways of looking at the city. If an American director sets his movie in Paris, he creates certain expectations, and he knows it. He can then proceed to confirm or confound those expectations or play with them in any way he wants, but the preconceived notions of the audience are real and must be taken into account. This is true of no other city in the world. Think about it.

A Hollywood director must think about Paris in the same way that he thinks about his stars. When a director works with, say, a Humphrey Bogart, he must be aware that this is not simply a somewhat sinister-looking guy of medium height with a lisp. Because that is not what the audience will see. The audience will see a mythical creature, the sum total of Bogey's previous incarnations. They will think: here he goes again, that tough old gumshoe, let's see how he handles *this*. That is something the director must not, and will not, ignore. If, after all, he had wanted a different reaction from his audience, he could have signed another actor, one with less, or different, baggage.

Paris is a movie star in much the same way, and a major one at that. A Hollywood movie set in Paris is always a movie *about* Paris. Paris may share the limelight, but it takes no second billing.

For French directors, the opposite is true. For them, setting a film in Paris is the most normal thing in the world. Why go anywhere else? It is practical, after all: This is where nearly all the writers, actors and, of course, the directors themselves live. For Americans, Paris may be the city of romance; for the French, it is their political, economic, and entertainment capital—Washington, D.C., New York, and LA. all rolled into one. So Paris it is, unless they have a reason to look for something specific that Paris can't offer: northern grime, rural settings, the sea, the sun, the mountains.

There is, however, one part of Paris which is used by French directors in much the same way in which the whole of the city is used by their Hollywood counterparts. This is the old working class Paris east of the place de la République and the Bastille. The rest of Paris is generally photographed in a casual, not to say lacklustre way. There are few scenic shots of Paris in French movies, and famous landmarks put in rare appearances. Whereas American movies tend to proclaim their Parisian locations, the tone in French movies is conversational. Where Hollywood shouts out THIS IS PARIS, native directors quietly reference streets, shops, and office buildings. If you didn't know that this was Paris, you often wouldn't be able to guess.

Eastern Paris, however, is different. It is full of mythical places: the square des Récollets, the quai des Jemmapes, rue du Transvaal and rue Vilin. These places may not mean much to an American audience, but in a French movie theatre, they will invariably trigger certain emotional responses. Eastern Paris is a star in the French cinema—not one that is in particularly high demand these days, admittedly, but one that is still very close to the audience's heart. Think Marlene Dietrich in the last years of her life, dragging her tired old bones through a series of glamorous cameos, and you've nearly got there.

Because, you see, the heyday of this particular "star" was a few years back, but, boy, what a heyday it was. If you were to put together a list of the ten greatest French films of all time, seven or eight would come from the 1930s and early 1940s while three or four more would have been inspired by them to some degree or another.

Note that we are not talking about movies praised only by a small and exclusive circle of *cinéastes*, but movies that have become a part of the national consciousness. These are films everybody has either seen or is so familiar with from countless references in popular culture that he knows them even if he has never actually watched them—the French equivalent of, say, *Jaws* or *Psycho*.

I don't know why the 1930s were such a great time for French movies, but I think I can tell why eastern Paris featured so prominently in many of the most celebrated films of the era. The 1930s were, after all, a period with a widespread appetite for realistic stories, in France and elsewhere. Hollywood produced films such as *The Grapes of Wrath* and *I Am a Fugitive from a Chain Gang*, which can still shock modern audiences with their gritty social realism. In French cinema, the realism was no less pronounced but not quite as gritty and more, well, poetic. Which is why the cinematic style of the period is often referred to as, aptly enough, Poetic Realism. If directors wanted the salty air of the Atlantic, they snubbed the bourgeois holiday resorts and went for the industrial harbors of Le Havre (*Quai de Brumes / Port of Shadows*). If exotic scenery was required, they preferred the narrow lanes of the *quartiers populaires* in France's colonial capitals to the airy residences of the rich (*Pépé le Moko*). And if a movie was set in Paris, it could only be in the Paris of the working class, Belleville, Ménilmontant, and La Villette.

Beside their settings, many of these films share certain features of their storylines: they often deal with the attempts of ordinary people to contend with the unalterable nature of destiny, sometimes overcoming the odds, sometimes succumbing to them. Not exactly cheery stuff then, but the 1930s were not exactly a cheery period.

Much of the Paris that provided the atmospheric backdrop for these films has disappeared, but much of it is still there. And more can be reconstructed in the imagination from what's left. For the next two walks, I invite you to follow me on a fascinating journey to explore a place where myth and reality coexist and collide.

ARRONDISSEMENTS: 11, 10, 19
DURATION: about 2 ½ hours

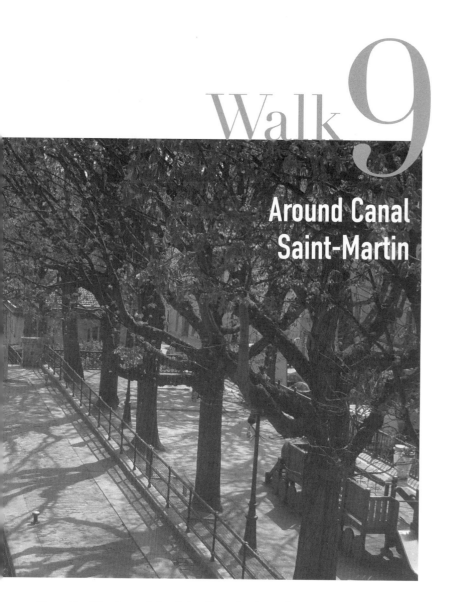

Walk 9

Around Canal Saint-Martin

From the "Boulevard du Crime" north along the Canal Saint-Martin

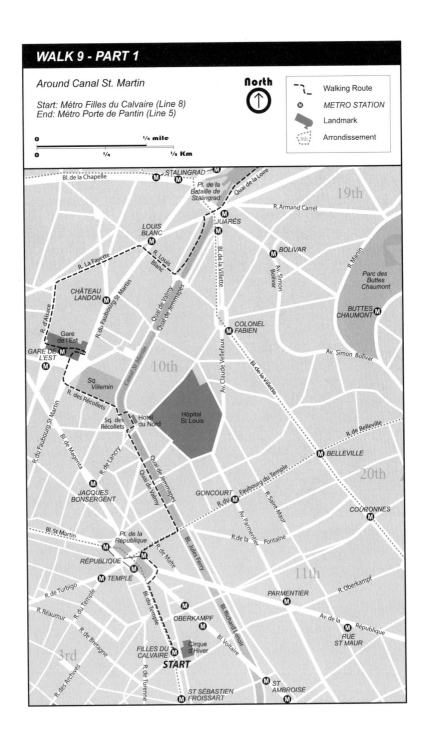

WALK 9 - PART 1

Around Canal St. Martin

Start: Métro Filles du Calvaire (Line 8)
End: Métro Porte de Pantin (Line 5)

North

Walking Route
METRO STATION
Landmark
Arrondissement

¼ mile

½ Km

Bl. de la Chapelle
STALINGRAD
Pl. de la Bataille de Stalingrad
Quai de la Loire
R. Armand Carrel
19th
JUARÈS
LOUIS BLANC
R. Louis Blanc
R. La Fayette
BOLIVAR
Av. Simon Bolivar
R. Manin
Parc des Buttes Chaumont
Bl. de la Villette
CHÂTEAU LANDON
R. du Faubourg St Martin
Quai de Valmy
Quai de Jemmapes
BUTTES CHAUMONT
R. d'Alsace
Gare de l'Est
COLONEL FABIEN
Av. Simon Bolivar
GARE DE L'EST
Canal St. Martin
Av. Claude Vellefaux
Bl. de la Villette
10th
Sq. Villemin
R. des Récollets
Hôtel du Nord
Hôpital St Louis
R. de Belleville
Sq. des Récollets
BELLEVILLE
R. du Faubourg St Martin
Bl. de Magenta
R. de Lancry
Quai de Jemmapes
Quai de Valmy
20th
JACQUES BONSERGENT
GONCOURT
R. du Faubourg du Temple
R. Saint-Maur
COURONNES
Bl. St Martin
Pl. de la République
Av. Parmentier
R. de la Fontaine
RÉPUBLIQUE
R. de Malte
Bl. Jules Ferry
11th
TEMPLE
R. de Turbigo
R. du Temple
PARMENTIER
R. Oberkampf
R. Réaumur
OBERKAMPF
Bl. Richard Lenoir
Av. de la République
RUE ST MAUR
R. de Bretagne
Bl. du Temple
Bl. Voltaire
3rd
FILLES DU CALVAIRE
Cirque d'Hiver
START
R. des Archives
R. de Turenne
ST SÉBASTIEN FROISSART
ST AMBROISE

Go to the Métro station Filles du Calvaire (Line 8) and leave through the exit boulevard des Filles-du-Calvaire.

This is the exit from which we see Tony Curtis emerge in the opening scene of **Trapeze**. Follow in his footsteps across the busy street, sprinting like him, full of energy (he needs it for his circus act and his affair with Gina Lollobrigida, you'll need it for the rest of this walk) to the Cirque d'Hiver where much of the action in **Trapeze** was filmed. (Also look at the shops and restaurants on either side of the building where some of the street scenes were shot.)

Turn left into the boulevard du Temple.

This stretch of the lively street—mainly the very last bit from no. 42 on, where a plaque tells us that the famous French writer Gustave Flaubert lived for 13 years—was known as the "Boulevard du Crime" from the late 17th century until 1862, when it was demolished in the wake of Baron Haussmann's urban renewal schemes. The name had nothing to do with any local preponderance of unlawfulness: "crime" was merely the bread-and-butter subject for most of the theaters that operated here at the time.

For this was where the theatrical genre of melodrama was invented and developed. Treacherous villains, cruel domestic tyrants, bloodthirsty brigands (their stage entrances announced by distinctive tunes from particular instruments) drew Parisians by the thousands. Crime was what they wanted to see and what they came here for, although some of the theaters also featured mimes, acrobats, tamed animals, and other types of circus acts.

Of all the theaters that once stood here, only the Théâtre Dejazet (no. 41, originally called the Folies Mayer) has survived, merely because it happened to be the only one built on the western side of the street (the odd-numbered side). The buildings on the other side were razed by Haussmann to allow for a widening of the street. As a result, the popular theaters moved west—like much else in Belle Époque Paris—to establish a new base along Haussmann's Grands Boulevards, mainly the boulevard des Capucines and the boulevard des Italiens (see Walk 7).

The "Boulevard du Crime" is immortalized in Marcel Carné's melancholic masterpiece **Les enfants du paradis / Children of Paradise**, voted "Best French Film of the 20th Century" by 600 French critics and movie profes-

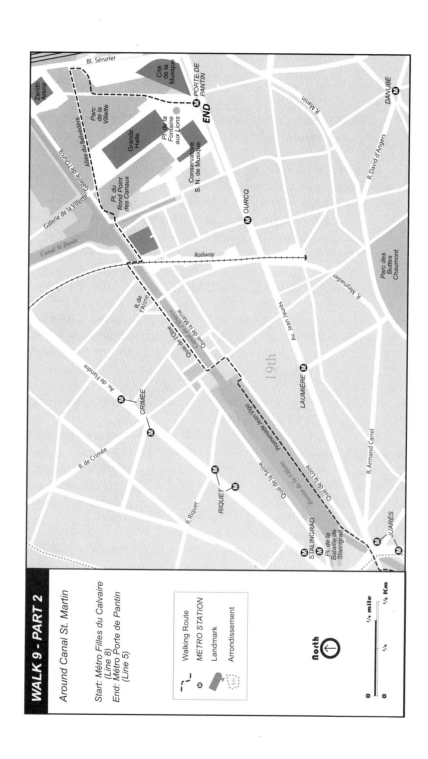

WALK 9 - PART 2

Around Canal St. Martin

Start: Métro Filles du Calvaire
(Line 8)
End: Métro Porte de Pantin
(Line 5)

Walking Route
METRO STATION
Landmark
Arrondissement

north

¼ mile
¼ Km

Bl. Sérurier
Zénith Arena
Parc de la Villette
Cité de la Musique
DANUBE
R. Marin
PORTE DE PANTIN
END
Allée du Belvédère
Galerie de l'Ourcq
Grande Halle
Pl. de la Fontaine aux Lions
R. David d'Angers
Galerie de la Villette
Pl. du Rond Point des Canaux
Conservatoire S. N. de Musique
OURCQ
Canal St. Denis
Railway
Parc des Buttes Chaumont
R. de l'Aisne
R. Meynadier
Canal de l'Ourcq
Quai de la Marne
Quai de l'Oise
Av. Jean Jaurès
LAUMIÈRE
19th
Av. de Flandre
CRIMÉE
Promenade Jean Vigo
R. Armand Carrel
R. de Crimée
Bassin de la Villette
Quai de la Loire
RIQUET
Quai de la Seine
STALINGRAD
Pl. de la Bataille de Stalingrad
JAURÈS

sionals in 1995. ("Paradise" is a theatrical term for the cheapest seats in the house, just under the rafters.) Set in the late 1820s and early 1830s, the film follows the interconnected lives of a beautiful young woman, played by the legendary French actress Arletty, and four of her admirers: a mime, a young actor, a criminal, and a rich aristocrat. It was made under difficult circumstances during the last years of the Nazi occupation and released in early 1945, after the liberation of Paris. (Most of the Boulevard du Crime was re-created on a set, but some of the movie's interiors were shot in the Théâtre Dejazet.)

> *At the end of the boulevard, walk into the place de la République, but stay on the right-hand side, crossing boulevard Voltaire and avenue de la République. Turn left, cutting across the front of the Holiday Inn on your right, and then take a right at the next corner into rue du Faubourg-du-Temple. Continue across rue de Malte and turn left at the large intersection into the quai de Valmy. Stay on the near side of the waterway, but cross over to the right side of the quai de Valmy (by the water) as soon as the canal comes into view.*

This is the Canal Saint-Martin, utterly beloved by Parisians and Parisian filmmakers in particular. It stands for a certain type of Paris: a Paris which is neither as grand as the big monuments on the Rive Droite nor as cool and self-consciously intellectual as the Rive Gauche. And while being picturesque (this is the movies, after all), this area is certainly not as quaint as Montmartre. This is the workingman's Paris without the grime, so to speak.

Americans are blissfully unaware of all this, of course, and if a Hollywood director needs a bit of water in his movie, he will go for the Seine any day because it's bigger and it's got more landmarks on it that are easily recognizable by the folks back home. So, as a rule of thumb: if you see the Seine flow across the screen, the film could come from anywhere in the world, but if you spot the stagnant pond of the Canal Saint-Martin, the film has got to be French.

> *And to illustrate this point, let's start our cinematic journey along the Canal Saint-Martin by walking north along the quai …*

... with the Chinese-American co-production of **Kiss of the Dragon** (but you see, it was directed by Chris Nahon, a Frenchman). We see Jet Li and Bridget Fonda quarrel at the foot of the first of the famous footbridges where the canal disappears underground towards the Port de l'Arsenal, to meet the Seine near the Bastille. On the sluicegate just behind, Amélie indulges in one of her favorite pastimes, skipping stones across the water in **Le fabuleux destin d'Amélie Poulain / Amélie**.

Continue to the next footbridge.

Thierry Lhermitte's girlfriend in **Les ripoux / My New Partner** a.k.a. *Le Cop* has a flat nearby. A footbridge also provides the backdrop for the scene in Julie Delpy's amiable if uneven directorial debut **2 Days in Paris** where the French-American couple quarrels about her "anger management problem," which has just got them kicked out of a restaurant.

Continue down this particularly pretty section of the Canal until you come to the crossing with rue de Lancry on your left (at the level of the fourth footbridge). Walk up the footbridge on your right— immediately behind the sign showing the way to the Hôpital Saint-Louis—and cross over to the other side of the canal to the quai de Jemmapes.

Right in front of you at 102 quai de Jemmapes is the legendary **Hôtel du Nord**, scene of another classic Marcel Carné movie of the pre-war era which, incidentally, features the most famous and most frequently quoted French movie line of all time. After her pimp has told her that he "needs a bit of a change in atmosphere, and my atmosphere, that's you," Arletty's prostitute explodes: "*Atmosphere, atmosphere, est-ce-que j'ai une gueule d'atmosphere*"— "Atmosphere, atmosphere, does my face look like it's made of atmosphere?"

The scene takes place under the bridge you have just crossed. The 1938 movie, a set of loosely connected episodes about people who have come here to live, love or kill each other, was entirely filmed on a set and merely took its inspiration from the hotel and its surroundings by the side of the canal. Nevertheless, the Hôtel du Nord, having fallen badly into disrepair, was declared a National Monument in 1989 to protect it from greedy developers.

Soon after, it was acquired by one of Carné's former assistants, who then proceeded to re-create the hotel in the image of the film. Arletty and her pimp share room 14 if you want to relive the experience.

Turn left into the quai de Jemmapes and cross back to the other side of the Canal again at the next footbridge. At the top of the bridge, look to your left.

The area between this footbridge and the one you have just crossed, called the square des Récollets (photo page 207), provides the background for the "film within a film" in **Le dernier tango à Paris / Last Tango in Paris** where Jean-Pierre Léaud's clueless moviemaker uses the "cover" of the film to propose to Maria Schneider.

We shall leave the Canal for the moment, returning later, but for the time being we turn left into rue des Récollets, about 20 yards further down the quai de Valmy. Continue past the Hôpital / jardin Villemin …

… used in **Julia** to stand in for the Vienna Hospital—one of the rare cases where Paris stands in for something else. Normally, this is way beneath the city's dignity.

> *At the end of the street, cross both sides of rue du Faubourg-St-Martin (there is a fairly large traffic island in the middle of the two lanes), turn right and, crossing rue du 8-Mai-1945, walk straight through the gates into the Gare de l'Est, the station for all rail traffic to the Alsace and southern Germany.*

This is the station where Little Zazie arrives with her mum from the provinces at the start of **Zazie dans le métro / Zazie in the Metro** and where her taxi ride through Paris begins. In **102 Dalmatians**, the Gare de l'Est stands in for the (non-existent) "Gare de Paris."

Walk through the small vestibule into the main entrance hall.

Immediately to your right, and more or less wedged into the near corner, is the site of the photo booth where **Amélie** solves the puzzle of the "mystery man" (the guy whose ID photos repeatedly appear in Mathieu Kassovitz's scrapbook) and where she eventually lures Kassovitz to find out for himself.

There is a nearly identical, yet subtly different entrance hall to your left in the same station, but believe me, this is the one. The photo booth was only put in for the movie. You will also search in vain for the restaurant in the station's lower level from which **Amélie** observes Kassovitz. It was added through clever editing.

The left side of the entrance hall, a section that's now blocked off, used to accommodate the lockers used by Jet Li in **Kiss of the Dragon**. (The Gare de l'Est was among the last French railway stations to retain lockers. In the England of the 1980s, lockers used to be one of the favorite places for IRA terrorists to hide their bombs, and when France was hit by a wave of terrorism in the 1990s, the French railway authorities, like their British counterparts before them, ordered all lockers to be removed.)

Walk through the entrance hall to the platform area and turn right towards the exit rue du Faubourg-St-Martin. Just before you reach the exit ...

... look to your left to spot the place where **Amélie**, quite literally, bumps into Kassovitz for the first time. (She is hit by a *coup de foudre*, a case of "love at first sight," while he engages in hot pursuit of the seemingly ubiquitous "mystery man"—and almost runs Amélie right over).

Sitting down on the stairs outside this exit to the station (opposite), Amélie has her first close look at Mathieu Kassovitz's selection of discarded passport pictures.

In order to take a look at the place where he actually lost it, we must turn back and walk—the platforms to our right—towards the exit on the opposite side of the station, the one labelled "rue d'Alsace." Turn right out of the exit, walk up the stairway (photo page 4) and then into rue d'Alsace.

Roughly even with no. 27, halfway down the first block, Kassovitz hops on his scooter and flees, dropping the scrapbook that Amélie then picks up.

Continue down rue d'Alsace, casting a glimpse into rue de Dunkerque to your left just before you reach the busy main road, rue La Fayette.

From the door of no. 1, just opposite the Hôtel Bristol, we see the young woman emerge in Jean Rouch's Episode 2 of **Paris vu par... / Paris Seen By...** on her way to an encounter with a mysterious stranger.

We will follow her, turning right into rue La Fayette onto the bridge where the episode meets its somewhat puzzling end. But as we move on …

… take a good look to the right across the thirty or so platforms of the Gare de l'Est (opposite). One cannot say that this view is beautiful in any conventional meaning of the word, but it would be churlish to deny that it has a kind of poetry. (*All cities are mad: but the madness is gallant*, writes Christopher Morley, *all cities are beautiful, but the beauty is grim.*)

Follow rue La Fayette across the place Dulcie September and turn right at the next corner into rue Louis-Blanc. Follow it until you rejoin the Canal, crossing the quai de Valmy to walk down by the waterfront, through the arch past the old warehouse—now used as a garage by the Parisian fire brigade (a ten-year-old could go crazy)—and up to the street level where the Canal disappears underground (for a short while).
Turn left to cross rue La Fayette and then right to cross boulevard de la Villette under the railway bridge. Then head toward Le Jaurès Café. Just before you reach it, turn left to rejoin the Canal (called the Bassin de la Villette here) on the footpath to the left of the quai de la Loire.

We are now entering the section of the old network of waterways where the canal left its leafiness behind and got down to some serious work, one might say. From where you are now standing, you would have seen—as little as thirty or forty years ago—dozens of barges in the process of being either

loaded or unloaded with all types of goods. Nowadays, only pleasure boats pass this way, and there is a good chance that one of those will be "stuck" in the lock to your left as you are passing by.

Canal trips are wonderful entertainment for people who derive great pleasure from watching sluicegate technology in action, time and time again, over a period of several hours. The canal is short, but boats are slow, particularly if they are made to pass through a lock every hundred yards or so. If you fancy the experience, you have come to the right place, because both companies that offer such trips—Canauxrama and Paris Canal—have ticket offices in the building to your right, one on either side of the waterfront cinema.

> *Continue down this airy and modern, but still very charming stretch of the Canal.*

It does not attract as many tourists as the Seine, and the flats which overlook it do not carry price tags of more than a million Euros; so plenty of ordinary people live nearby, turning the Bassin—particularly on a bright and sunny day—into a showcase for multiculturalism in action. It's a great place to watch

Portuguese concierges walk their overfed dogs, Antillean mums exchange the latest rounds of gossip, and children of all races make new friends in the playgrounds while the old anglers watch them all (and the fish) go by.

The promenade on which all of this happens carries the name of Jean Vigo, the director of the dreamlike, yet strangely unsentimental **L'Atalante**, another candidate for the title of "Greatest French Movie of All Time." The film describes the lives and loves of a young ship owner and his capricious wife who lose each other in the streets of Paris (she is hungry for adventure and has a keen eye for the night life) before being eventually reunited on their barge. The film is partly set on the Bassin de la Villette and partly on the Canal de l'Ourcq, which is located behind the lock and bridge ahead of you in the far distance.

The entire place would be virtually unrecognizable to them nowadays—especially if you bear in mind that the "sandy stretch" between the two paved walkways, the one by the side of the canal and the other one a little further to your right by the side of the apartment buildings, was filled with a long line of warehouses at the time.

L'Atalante was first released in 1934 in a mercilessly butchered version. The producers had done such a shabby job—removing the entire original soundtrack and shortening the film and renaming it after a song that was doing well in the charts at the time—that most *cinéastes* boycotted the premiere. Also missing was the director Jean Vigo himself, who was at the time already dying of tuberculosis, aged only 29. The film was fully reconstructed only in 1990 when old footage previously presumed lost was found. Its Director of Photography, Boris Kaufman, was more fortunate than Vigo. He later went to Hollywood where his work for *On the Waterfront* won him an Academy Award.

Incidentally, the boat on which Léaud and Schneider are sitting in **Le dernier tango à Paris / Last Tango in Paris** and whose life belt they watch, ominously, sink to the bottom of the Canal, is called the Atalante, a clear hommage to Vigo's masterpiece.

At the end of the Promenade—where, if you were to continue, you would run straight against the wall of the warehouse—walk right past the building down the continuation of the quai de la Loire.

The warehouse, now used by the municipal rowing club and for some loft-style residences, was Richard Bohringer's stylish residence in **Diva**. The young mailman spends much of his time there and that's where the plot to rid him of his troublesome pursuers is eventually hatched.

Turn left behind the warehouse into rue de Crimée to cross the Canal over the drawbridge. Walk on the left-hand side of the bridge.

This is the place where Ed Harris crosses over into Paris in the somewhat underrated WWII thriller **Code Name: Emerald**. (Note the interesting optical contrast created by the proximity of the very industrial drawbridge winches and Church of Saint-Jacques-Saint-Christophe-de-la-Villette, which looks as though it had jumped straight out of a spaghetti western.

Turn right into the quai de l'Oise, leaving the Canal de l'Ourcq—as it is called from here on—to your right. As you walk toward the next bridge …

… you will pass no. 9 quai de l'Oise, where both the Studio Marcel Carné and the Conservatoire Libre du Cinéma Français are located.

A bit further down, beyond next bridge, you will come to the corner of the quai de l'Oise and rue de l'Aisne.

This is where Beatrice Dalle (the blind girl) is taken by the taxi in Jim Jarmusch's **Night on Earth**. Earlier on, we see her cross the canal via the easily recognizable rue du Crimée drawbridge that we have just passed.

Cross the Canal, one last time, over the big cast iron railway bridge in front of you (there is a stairway on the far side). Once on the other side, continue straight into the quai de la Marne, crossing the disused section of the Canal to your right, the grandly named Darse du Fond de Rouvray.

Take a closer look at this ungentrified section of the Canal, virtually the last one down this stretch: it gives you an impression of what most of the Canal must have looked like before it was done up in the 1970s and 1980s. Alternatively, watch or rewatch **Les ripoux / My New Partner** where we follow Philippe Noiret's corrupt cop on his escape route down the Canal, carrying away the one million dollars he has just snatched from a group of gangsters.

The buildings on the other side of the Canal belong to the Science and Industry Museum in the Parc de la Villette, which we are about to enter. Before their conversion in the late 1970s, those buildings housed the municipal slaughterhouses.

The park and museum were the "Grand Project" of President Valery Giscard d'Estaing. It is one of the country's unwritten laws that every French President must have at least one such project: Pompidou in the early Seventies had his cultural center, Mitterrand in the Eighties had the Louvre Pyramid and the La Défense district.

Walk straight on into the place du Rond-Point des Canaux, down the stone steps in front of you. Follow the path to the right of the wedge-shaped building and cut straight across the Galerie de la

Villette with its carousels and playgrounds into the park's allée du Belvédère. Continue down this leafy, quiet path until you reach, at the very end, the parking place of the Zenith arena.

The Zenith itself—where Olympic champion Katharina Witt appears as a Bulgarian figure-skating champion towards the climax of John Frankenheimer's 1998 **Ronin**—is to your left. But the car park is worth a look in its own right. Here, to your left in front of the large ramp that leads up to the main road, is the place where Robert De Niro and Jean Reno apprehend Jonathan Bryce's renegade IRA man in the film—and where Natasha McElhone drives away to leave him in the lurch.

Retrace your steps and take a left when you come to the allèe du Zenith. On reaching the end of this path, you will find yourself in the bottom left-hand corner of a large piazza called place de la Fontaine aux Lions (I leave it to you to work out where it got its name). Cross the piazza diagonally to the top right-hand corner where you will find the Métro station Porte de Pantin (Line 5). If you're looking for food, you'll find plenty of options just across the street.

ARRONDISSEMENTS: 11, 20
DURATION: 2 hours and 45 minutes, including a 30-minute walk
through Père Lachaise

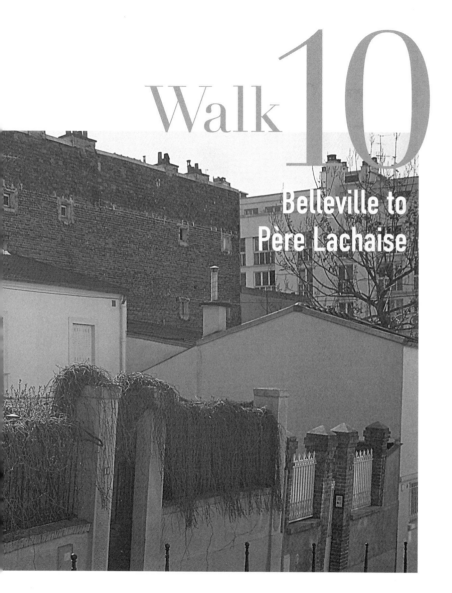

Walk 10

Belleville to Père Lachaise

Through the streets of the working-class quarters of Belleville and Ménilmontant (birthplaces, respectively, of Édith Piaf and Maurice Chevalier) to Père Lachaise Cemetery

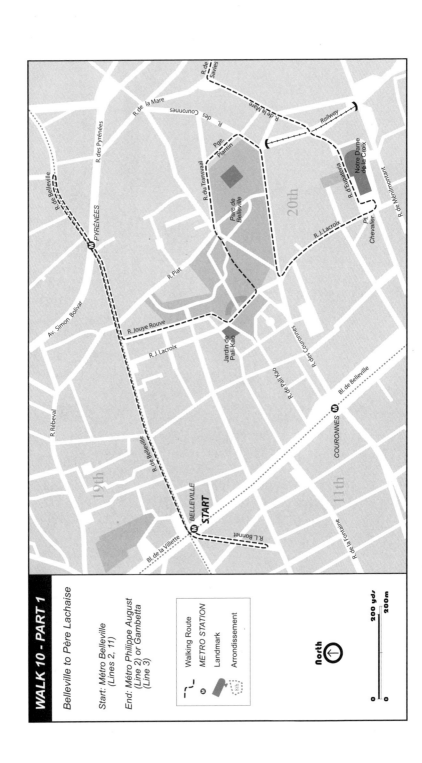

WALK 10 - PART 1

Belleville to Père Lachaise

Start: Métro Belleville
(Lines 2, 11)

End: Métro Philippe August
(Line 2) or Gambetta
(Line 3)

Walking Route

METRO STATION

Landmark

Arrondissement

north

200 yds
200m

0
0

R. de Savies
R. de la Mare
R. de la Mare
R. de Couronnes
R. des
R. de la Mare
Railway
Pge.
Plantin
Notre Dame
de la Croix
R. d'Eupatoria
R. de Belleville
R. des Pyrénées
R. du Transvaal
PYRÉNÉES
Parc de
Belleville
20th
R. J. Lacroix
Pl.
Chevalier.
R. de Ménilmontant
R. Piat
Av. Simon Bolivar
R. Jouye Rouve
R. J. Lacroix
Jardin de
Pali-Kao
R. Rébeval
R. de Pali-Kao
R. des Couronnes
Bl. de Belleville
R. de Belleville
19th
COURONNES
11th
BELLEVILLE
START
Bl. de la Villette
R. L. Bonnet
R. de la Fontaine

Take the Métro to Belleville (Lines 2, 11). Leave the station through exit no. 6 and turn right into rue Louis-Bonnet.

No. 4 near the end of the street on your left is the Hôtel de la Paix, under reconstruction as we go to press, where Franka Potente and Matt Damon are staying in **The Bourne Identity**. Some movie makers may get their locations wrong—suspiciously large numbers of people in movies live in the immediate vicinity of famous landmarks, for instance, and penniless students and artists, the staple characters of "Parisian" movies made in Hollywood, often have apartments with panoramic views over the entire town—but this one feels absolutely right. Whatever you might say about the Hôtel de la Paix, it is unquestionably the type of place where you would want to hide if the CIA were looking for you. It looks like a joint that has seen a lot over the years, where few questions would be asked and where you would have to do something pretty outrageous to raise an eyebrow, never mind make someone call the authorities. This, after all, is a part of Paris where the five corners of the world have been rolled into one, and such cheek-by-jowl multicultur-alism only works if everybody minds his own business without sticking his nose too much into anyone else's.

Retrace your steps to the station. Cross the main street, the boulevard de Belleville, and walk straight into rue de Belleville a few meters on your left.

We are now entering the heart of Belleville, the main working-class neigh-borhood of modern Paris (since the 19th century) and traditionally the first port of call—a kind of European Brooklyn—for each wave of immigrants who have sought refuge, shelter and work in the French capital, whether they came from rural France, the rest of Europe, or the French colonial empire. (In this part of Belleville, it is mainly the Chinese—or, more specifically, the Chinese from Vietnam—who seem to have stayed.)

When Belleville became a part of Paris in 1860, it was one of the five largest cities in France, and just like any other city, it had—and to some extent still has—its fine distinctions. For one, it is important to bear in mind that the town of Belleville in its pre-1860 boundaries comprised a few areas which, today, are known under different names, mainly the nearby neighborhood

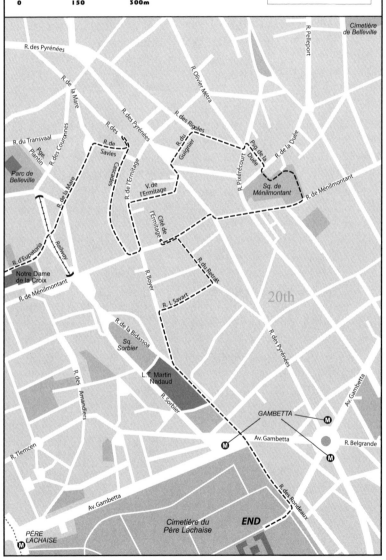

WALK 10 - PART 2

Belleville to Père Lachaise

Start: *Métro Belleville (Lines 2, 11)*
End: *Métro Philippe August (Line 2)*
   or Gambetta (Line 3)

North
↑

	Walking Route
	METRO STATION
	Landmark
	Arrondissement

0   300 yds
0   150   300m

R. des Pyrénées

R. de la Mare

R. du Transvaal

R. des Couronnes

Pge Plantin

Parc de Belleville

R. des

R. de Savies

Cascades

R. de l'Ermitage

R. des Pyrénées

R. des Rigoles

R. du Guignier

R. Olivier Métra

R. Pelleport

Cimetière de Belleville

V. de l'Ermitage

Cité de l'Ermitage

R. Pixérécourt

Pge de la Duée

R. de la Duée

Sq. de Ménilmontant

R. de Ménilmontant

R. de la Mare

R. d'Eupatoria

Railway

Notre Dame de la Croix

R. de Ménilmontant

R. Boyer

R. du Retrait

R. L Savart

20th

R. de la Bidassoa

Sq Sorbier

L. T. Martin Nadaud

R. Sorbier

R. des Pyrénées

R. des Amandiers

Av. Gambetta

GAMBETTA Ⓜ

Av. Gambetta

R. Belgrande

Ⓜ

Ⓜ

R. Tlemcen

Av. Gambetta

PÈRE LACHAISE
Ⓜ

Cimetière du Père Lachaise

END

R. des Rondeaux

of Ménilmontant. The old town of Belleville extended north almost all the way to the canal (the area known as La Villette) and south down to the Père Lachaise Cemetery, so the *quartier* which is currently known as Belleville was, at the time, only the downtown area of a larger entity, and the rue de Belleville served as the town's central shopping and entertainment street.

Walk down a few blocks to no. 72 on the right side of rue de Belleville.

This is where the famous French singer Édith Piaf was born (as Édith Giovanna Gassion on 19 December 1915), literally, as the story has it, in the gutter, when her mother's contractions began in the middle of the street and a policeman put his cloak around her to shield her from the curious eyes of the bystanders. In the 1960s, after Piaf's death, a plaque was put up here to mark the very spot. The ceremony was attended by Piaf's old colleague Maurice Chevalier, the other great popular singer of 20th century France, whose life and career provide an almost perfect reverse mirror image of Piaf's—from their origins in the same 'hood (hers destitute, his respectable) to their respectively bitter and sweet endings. Because, you see, "Belleville" in the modern sense—the "downtown" area of the old city around rue de Belleville—was always the shabbiest part of town, the area where the "irresponsible poor" and feckless lived.

People like Édith Piaf's parents, for instance, a street singer and a circus artist. Piaf's father was a contortionist, actually, and apparently a pretty good one at that, good enough to receive an offer from P.T. Barnum. But, of course, he turned the offer down—with the words, as legend has it: "Does this American think a man from Belleville can be bought with money?"

Édith Piaf grew up in a brothel in Normandy with her grandmother (who worked there as a cook), and when she returned to Paris to live with her father, they moved into rented accommodation a bit further up the street at no. 115. She was discovered and signed on the spot by the owner of a posh nightclub when singing in the streets around the place Pigalle. But—and this was to prove a leitmotif in poor Piaf's life—every time she dragged herself to her feet, she was about to get hit again, and the blows got harder through the years. The man who had discovered her, for instance, Louis Leplée, the owner of the posh Le Gerny nightclub near the Champs-Élysées, was killed in an underworld feud (she herself had to flee Paris after that), and the great love

of her life, the championship boxer Marcel Cerdan, was not only married but died in a plane crash. Piaf herself died at the age of 47, adored by millions but hopelessly addicted to morphine and virtually bankrupt. (Maurice Chevalier, on the other hand, seemed to spend his entire career "on the sunny side of the street." More of him a bit later on.)

> *Turn around and walk downhill again, stepping to the right edge of the sidewalk to get a clearer view of the Eiffel Tower in the distance.*

You can see the Tower so clearly from here because Belleville is located on a hill, one of an original seven hills on which the city of Paris was built—several of them, including the Montparnasse, however, were already flattened by the Middle Ages. (Which gives you an idea of how tall and mighty these hills must have been.)

The streets of Montmartre and Belleville, on the other hand, undoubtedly still require some degree of climbing, and although one would assume that land surveyors have by now had enough time to work this out, one still finds conflicting information as to which of these two Parisian hills is the higher. Most sources, however, go with Montmartre.

Turn left into rue Jouye-Rouve and walk past the bas relief on your left behind the first park gate, which marks the spot of an ancient nursery school. Continue down the street (it changes its name to rue de la Ferme de Savy), following the sweep to the right, and at the end, turn left into rue Julien-Lacroix.

Walk until you reach the corner with rue Vilin on your right. Now turn left into the park and climb the stairs all the way up to the "Maison de l'Air" under the canopy on top of the hill.

Come on, it's not that bad. Really. And you're being rewarded with a magnificent view over Paris that features the Eiffel Tower and the Invalides (two landmarks missing from most Montmartre views). Now you know what put the "belle" into "Belleville"—because the *quartier* almost certainly derives its name from *belle vue* (beautiful view). Belleville as a town was never beautiful and lost whatever beauty it may have had when it became a "ville."

But turn your attention to the view on the left and to the area right in front of you. When Richard Berri's tough cop drives his car to the top of this hill in the 1982 French crime classic **La balance** to talk Nathalie Baye's hooker into working with the police, neither the ugly housing estates on your left nor the trees and flowers on the slope in front of you were there. Instead, the entire area was a giant construction site—before which it had been covered with late-19th century homes, some of them ramshackle, some dark and grim, but all of them contributing to the area's—once—unique character.

Step out from under the canopy now and turn to your right, still on the right side of the street, opposite the house which points like a wedge into the intersection.

You are now standing in one of the legendary spots of ancient Belleville, the old corner of rue Piat (which extends behind you) and rue Vilin which you left—remember?—when stepping into the park at the bottom of the hill. There is a famous photograph by Willy Ronis of this corner where a group of boys is playing some game or another under the stairway. No collection of Belleville nostalgia would be complete without this picture. But the corner does not exist anymore, and neither does most of rue Vilin, which used to climb up all the way to the top of the hill. If you compare your present view down rue Piat with Willy Ronis's photo, you can just about recognize the sweep of rue Piat's right side. Think of the rue Vilin that you left at the bottom of the park: it is pleasant, green, and pretty. And the only people who yearn for the romance of the old tenement halls are those who would not have to live in them if they were still standing. So it would be churlish to deny that something has been gained, but it would be equally churlish to deny that something has been lost.

(Rue Bisson, a side street of rue Vilin at the bottom of the hill, provides the scene for a major chase in **La balance**, but at the time the movie was made, it was already under reconstruction. For a better view of old Belleville, try the 1933 **Quatorze Juillet / Bastille Day** and Albert Lamorisse's Oscar-winning short **Le ballon rouge / The Red Balloon**, which won the Palme d'Or at the Cannes film festival in 1956.)

> *Continue onto rue du Transvaal, to the right of the wedge-shaped building (photo page 10), pausing at no. 15 …*

… where we see Serge Reggiani and Simone Signoret exchange a passionate kiss in **Casque d'or / Golden Helmet**, a kind of *Gangs of New York* set in 19th century working-class Paris, one of the truly great French movies of the post-WWII era.

> *Continue down rue du Transvaal past the picturesque villa Castel at no. 16. Turn right just past it into the narrow passage Plantin …*

… which shows you a different Belleville, immaculately kept little homes with tiny back gardens behind high walls. (We shall see more of that a little further in our walk when we reach Ménilmontant.)

> *Take the stairs down to rue des Couronnes.*

No 83, immediately on your left at street level, is the house where **Jules et Jim / Jules and Jim** first meet Jeanne Moreau. Passage Plantin and the stairway also feature prominently in the car chase from **The Bourne Identity**, which was largely shot in the side streets of Belleville: we see Matt Damon crash his car down the steps behind you. (And, yes, it fit; it was a very small car.)

Turn right into rue des Couronnes—past the gardens of the villa Castel on your right—and follow the street as it sweeps to the right, with Belleville Park to your right and a modern housing project on your left.

Somewhere along this stretch of the walk, we cross the frontier from Belleville into Ménilmontant. This is not and has never been an administrative boundary and is therefore ill defined in geographical terms. But, although one must be careful not to overemphasize the dissimilarities, there are nevertheless clear distinctions between the two. Working-class quarters they may both have been—and still are in a way. But Belleville has always been the more profligate and carefree of the two, a place for, well, street singers and circus artists. While "Ménilmouche" has generally tended to house the "lace curtain" working classes, their working men's libraries and working men's clubs.

Turn left at the next corner into rue Julien-Lacroix (there is no street sign). Follow this street all the way down until you are standing right in front of the church, called Notre-Dame-de-la-Croix.

This is the church into which Rebecca Romijn-Stamos escapes from her pursuers in Brian De Palma's **Femme Fatale** and where she stumbles upon her new identity. The bakery straight in front of you is another key location of the movie. In **Femme Fatale**, it was made up as the Bar du Paradis where Rebecca Romijn-Stamos, her hair dyed black, meets her accomplice from the heist who is subsequently killed by a truck on rue Étienne-Dolet (the street which leads straight away from the church).

Also cast an eye on the leafy little square to the right of rue Étienne-Dolet with the small restaurant and tables under the trees. This area used to be dotted with squares such as this where working-class people went to take their Sunday lunch and listen to open-air concerts by local bands and singers. It was in places like these that singers like Maurice Chevalier—after whom, incidentally, this place has been named—cut their teeth on their way to greater triumphs.

Walk back a few steps to the rue d'Eupatoria by the side of the church and turn right, past the house at no. 11 where Antonio Banderas's penthouse flat is located in **Femme Fatale**. *Continue to the end of the street and turn left into rue de la Mare.*

All the houses here are new, but the low steel bridge (opposite) is easily recognizable from a scene in the 1955 heist classic **Du rififi chez les hommes / Rififi**. (The son of a friend of Jean Servais's aging gangster Tony has been kidnapped, and Tony asks his former lover to assist him in the search. It is right in front of this bridge that she promises to help him.) We actually see quite a lot of old Belleville in **Du rififi chez les hommes / Rififi** when Tony drums up support for his quest among his pals in the Parisian underworld, including a few shots of rue Vilin which we visited earlier.

Walk up the iron stairway and cross the railroad tracks …

… remnants of an overground city rail system which was eventually made redundant when the underground train system was established in the early 1900s. (The Ménilmontant station, opened in 1862, was originally located a few yards to your left.)

Continue down rue de la Mare, on the other side of the viaduct, across rue Henri-Chevreau, to rue de Savies, where you turn right. Walk to the end of rue de Savies and turn left into rue des Cascades.

The corner with nos. 42bis and 42ter was recreated for the movie **Casque d'or / Golden Helmet**, where it provides the setting for several street scenes. No. 44 just one house down the road is the house of Felix Leca, the great rival of Serge Reggiani's character of Georges Manda. (This is also the address where the real Felix Leca lived. It was Leca's fight with Georges Manda over the love of a beautiful girl that inspired the movie. Both Leca and Manda were leaders of street gangs, so-called Apaches. They led their thugs into a fullscale pitched battle on rue des Haies south of Père Lachaise, sparing neither knife blades nor guns. To the inquisitive public prosecutor, Manda retorted during his trial: "We fought each other, the Corsican and myself, because we love the same girl. We are crazy about her. Don't you know what it is to love a girl?"

Eventually, both Manda and Leca were deported to a penal colony. The girl with the "golden helmet" of blonde hair wasted no time bewailing her unfortunate suitors, turning for solace to the world of entertainment and the company of wealthier men. But this was true only in real life. The movie ended on a somewhat more romantic note.

Retrace your steps to the corner of rue de Savies and rue des Cascades, passing the "Regard Saint-Martin" (the small stone hut on your left) …

… which is one of the places that supplied the Parisian population with drinking water for 500 years.

Continue down rue des Cascades to rue de Ménilmontant.

Slopes like the one to your right were used to grow wine until the 19th century. In fact, Paris produced its own wine until fairly recently, and it is said that during the 1870 siege when people were reduced to eating insects and rats, the wine never ran out.

The local Belleville wine was called the "guinguet" from which the *guinguettes* deriveds their name: bars, often located by the riverside, where Parisians went on weekends to have some fun. They've been immortalized in the impressionist paintings of Auguste Renoir and, of course, in the movie **Casque d'or / Golden Helmet**.

> *Turn left and immediately left again into rue de l'Ermitage. After passing the Studio de l'Ermitage on the right side of the street, turn right into the villa de l'Ermitage …*

… a passage with quaint little bungalows and front gardens on either side, some extremely well kept, some far less so, thus giving you a pretty good idea what much of this area would have looked like a hundred years ago.

> *Walk to the bottom of this little settlement's main thoroughfare where you will find a passage to your left, leading you into rue des Pyrénées. Cross this street, turn left and then—after a few steps—right into rue du Guignier, leaving the picturesque little place du Guignier to your left.*
> *At the bottom of rue du Guignier, turn right into rue des Rigoles which leads you into a three-street junction. Cross rue Pixérécourt straight ahead of you. Turn left and immediately take a sharp right at the next corner into the passage de la Duée, the narrowest street in Paris. (There is no sign for it.)*

Sadly, the house on the left side recently disappeared thus irrevocably altering the passage's character. The houses on either side used to deprive the passage of direct natural sunlight and made it impossible to pass through without touching at least one of the walls with your shoulders, giving this alleyway its unique and slightly sinister character. Yet another reminder that this part of Paris is in a constant state of flux and that we have to hurry to experience any of its old-world charm. Who knows how much of old Belleville will still be standing in five or ten years time?

Cross the street in front of you into the little public garden, the square de Ménilmontant. Walk straight across the park and exit on the other side, along the pathway lined by thin trees, straight into rue de Ménilmontant. Turn right, crossing first rue Pixérécourt …

(Rue de la Chine, the continuation of rue Pixérécourt, on your left, was the birthplace of the popular French singer and songwriter Serge Gainsbourg. More about this extraordinary character in Walk 8.)

… and then the busy rue des Pyrénées. Continue down rue de Ménilmontant for about a hundred yards until you come to no. 113, on your right side just past the cité de l'Ermitage.

This little house (below) on the corner of the cité de l'Ermitage is where Garance and the mime declare their love for each other in **Les enfants du paradis**, a grand view of Paris at their feet, albeit without the Centre Pompidou. Now you can also see what put the *mont* into Ménilmontant.

Belleville and Ménilmontant are twin hills, actually, both located on a—somewhat—elevated plateau.

Walk a few steps back now and turn right into rue du Retrait ...

... the street where Maurice Chevalier was born and grew up. Whether his birthplace was no. 29 or 31 (the sources disagree) does not really matter, because all houses between 25 and 31 have been torn down anyway. New houses were erected in their place, but if you look into their open-plan backyard, you will appreciate that the architects have tried to preserve some of the intimacy of early 20th century working-class housing estates.

To many people who know Maurice Chevalier mainly or exclusively as Louis Jourdain's friendly uncle in *Gigi*, it may come as a surprise that he was a Parisian working-class lad. After his early triumphs in local vaudeville, he went to Hollywood to become one the world's first global celebrities, starring in a string of highly successful musicals from the late 1920s to the early 1930s. Most famously, he played Prince Danilo in Ernst Lubitsch's 1934 version of *The Merry Widow*, a role that stayed with him for the rest of his life.

More to the point, however, Chevalier was the original "Teflon" man long before the stuff was actually invented: no scandal, no matter how serious, ever stuck to his sunny reputation—from his early affairs with much older showbiz divas whom he dropped as soon as they became more of a headache than a useful stepping stone, to his declared admiration for the (Nazi puppet) regime of Marshall Pétain during WWII, to his brush with Joseph McCarthy's House Committee on Un-American Activities (HCUA). He just kept smiling and embedding himself ever deeper into the world's common subconscious as the quintessential Frenchman, while his career went from strength to strength.

His alleged Communist sympathies did not prevent Chevalier from acquiring a taste for the high life that included a castle-like property near Paris where he spent, on and off, the last years of his life and where he died in 1972, aged 83.

You will get an even better idea of what distinguished "Ménilmouche" from the nearby Belleville after you ...

... turn right into rue Laurence-Savart ...

… with its 2-ups-2-downs and their tiny but carefully tended "manicured" front gardens (photo page 223).

At the bottom of this street, turn left into rue Boyer. Follow this street when it joins rue de la Bidassoa, past the public baths (a remnant from the times when indoor plumbing was considered an inappropriate luxury for working-class homes) until you reach the far side of the street on the corner of rue Villiers-de-l'Isle-Adam, with the children's playground on your right.

Turn round now to look down rue de la Bidassoa which you have just come from, the rue d'Annam climbing to your right.

You are standing in the exact spot where Jean Servais's Tony Le Stephanois snuffs it in **Du rififi chez les hommes / Rififi**. (2 rue d'Annam is the house where Tony's friend lives—the one whose young boy has been kidnapped. Tony frees the boy, but is mortally wounded in the process, and then drives the kid all across town, slowly dying at the wheel before making that last erratic climb halfway up rue d'Annam.)

Now continue down rue de la Bidassoa, crossing rue Orfila and the busy avenue Gambetta.

The trees on your right belong to the garden fronting Père Lachaise Cemetery. If graveyards aren't your thing, you can end the walk here and turn left to the next Métro station (Gambetta). But if you're in the mood to visit a few famous graves, resist the temptation to walk right into the jardin Samuel La Champlain—lush and leafy it may be, but it won't lead you anywhere.

Walk instead straight into rue des Rondeaux ahead of you. You'll find an entrance to the cemetery on your right after you've walked about a block (200 meters). Walk straight in.

A map at the first corner inside the compound will tell you where to find the graves of all the famous people who are buried here. Each and every path in Père Lachaise is named, just like the real streets beyond its walls. It's really a little city here, a city of the dead.

You are, of course, free to plan your own walk, but in case the map fails to inspire you, I recommend the following route:

Turn left down avenue Circulaire immediately behind the entrance gate and right at the first corner into avenue Carette.

Look for a grave with a huge modernist angel on it (sculpted by Jacob Epstein in 1911, originally complete with male genitals which were later broken off—having been found to be "obscene"—and kept as a paperweight by a succession of Père Lachaise Cemetery gardeners). This is the final resting place of Oscar Wilde, where Rufus Sewell wins back his fiancée in **Paris, je t'aime**, helped by a few words of characteristically pointed advice from the old wit and sage. (Wilde is now all the rage again in England, but for 50 years after his death, not a single boy in the country was baptised Oscar.)

Stay on avenue Carette. Cross avenue Transversale 3 then turn left into avenue Transversale 2. About halfway to the next corner ...

... you will find the grave of the journalist Victor Noir who, if the bronze statue on his grave is anything to go by, must have been buried with a massive erection. The statue's, ahem, most prominent feature did not go unnoticed for long, and the grave has become some sort of a pilgrimage site for giggly young girls. I think you can work out for yourself which part of poor Victor's anatomy has attracted their particular attention. A small clue: Look for the most lovingly polished part of the bronze statue. (Or follow the tour guide in Alain Resnais's **On connaît la chanson / Same Old Song** who explains why this grave—of an otherwise undistinguished journalist—has become the cemetery's most famous.)

Turn left into avenue Greffulhe and then rejoin avenue Circulaire, turning right.

Where the avenue takes a 90-degree turn to the right, you can spot the Mur des Fédérés on your left, the wall against which the last fighters of the Commune de Paris were lined up and shot in 1871. This is another pilgrimage site, although for a different crowd. Opposite the wall, you'll find the graves of many leading personalities from the French left including most chairmen of the French Communist Party.

A little further on, just after passing the monument for the victims of the Mauthausen concentration camp, turn right.

The grave of Édith Piaf is located in the second row, a little hidden, but you can't miss it. Just look for the usual "tragic woman crowd": gay men, cleaning ladies, and unmarried French lit teachers from sad little provincial towns.

Now it gets a bit more complicated. Rejoin avenue Circulaire and, where it forks, turn to the right into the chemin de la Guérité. Follow this path (it changes its name to chemin de la Badoyère), keeping straight, and just before you reach the Rond-Point—don't worry: you will recognize it when you see it—turn left into chemin de Lauriston and again left into chemin de Lesseps.

Ten or fifteen years ago I would have said: from here on, just follow the smell of cheap booze and marijuana. But the days when Jim Morrison's grave was surrounded all day by a flock of latter-day hippies are long gone. You get an impression of what it was like in **2 Days in Paris** when Julie Delpy and her American boyfriend visit the grave—although Jack, as he freely confesses, "doesn't even like The Doors." These days, you are more likely to come across mature American women, showing their female offspring the grave of the man they used to have a terrible crush on when they were about their daughters' age. The grave also features briefly in Oliver Stone's **The Doors**, but the statue you see in the movie was chipped off, little by little, by admirers, and the gravestone was replaced in the 1990s.

This is the end, beau-ti-ful friend, of our elaborate plans, the end—well, at least as far as this particular walk is concerned.

The nearest Métro stations are Philippe August (Line 2) straight ahead to your right, and Métro Gambetta (Line 3), which you can reach by retracing your steps in the opposite direction. And, just in case you feel that the blue bus is calling you: yes, Gambetta has buses, too.

Further Afield

The ten walks I have laid out are, to a certain extent, based on convenience. I have tried to make them as entertaining as possible, avoiding long stretches of nondescript residential streets with nothing to show you at the end but a second-rate sight from a second-rate movie, such as a door to an inaccessible flat. While I think this has, by and large, worked out fairly well, such a strategy comes at a price.

This price is a certain lack of balance: while some minor sites have slipped in because they happen to lie between two major locations, I had to discard quite a few places of interest that would have required rather lengthy detours to include them in one of the ten walks. The price is also a certain lack of thematic congruity: in the midst of an occasionally relentless succession of visual impressions during our walks, we hardly ever got the chance to follow a particular theme or explore a single movie or genre in depth. And finally, the price is a lack of breadth: by their very nature, our walks have tended to focus on a fairly small area of central Paris. But Paris, even the Paris of the movies, is much larger than that. It also comprises the residential areas near the inner ringroad (the *périphérique*), the suburbs, and even, believe it or not, the occasional large park.

Now is the time to set all of these things straight. In this chapter, I'll call your attention to a number of scattered locations that are interesting in themselves and that some of you may well find either worth a special trip or worth adding to one of the walk itineraries. I'll start with some sights that did not fit in any of the ten walks and then move on to ones that fit a particular theme or could be added to one of the ten walks. I'll also note the nearest Métro station for your convenience.

Odds and ends

I have about fifty sights on my list that could not be accommodated in any of the walks, but listing them all would be completeness for completeness's sake. The question I had to ask myself was: would anybody out there want to make a trip of maybe thirty minutes just to see *this*?

- First up in this deliberately pared-down list is Julie Delpy's flat in **Before Sunset** at 18 passage des Petites-Écuries. It is about a ten-minute walk away from the Métro station Strasbourg-Saint-Denis (Lines 4, 8, 9) where Walk 7 ends.

  Just turn left on boulevard de Strasbourg and left again into rue du Chateau-d'Eau, which changes its name after the first intersection to rue des Petites-Écuries. The passage is the next street on your left.

- It's a similar story with Naomi Watts's home in **Le divorce**: close to one of the routes, but not really interesting enough to most people to merit a detour, since all you can see from the street is the door to the courtyard. If, however, you love the movie and want to see it anyway, you can work a visit into Walk 2.

  Fairly early on, you are instructed to turn right into rue des Francs-Bourgeois coming from rue des Archives. What you will do instead is continue on rue des Archives to the corner beyond the National Archives. Turn right there into rue des Quatre-Fils and then left into rue Vieille-du-Temple. At the next corner, turn left into rue du Perche opposite the Bar St-Gervais …

… following Naomi Watts and her new boyfriend on the way to her place—where they find the police at her home and her husband's corpse in the trash bin.

  At the end of rue du Perche, cross rue Charlot—leaving the Church of Sainte-Croix on your left—and walk towards the door immediately to your left on the other side of rue Charlot.

This is the door you have been looking for.

After which you continue down rue Charlot, the church to your left. Turn left into rue des Quatre-Fils, then right into rue Vieille-du-Temple, and left into rue des Francs-Bourgeois. You are now back in Walk 2. Turn right at the next corner into rue des Hôpitalières and continue Walk 2.

• Next up is the Sorbonne, Paris's largest (and, of course, oldest) university which, strangely enough, does not seem to attract a lot of attention from moviemakers. In fairness it must be said that all of its medieval buildings have been long destroyed. The oldest part of it still standing is the chapel which dates from the 17th century and is therefore not remarkably old by Parisian standards. The entrance to this chapel on the place de la Sorbonne (near boulevard St-Michel, about 250 yards down from the Métro station Cluny-La Sorbonne, Line 10) stood in for the police HQ in the Steve Martin remake of **The Pink Panther**. To visit it as a detour from Walk 2 …

*… instead of turning right into rue Racine from boulevard St-Michel after visiting the **Mephisto** spot, stay on the boulevard for a block or so to reach place de la Sorbonne (on your left). Then retrace your steps and turn left into rue Racine to continue the walk.*

• Another "neglected landmark" is the UNESCO headquarters building on avenue de Ségur (behind the École Militaire, which is itself located behind the Eiffel Tower). Apart from an establishing shot in **Charade** (Audrey Hepburn works for UNESCO as a simultaneous translator), the only movie reference to it I could find is the chase sequence in **Rush Hour III**: you see a brief flash of the building in the background of the Chris Tucker tug-of-war with the biker who is trying to pull him out of the cab. Even then, you have the impression the film is more interested in the nearby Valentin Haüy monument at the corner of rue Valentin-Haüy and rue Bouchut, around which much of the remaining chase takes place. The nearest Métro station is Ségur on avenue de Suffren (Line 10).

- Finally, two more home addresses, both in the bourgeois south of the 16th arrondissement, which we do not visit in any of our walks. In **The Truth About Charlie**, Thandie Newton lives at 12 rue Desbordes-Valmore, north of the Métro station La Muette (Line 9) and only a couple of blocks away from Maria Callas's former flat in the even tonier neighborhood north of avenue Georges-Mandel. The gated community of Hameau Boileau at 38 rue Boileau (just off the Métro station Michel-Ange-Molitor, Line 9) is the place where the four middle-aged gourmets have decided to eat themselves to death in Marco Ferreri's bitter satire **La grande bouffe / Blow-Out**. You could visit both as (long) detours from Walk 5, when you are in the vicinity of the place de Trocadéro.

Green Spaces

One point that visitors to Paris often make is that the city has practically no green spaces. While it is true that it has nothing that compares with New York's Central Park or London's green belt of Hyde Park, Regent's Park, Kensington Gardens, and so on, Paris is not completely devoid of large expanses of greenery. You just have to know where to find them.

The biggest and certainly best known of Parisian parks is the Bois de Boulogne on the city's western outskirts. In fact, it is more a small forest than a conventional park. The best way to explore it is to go by Métro to the station Porte Dauphine (Line 2) and walk from there to the *Lac Inférieur*. (you'll find maps everywhere along the footpaths). This is where—down the Ceinture du Lac path around the lake—the opening scene of **Gigi** was shot, complete with Maurice Chevalier's merrily debauched "Thank Heaven for Little Girls." (Nowadays, he would be arrested for that, famous Frenchman or not.)

Other points of interest in the Bois de Boulogne include the restaurant La Grande Cascade. Catherine Deneuve meets the necrophiliac Duke there in Luis Bunuel's **Belle de jour**. And in **Paris When It Sizzles**, the screen characters in William Holden's movie-within-a-movie (impersonated by Audrey Hepburn and himself) have lunch at the Grande Cascade. (The scene includes one of the worst pieces of editing in a major Hollywood movie: a studio sequence with Tony Curtis—who obviously did not want to or could not shoot his scenes on site in Paris—is cut into the film in the most brutally obvious of fashions.) Further to the north, you'll find the Parc de Bagatelle where the eponymous lovers play polo in Louis Malle's **Les amants / The Lovers**. (The film is mainly famous in the U.S. for its role in a landmark definition of obscenity delivered by the Supreme Court, generally known as "I know it when I see it," the phrase used by Justice Potter Stewart to acquit the film and its producers of all charges brought against them.)

But whatever you fancy doing in and around the Bois de Boulogne, be aware that the atmosphere of the area, mainly but not exclusively its eastern rim near residential Paris, drastically changes after dusk. Streetwalkers abound, many of them of the transsexual variety. If that is not your idea of good entertainment, you should stay well clear of the Bois de Boulogne after dark. The movie **Diva** gives a good impression of what the area—in particular the *quartier* around the place Dauphine—looks like late at night.

Less known—and less often visited by tourists and foreign filmmakers (and streetwalkers)—is the Bois de Vincennes at the opposite end of town. But the chateau here puts in an appearance as the Nazi prison in **Code Name: Emerald**, the one where the American POW is interrogated (Château de Vincennes Métro stop, Line 1). And the harness racing track of Vincennes plays a key role in the French cop caper **Les ripoux / My New Partner**.

There are, of course, parks within the city limits of Paris, most notably the Buttes Chaumont where Camille meets with her lover (and where we first meet her when she shows a group of tourists around) in Alain Resnais's **On connaît la chanson / Same Old Song**. Foreign moviemakers may have yet to fall for the Buttes Chaumont's charm, but chances are that you will like it if you are a movie fan, because this is certainly the most theatrical of Paris parks, complete with grottoes, wooden bridges, and carefully arranged vistas across the artificial landscape. So just stroll around, enjoy, and avoid the dog turds. (This is the only city park that dogs are allowed in). The park is in the 19th arrondissement. Métro Line 7bis stops at the Buttes Chaumont station.

The park most movie buffs will want to see, however, is probably the Promenade Plantée (photo page 244), not—in the strictest sense—a park at all, but rather a two and a half-mile walkway constructed on an abandoned railway viaduct. It is one of the main locations of the movie **Before Sunset** and can be most easily reached from the Line 1 Métro stations Gare de Lyon or Reuilly-Diderot. Walk in—just like Julie Delpy and Ethan Hawke— through the main entrance opposite 90 avenue Daumesnil and continue in the direction of the place de la Bastille.

Finally the Musée Rodin. It is, strictly speaking, not a park at all but rather, as you may have guessed, a museum. Its sculpture garden can nevertheless serve very well in lieu of a park as a space of repose and tranquillity in the midst of the city's hustle and bustle. Musée Rodin is centrally located (near the Métro station Varenne, Line 13, right next to the Hôtel des Invalides; see Walk 6) and has been used several times in major movies, most notably as Thomas Jefferson's U.S. Embassy in **Jefferson in Paris** and as the meeting place for Marcello Mastroianni and Sophia Loren in Robert Altman's **Prêt-à-Porter**. It is one of the few museums one could recommend to visitors who have no genuine interest in art, because, in addition to its tranquil garden, it comes equipped with a modestly priced cafeteria and is therefore one of the few places where you can work simultaneously on your culture and your tan while getting quietly smashed. Unless it rains, of course—in which case I recommend the nearest pub.

If you want to combine a visit here with Walk 6, I suggest visiting the museum first and then walking up boulevard des Invalides to the esplanade until you reach rue de l'Université. Turn right into rue de l'Université. The Foreign Office (our first sight in Walk 6) will be right across the street.

Markets

One of the things most foreign visitors to the French capital want to see is a real Parisian street market. Here are a few possibilities, some of which have also served as movie locations:

- The market along rue Lepic and rue des Abbesses in Montmartre (Métro station Abbesses, Line 12, or Blanche, Line 2) is lively and colorful—many scenes from **Le fabuleux destin d'Amélie Poulain / Amélie** were shot here (see Walk 4). But it has shops instead of stalls, so it probably won't count as "real" enough in many peoples' eyes. On the plus side, the market is open for business throughout the week. Don't go on Mondays, however: many shops are closed.
- The rue Mouffetard street market (Walk 2; Métro station place Monge, Line 7) is also highly recommended.
- Apart from those, most interesting are probably the markets on the rue de Buci in the St-Germain quarter (*haut bourgeois*, open daily in the mornings; Métro station Mabillon, Line 10) and the Marché Aligre around place d'Aligre near the Métro station Ledru-Rollin, Line 8 (multi-cultural, open daily except Mondays; closed Sunday afternoons).
- Less famous but equally interesting in its own way is the Marché de la Convention in the southwest of the city (Métro station Convention, Line 12; open Tuesdays, Thursdays, and Sundays—when it is most lively—until mid-afternoon). It also happens to be the place where the French actress Julie Delpy does her grocery shopping in real life. Which is why she used it as the location for the market scenes in her directorial debut, **2 Days in Paris**. In the film, the market with its dead baby pigs—"look what the French have done to Babe"—milk-fed lambs and, the clincher, a baby calf's tongue, turns out to be her American boyfriend's chamber of horrors.

As an added attraction, once you have finished exploring this market, you can take some refreshment at the nearby Café du Marché at 238 rue du Convention, which also puts in an appearance in Delpy's film.

Suburbs

The French word for suburb, *la banlieue*, has totally different connotations from its English and American counterparts. *La banlieue* is not a place of leafy avenues and spacious gardens. It is gray, mean, and menacing. This is where people live who cannot afford a ticket into polite society, i.e., a flat—at least a rented one—in one of the respectable areas of downtown Paris. Think of Paris and its suburbs as a series of concentric circles. Leafy avenues and spacious gardens begin only beyond the dreaded *cités*, the concrete belt of run-down 1960s' housing projects that surround central Paris. But even most of their inhabitants would gladly trade in a spacious garden for a share in the hurly-burly of the central city. For the French, *la banlieue*, even in its idyllic version, has overtones of misery and frustration—of exile.

Saint-Denis, north of Paris, is one of the most notorious banlieues around the French capital. The most famous celebrity to come from Saint-Denis is the porn actress Tabatha Cash, a fact that alone speaks volumes. But Saint-Denis also happens to be the home of the Abbey of Saint-Denis, the ancestor of all Gothic churches anywhere in the world and the place where (nearly) all French kings since the early 6th century Clovis I have been buried. It is in this capacity that it attracted the makers of **Jefferson in Paris**. Nick Nolte as the eponymous ambassador and Greta Scacchi have their first intimate conversation at the Basilique de Saint-Denis, where they inspect some of the royal tombs ("overloaded monstrosities," Nolte's Jefferson calls them). The nearest Métro station is Basilique de Saint-Denis (Line 13).

Versailles, 22 kilometers southwest of central Paris, is at the other, *petit-bourgeois* end of the suburban spectrum and on the other, safe side of the concrete belt as well. It is, however, famous for its distinctly non-*petit-bourgeois* palace, Louis XIV's 1,500-room mansion, which at some stage devoured about 25 percent of the country's entire budget—and that only covered the cost of running it, never mind the expenses required for the actual construction. It is actually quite rare for the French Government, which owns the place, to grant permission to film on the palace grounds, but they made exceptions for **Jefferson in Paris**—where, historically correct, Jefferson watches a balloon take off from the palace gardens—and, more recently, for Sophie Coppola's **Marie Antoinette**.

Finally, if you are determined to see how tough life in the 'hood can be for a Parisian *banlieusard*, you could do worse than visit Chanteloup les Vignes. This is where director Mathieu Kassovitz—yes, believe it or not, the clueless passport pic collector from Amélie—shot his unflinchingly realistic **La haine / Hate**. If you really want to go there, take the train from the Gare St-Lazare (a journey of about forty minutes on the RER network, with around three departures per hour). But don't expect any further clues. From Chanteloup central station onwards, you are completely on your own, pal.

Microwalks

Sights come in clusters. Stroll through Montmartre, and you can spot a movie location on practically every street corner; travel the streets of the 13th or the 17th arrondissements, and you can walk around endlessly without stumbling on any familiar site. What's more, most of the time even the clusters come in clusters—which has enabled us to visit fairly disparate areas in the same Walk, such as, in Walk 7, the fashionable rue de la Paix in the Opéra *quartier* and the rue St-Denis. It does not always work that way, however. Some clusters are relatively isolated. In the following "microwalks" we shall pay a visit to a few of them.

Flea market / "Marché aux Puces"

Let's begin with one cluster that is quite a long way out, so far out actually that it is not, strictly speaking, a part of Paris anymore. The "Marché aux Puces" was established 200 years ago when traders of secondhand goods were kicked out of Paris. It has since developed into the largest flea market in Paris and presumably the world, welcoming 200,000 visitors each weekend (most shops and stalls are open only from Saturday to Monday).

From the Métro station Porte de Clignancourt (Line 4), follow the street signs that lead you to the flea market and walk underneath the flyover that marks the city's boundary into avenue Michelet.

You're now in the municipality of Saint-Ouen. Roy Scheider's car is blown up in **Marathon Man** in front of the restaurant Le Soleil at 109 avenue Michelet.

Cross the street and turn left into rue Biron.

At no. 55/56, we see Roy Scheider stroll around in **Marathon Man** just before he returns to his car.

Follow rue Biron to the end to rue des Rosiers.

At 8 rue des Rosiers, Mark Wahlberg and Thandie Newton are meant to meet their contact, an antiques dealer, in **The Truth About Charlie**. And it is somewhere on rue des Rosiers, too, with the Marché Paul Bert in the back, that we see Edward Fox kit himself out like a French army veteran with beret and black jacket in **The Day of the Jackal**.

But we owe the most extended *puces* sequence to the *nouvelle vague* classic **Zazie dans le métro / Zazie in the Metro**. Here is where Zazie makes her decidedly creepy companion buy her a pair of jeans while he himself purchases a pair of sunglasses—from a market trader who looks suspiciously like himself—before she runs away from him and they lose each other between the stalls.

Actually, the best way of experiencing the market is probably to lose yourself between upmarket antiques shops (of which there are quite a few) and street traders—as long as you don't lose your valuables along the way. Which is why you should make sure that they are safely tucked away before you arrive.

On the way back to the Clignancourt Métro station …

… cast a glance to your left: Here, at the intersection between the Porte de Clignancourt and boulevard Ney, one of the largest (real-life) manhunts in post-WWII France came to an end when gangster Jacques Mesrine—a sort of French John Dillinger—was gunned down by police sharpshooters on November 2, 1979. A two-part movie about Mesrine's life featuring Vincent Cassel, the French super-thief Jacques Toulour in *Ocean's Twelve*, is due to be released in 2009.

La Défense

La Défense is another business district that was, for reasons of convenience, moved outside the city limits (although this one has remained, in strict administrative terms, a part of Paris). You can see its high-rise buildings from almost anywhere in western Paris, and Parisians are mighty proud of their "Manhattan-sur-Seine." In truth, however, nobody who has ever walked in midtown Manhattan would be in any danger of confusing the two. "Milwaukee-sur-Seine" would seem to be a much more accurate if much less flattering epithet.

If you watch a lot of French movies, you are sure to have seen La Défense a few times because it is regularly used by local directors—mainly, though by no means exclusively, as a cheap stand-in for American street scenes. The *quartier* is easy to reach by Métro: Line 1 takes you straight to the district's top landmark, the *Grande Arche* (above). Leave through the main exit, following Bruno Ganz in **The American Friend**, who walks out onto the large courtyard, the place de la Défense, after he has performed the "hit" on the escalator of La Défense Métro station.

A number of other films include scenes shot in La Défense. For example:

- Rowan Atkinson arrives under the futuristic *Grande Arche* believing that he is entering the Gare de Lyon. This after his taxi takes him to the wrong address, thanks to a typically Mr. Bean mix-up—and to make sure that **Mr. Bean's Holiday** starts on an appropriately confused note.
- Matt Damon comes to the area to conduct some inquiries about his past in **The Bourne Identity**.
- The basement of the huge *Centre Commercial* provides the setting for the bank robbery (at the non-existent Banque de l'Union) in the notorious French heist movie **Dobermann**. This film caused quite a stir in the late 1990s due to its graphic violence, almost becoming a *cause célèbre*. Nowadays, it just looks rather cartoonish and silly.

Bastille

Next to the lack of expansive green spaces, the seeming lack of any major building activity is the point visitors make most frequently about Paris. If you're coming from London, for example, you're used to seeing dozens of cranes as a semi-permanent feature of the city's skyline. Thus you may conclude that while London is forever in the process of becoming, Paris is happy with what she is, or perhaps what as she once was, self-contentedly in love with her own image. While there is probably a grain of truth in this, it is an over-simplification because the basic assumption is flawed. It is simply not true that Paris is a no-change-zone, an urban museum—beautiful, but dead—like inner-city Venice. And to prove this, we shall visit the lively inner-city quarter around the Bastille.

This walk will be of most interest to those of you who have seen the French movie **Et chacun cherche son chat / When the Cat's Away**. The film is a sort of a proto-*Amélie*, with a cast of loveable locals and a charming young girl whose story—of her search for her cat and a love life that deserves its name—holds it all together. There is one big difference between the two movies, however: whereas Amélie celebrates "the eternal Montmartre," **Et chacun cherche son chat / When the Cat's Away** is all about change, both the change in people's lives and, at a more visual and cinematic level, change in a particular area of Paris—the formerly working-class area east of the place de la Bastille—from grime to gentrification.

Start at the Métro station Bastille (Lines 1,5,8). Head toward exit "rue St-Antoine," and, when the signs get more specific, to exit "rue du Faubourg-St-Antoine." Walk straight ahead out of the exit (to the left of the fork) into rue du Faubourg-St-Antoine. After about 500 yards, take leafy avenue Ledru-Rollin to your left.

We see Chloé—the movie's main protagonist—put up a search note for her missing cat (the eponymous one that is "away") in the bakery at no. 109, setting the entire neighbourhood on a search. The bakery, in real life, seems very popular; there is always a queue in front, a good sign. They also offer *sandwiches a toutes heures*. So this may be a good place to stock up for wherever you are heading for the rest of the day.

Cross the avenue at the corner of rue de Charonne. Turn left and immediately right into rue Keller—just before the Café Pause at the corner of rue Keller and rue de Charonne, the place where all the chi-chi people Chloé so heartily detests take their coffee. (It isn't quite that bad, actually, but one understands what she means.) On rue Keller, between nos. 15 and 29 …

… the old women recapitulate what this and that shop once used to sell before all the fashion designers and advertising executives moved in. But, in a further elaboration of the *leitmotif* of change (you couldn't make this up), neither the "Terrain Vogue" nor the "Manga Tonga" boutique (where their particular bemusement is focused on a bra with pointed steel tips) still exists, having made way for a colorfully diverse row of shops ranging from the almost-if-not-totally conventional (an art gallery, a shop that prints customized T-shirts) to the downright weird (a shop selling fantasy figurines, chiefly, it seems, of Sir Ian McKellen as Gandalf in *Lord of the Rings*, and a shop of manga accessories that offers only stuff for girls). By the time you pass by, of course, all of those may be gone, too, which only goes to show how life imitates art.

Follow the street to its end.

The new church to your left is Notre-Dame-d'Esperance. The ongoing demolition of its predecessor was one of the central metaphors of **Et chacun cherche son chat / When the Cat's Away**.

Turn left and immediately left again, going back in the direction you have just come from.

The Bar des Taillandiers at 22 rue des Taillandiers is the place where the "real" people in the movie meet. It has since become the restaurant La Griaude, but still looks very much the same. More change at no. 16-18, the house where Bel Canto lives (the man with whom Chloé finds what she has been looking for, besides the cat, throughout the film), which has since received a new coat of paint. The record store TECHNO IMPORT next door on the ground floor is still there as we go to press. But a row of chic offices has gone up at no. 20.

A short way farther down, turn right into passage des Taillandiers where, at no. 5 …

… we find—reassuringly unchanged—the place where Chloé shares an apartment with her gay flat mate. They have a deal: He pays most of the rent, she comforts him when something goes wrong in one of his relationships, which is pretty often. This is also where Chloé finally finds Grisgris the cat, wedged between the wall and the stove, alive and well if slightly thinner than before.

Follow this street to the end and turn left into passage Thiéré. At the end of this narrow lane, turn right into rue de Charonne, past the rue de Lappe, the center of much of the entertainment trade—bars, discos, restaurants—that has entered the area over the last 15 years.

The Café des Entre Potes at 14 rue de Charonne is the place where Chloé is chatted up first by Mr. Awful and then by the lesbian barmaid for a truly great night out.

Continue down rue de Charonne and right into rue Faubourg-St-Antoine to return to the place de la Bastille.

Throughout Paris's history, this area has attracted craftsmen and artisans, the respectable working class of its day so to speak. The furniture trade in particular has always prospered here and has stayed in the area to this very day (look left and right into the courtyards for confirmation.) In the late 18th century, this was a hotbed of discontent, and it must have been down this street—the ancient rue Faubourg-St-Antoine—that the angry men and women came on their way to the Bastille on July 14, 1789.

The street is rarely used in the movies, however, because it is quite difficult to avoid an anachronistic glimpse of the Bastille Monument (erected in honor not of the 1789 storming of the Bastille but of the revolution after that, the one in 1830 which also provides the background for Victor Hugo's *Les Misérables* as well as the stage musical of the same name). The Monument does, however, put in an appearance in **Et chacun cherche son chat / When the Cat's Away**. In the dream sequence, Chloé stands on top of the Bastille column shouting for Grisgris. Don't bother, however, to search for the picturesque Métro pavilion on whose locked doors Zazie is rattling in **Zazie dans le métro / Zazie in the Metro**: that one fell victim to a refurbishment of square and station in the 1970s.

Finish this microwalk on a movie theme in the Café le Bastille, on your right as you leave rue du Faubourg-St-Antoine. In **Place Vendôme**, Catherine Deneuve meets Jacques Dutronc here before she is to lure him into the trap that's been prepared for him by the police at the Gare de Lyon. In the movie, through clever editing, the Café le Bastille is made to overlook the station.

The passages

There are worse ways of spending a rainy afternoon than strolling through the *passages couverts* of Paris, the indoor shopping arcades that were all the rage in the early 19th century. They were meant to give shoppers, mainly ladies, an opportunity to stroll through genteel surroundings in comfort and safety—much like the modern shopping mall, if you think about it. About twenty *passages couverts* are left out of a total of 150 at the peak of their popularity. Most are in the 2nd and 10th arrondissements.

The first of these shopping streets was the passage des Panoramas, named after a scenic picture, which they thought at the time necessary to attract customers. The picture has long since disappeared, unlike the passage itself

and the shop of the engraver Henri Stern, which has been in continuous existence here since 1834. The passages Verdeau (above) and Jouffroy came later, during the 1840s. They were constructed in steel and glass, cutting-edge technology at the time, and celebrated by the French surrealists. (One can't help wondering what would they would have made of Edmonton Mall.)

You can reach the passages easily from Métro stations Richelieu-Drouot and Grandes boulevards (Lines 8, 9). I deliberately refrain from giving you a fixed itinerary, however, because part of the fun is simply losing yourself in the narrow hallways of successive passages between fashion boutiques, bookshops, and stamp dealers. The passages are a lot less fashionable nowadays than they once were. But you will like them if you appreciate the slightly musty air of faded grandeur. As you walk, be on the lookout for two sights, the toyshop Le Pain d'Epice at 29-33 passage Jouffroy where Mark Wahlberg does some shopping in **The Truth About Charlie** and Le Bistrot at 7 passage Verdeau where Matt Damon has a coffee in **The Bourne Identity**. This is where Franka Potente tells Damon that the corpse of Kane, one of his aliases, has just been found.

"Gangland"

Finally, a personal favorite of mine:

I used to work more or less regularly at a broadcasting studio in the south of the 13th arrondissement and came across—purely by chance—the iron walkway across the platforms of the RER station Massena where Alain Delon's hitman nearly gets killed in **Le samouraï / The Godson**. Delon meets his contact, expecting to get paid for a hit he has just performed, but the contact tries to shoot him. So every time I walked down this way, I played the scene in my mind, going BANG BANG BANG near the station house on the other side—riddling with bullets the dirty bastard who just tried to cheat me out of my hard-earned pay—and then walking down the stairs to street level while readjusting the collar of my trench coat. That always made me feel very cool indeed and got me into the right mood for a hard session at the office. (Nobody ever tried to cheat me out of my pay—so it must have worked.)

Unfortunately, however, the RER station Massena no longer exists; it was merged into the large RER-Métro interchange at the new Bibliothèque François Mitterrand a couple of hundred meters up the track. Worse, the entire area, once something of an "urban reservation" of endangered architectural species such as dishevelled shops, semi-derelict tenement halls, and abandoned warehouses, is now littered with spanking new office buildings and has totally lost its romantic air of genteel neglect.

But it's not all gone. The freight terminal of the Gare d'Austerlitz still occupies much of the area around the railway tracks. If you walk down rue Watt with the freight trains running overhead, you can imagine how scary and godforsaken the entire area once must have been.

Jean-Pierre Melville used this part of town a few years before he made **Le samouraï / The Godson** in the equally splendid **Le doulos / The Finger Man**. In the opening sequence, we see Serge Reggiani walk past rue Watt on his search for the guy who buys and sells stolen jewelry. And although the Massena walkway from **Le samouraï / The Godson** has been dismantled, the station house where Delon arrives and walks down to street level is still there, abandoned and semi-derelict, wedged into the extreme bottom corner of rue du Loiret next to the stairs.

While you are here in the 13th arrondissement, why not take advantage of the opportunity to take a look at some other movie sites in this district, by far the city's least fashionable.

Take tramway line T3 (the only tram line that circulates within Paris city limits) from the nearby Métro station Porte d'Ivry (Line 7) in the direction of pont de Garigliano and alight at Stade Charlety.

This 20,000-seat stadium, nowadays used by a lower-division soccer club and for concerts and political rallies, provided the background for the eventually discarded duel sequence in Alfred Hitchcock's somewhat jinxed 1969 Cold War thriller **Topaz**. In the first version of the film, secret agent Frederick Stafford and his old friend-cum-rival-in-love Michel Piccoli (who has just been exposed as a Russian spy) decide to settle their unresolved matters in—get this—a duel, pistols at dawn. This is, quite unbelievably, the ending Hitchcock and his equally experienced screenwriter Samuel A. Taylor wanted for the movie before the preview audiences intervened. Almost to a man and woman, they said that they hated this scene more than any other in the movie.

So Hitchcock scrapped his preferred ending and replaced it with the one you can see on the restored version of the DVD (where we see Piccoli, like the real-life spy British Kim Philby, escape on a plane to Moscow). But the preview audiences didn't like that ending either, so the final scene the cinema audiences actually saw at the time (Piccoli killing himself) had to be cobbled together from existing shots.

Still, Stade Charlety may very well be the only place Hitchcock actually directed in Paris, because the scene from *Topaz* described in Walk 6 was probably, by the looks of it, shot by a second-unit crew.

To continue, turn left—Stade Charlety at your back—into boulevard Jourdan and then right at the next corner into rue l'Amiral Mouchez. At the three-street junction, take the "two o'clock" turn into rue Auguste-Lançon and then the first street to your right, rue Brillat-Savarin (like the cookbook writer).

The house at no. 49 on your right plays a major role in the French film **Caché**, Michael Haneke's essay on post-colonial guilt. The film opens with a three-minute-long take of the entrance door, showing people walking in, walking out, and walking past, a little like an abridged version of Andy Warhol's *Empire*. It is only at the end of the scene—when the images suddenly begin to fast forward—that we realize that this has been a video, one made by Daniel Auteuil's mysterious foe and tormentor as it turns out.

Once you have come all the way to see this, you may also want to walk down rue des Iris, opposite the building from which the videos have apparently been shot, and explore. You'll find the area an idyllic and village-like development in an otherwise fairly unattractive part of the town.

Métro Stations

The Paris Métro system puts in a great many movie appearances. Most movies set in Paris feature at least one Métro scene, and the stations seem easy to identify. But not everything is as it seems. For some years, the Paris Transport Authority has restricted the access of film crews to the stations under its control, and it has made it more and more difficult to get a permit to film at one of the busy stations.

Most crews are re-routed to the station Porte des Lilas in the east of the city—a large and somewhat underused station that features correspondingly often in films, if not always under its own name. In **Ronin**, however, either because of an oversight or because the director saw no reason to pretend the station was any other, the real name of the station appears in the scene where Natasha McElhone meets Jonathan Pryce.

Famous scenes shot in the Paris subway over the years include Cary Grant's chase after Audrey Hepburn in **Charade** (on Line 1 to the Palais Royal), the daring escape of the young mailman on his scooter in **Diva** (featuring the Concorde and Opéra stations, Lines 1, 8,12 and 3, 7, 8, respec-

tively), and Alain Delon's attempt to shake off a police tail in **Le samouraï /
The Godson**, centering on the Télégraphe station on Line 11.

The Coen Brothers shot their contribution to **Paris, je t'aime**, featuring
a wonderfully clueless Steve Buscemi, at the Tuileries station (Line 1). And
for real Métro devotees, there is a French movie called **Subway** shot entirely
in the Paris Métro system. Made by Luc Besson in 1985, the film stars
Christopher Lambert (Tarzan in *Greystoke*) and Isabelle Adjani. It was very
successful in France and won Christopher Lambert a *César* (French Oscar)
for Best Actor.

Restaurants

Many restaurants with a movie connection feature in our ten Walks, but few
of those that are out of the way merit a detour. One that does is La Grande
Cascade in the Bois de Boulogne, which we have already mentioned above
under "Green Spaces." Of the remaining few, top of the list is Le Train Bleu.

Built during the heyday of rail travel within the confines of the Gare de
Lyon in the more-is-not-nearly-enough architectural style of the era, Le Train

Bleu has, unsurprisingly, attracted the attention of moviemakers ever since. This is the place the "hitwoman" **Nikita** is treated to a birthday dinner by her sadistic boss (to carry out her first assignment, right there and then) and where the trap is laid for Jacques Dutronc's jewel thief in **Place Vendôme**. Le Train Bleu also puts in an appearance in **Travels with My Aunt** as the restaurant where Maggie Smith experiences a flashback to her youth. And in **Mr. Bean's Holiday**, Rowan Atkinson walks in, apparently expecting some sort of burger-and-fried-chicken railway buffet, as a sort of second choice after he has failed to get a sandwich out of the vending machine (his tie got caught in the money slot).

Somewhat at the other end of the spectrum is Le Pure Café (opposite and page 240) at 14 rue Jean-Macé, near Métro Charonne (Line 9) in the 11th arrondissement. A modest little café—with much to be modest about—it is frequented by a predominantly young and local clientele. It owes its worldwide renown (and its place on our list) solely to the fact that Ethan Hawke and Julie Delpy have a long chat over a cup of coffee here in **Before Sunset**. The café is fairly close to the Bastille microwalk, so you could combine the two excursions.

If Le Train Bleu is a James-Bond-kind of place, Les Bains at 7 rue du Bourg-l'Abbé is distinctly Austin Powers. A restaurant-cum-nightclub conversion built in the cavernous spaces of the old municipal baths, it's simply shagadelic, baby. For a while (in the 1980s), it was so popular that it became the studio for a late night TV program. In **Frantic**, this is the club—called the Blue Parrot—where Harrison Ford naively thinks the "white lady" the Rasta man is talking about is his wife. (Innocent boy.) If you want to check it out, rue du Bourg-l'Abbé is a side street off boulevard Sébastopol. It's less than half a mile south of the end of Walk 7 or can be reached via the Étienne-Marcel (Line 3) or Réaumur-Sébastopol (Lines 3 and 4) Métro stations.

The one Paris restaurant most of you will want to visit, however, sadly does not exist. Gusteau's, where they serve an excellent **Ratatouille** I hear, is an amalgam of several famous Parisian restaurants, including Taillevent, Le Tour d'Argent (see Walk 1) and Le Train Bleu (see above). A five-man crew from Pixar, among them the director and production designer, spent a week in Paris, dining in a different luxury restaurant every night so they could get "the feeling of the place right." A terrible sacrifice but one they were apparently willing to make.

What to Watch Before You Come

This chapter is for all of you who are planning a trip to Paris and want to develop a sense of the place before you leave. Ditto for those of you who've been to Paris and are interested in pinpointing some new neighborhoods to explore. Why go through piles of books that rattle on endlessly about what king followed what queen and what building was built in what style when you can let Hollywood's finest whet your appetite much more entertainingly?

Each of the films I recommend to you includes a number of interesting locations that aren't overrun with tourists and will be found in one or more of the ten Walks in this book. My recommendations come in two groups, wholehearted endorsements and movies I recommend with reservations. That's because I picked them primarily for their Paris locations and only secondarily for their cinematic quality. On the other hand, every movie is at least watchable and most are very enjoyable. After all, if it's boredom you're looking for, I might as well just send you back to that dusty 14-volume History of France.

The top three

Let's start with my three unqualified recommendations. These films have all the right ingredients: great locations and high-quality entertainment. They're listed in order of the number and range of locations they include.

- **The Bourne Identity** (2002) is unbeatable as both a fun film and an antidote to the overdose of saccharine that's an occupational hazard for people who watch too many movies about Paris. Rare for a movie of its genre, it appeals even to people who are in general not too keen on action thrillers. The film was a surprise hit when it came out in 2002; nobody had expected it to be so successful. It's since spawned a budding franchise for its protagonist, Jason Bourne a.k.a. Matt Damon (for whom this film was the springboard to superstardom) as a James Bond for the 21st century. *The Bourne Identity* features good locations that haven't been overused, straying far beyond Sacré-Coeur, the Arc de Triomphe, and the pont Alexandre-III to give you a real feel for the city. Its locations can be found in seven of our ten Walks—more than any other film in the book.

- **Amélie** (2001) is the most popular French film ever released in the U.S., and it is easy to see why. It's simply a perfect piece of cinema—funny, warm, and utterly delightful. On top of that, it is original and French, too, in an understated way, no striped sweaters or berets in sight. It does not cover the whole of Paris, admittedly, being mainly, though not exclusively, set in Montmartre. Still, it gets around enough to be found in five of the ten Walks.
- And finally, there is **Charade** (1963), the best Hitchcock film that Hitchcock never made, or so they say. *Charade*, directed by Stanley Donen, is witty, well-paced, and so full of unexpected twists and turns that you can barely follow the plot and will still discover something new no matter how many times you have watched the movie before. More to the point, *Charade* gives you an idea of Paris in an almost subliminal way. It deals, lest we forget, with serious things: a murder right at the start and a murderer on the loose who scatters the corpses of his victims all over the place, but, more seriously, with a subject of truly tragic dimensions, the betrayal of innocence by experience. This is the stuff of Greek tragedies, but *Charade* treats this enormously heavy subject matter with the lightest of hands, frivolously, one might say. And what could be more quintessentially Parisian than that?

More qualified choices

The following movies aren't up to the level of the three above. But you'll see a number of interesting Paris sights as you watch and will most likely enjoy the films as well.

Inevitably, ROMANTIC COMEDIES are well represented among movies set in Paris. You could definitely do worse than the following two:
- **French Kiss** (1995) gives us Meg Ryan and Kevin Kline at the top of their form. My reservation is that as far as its Paris content is concerned, you could switch off after the first 30 minutes or so because the movie relocates to the south of France.
- **Sabrina** (1995 version) also has only about 30 minutes worth of Parisian scenes, but they are located at opposite ends of the movie. Yet even when the film is set in New England, Paris hovers just "off-stage," rather like a

central character who may not be physically present at the moment but who, you are made to feel, will return to play a key role in the *denouement*. Watching it again recently, I found it surprisingly funny, too.

On balance, there is not much to choose between *French Kiss* and the 1995 *Sabrina*. If you like this sort of thing—lightweight, charming, and predictable—you will almost certainly like them both.

- **Before Sunset** (2004) is a somewhat different kind of romance. It features some lovely and infrequently used locations, shown "in depth" rather than fleetingly—which is always nice. As a movie, however, it isn't particularly cinematic, and little attempt is made to connect dialogue and picturesque scenery. You could perform *Before Sunset* on a theater stage or even on radio without losing much. That said, the movie keeps you engaged, and even if you don't fall in love with the two protagonists, you will want to know what happens to them at the end.

Which brings us straight to the related genre of the **SCREEN MUSICAL**. The first two of the following offer some good—even great—locations, but will probably strike you as dated, at least in part. The third is the best cinematically but it focuses less on its Paris locations.

- **An American in Paris** (1951) was hailed in its time as a masterpiece, the ultimate achievement in the history of the "seventh art." But as cinema, it buckles under the weight of its own artistic ambition. Nonetheless, while you will certainly want to keep the remote at hand to zip through the film's interminable dancey bits designed in the style of various impressionist painters, much of the movie and most of its musical numbers still work rather well.
- **Funny Face** (1951) hasn't aged well, either, and the screen relationship between Audrey Hepburn and Fred Astaire certainly doesn't crackle. But the film shows great locations, and Audrey Hepburn's charm papers over some cracks in its narrative structure.
- **Gigi** (1958) is a slightly different matter, a costume drama that fails to make the best use of its Paris locations. Most of the time, director Vincente Minelli seems in a hurry to move indoors where he can recreate the Belle Époque without having to compromise and cut corners. Still, *Gigi* provides atmosphere and has a certain period charm, a combination that can more than make up for a lack of powerfully driven narrative.

And don't forget **THRILLERS**, another genre that's thick on the ground in Paris. Many excellent French and American thrillers are mentioned in the Walks. If I had to suggest just one French thriller to watch before you come, I would pick:

- **Du rififi chez les hommes / Rififi** (1955). It tops my list as an introduction to the city because you get to see some dark side streets around the place Pigalle as well as quite a bit of the areas covered in Walks 9 and 10, around the Canal Saint-Martin and the neighbourhoods of Belleville and Ménilmontant. These interesting parts of town are otherwise underrepresented in this list of recommended movies.

Two American thrillers also make my "recommended with qualifications" pre-trip viewing list:

- **Ronin** (1999), the better of the two, is craftily directed by John Frankenheimer—who, as an ex-racing driver, directed all the stunts and car chases with apparent gusto, and written by David Mamet—who is credited under the alias Richard Weisz after having fallen out with the film's producers. My qualification: it absents itself from Paris for much of its middle section.
- **Frantic** (1988) offers some good locations and keeps going at a brisk pace, but it doesn't rank among director Roman Polanski's best work. Still, Harrison Ford is perfectly cast as the middle-aged American businessman who discovers that he is a much tougher cookie than he himself would have dared to think.

My strongest reservation ...

... applies to **Paris, je t'aime** (2006). This anthology of eighteen short films by different directors is set in various areas of the city, making it sound like the perfect introduction to Paris. It's not. All too often, the directors follow the pattern "establishing shot segue to interiors." And many of the remaining exteriors were shot at night, ensuring that you don't get to see all that much. So while you might well enjoy it, you won't find it too helpful in planning your vacation itinerary.

Index of Films

C

D

About the Author:

Michael Schürmann is a journalist, broadcaster, and translator.
He has lived in Paris since 1993.

Photo by Marlys Schürmann

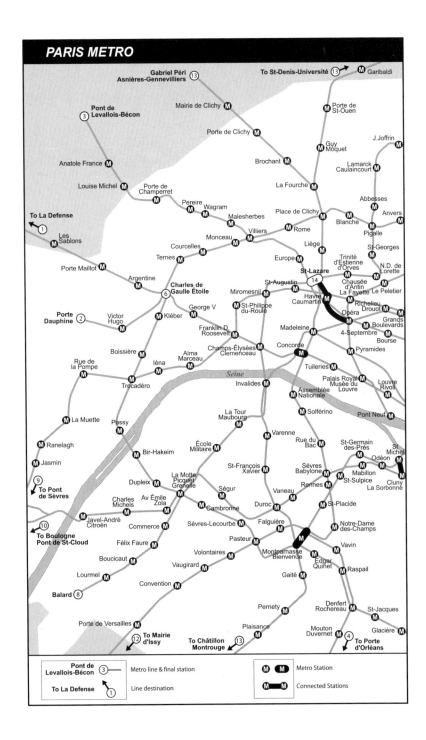

PARIS METRO

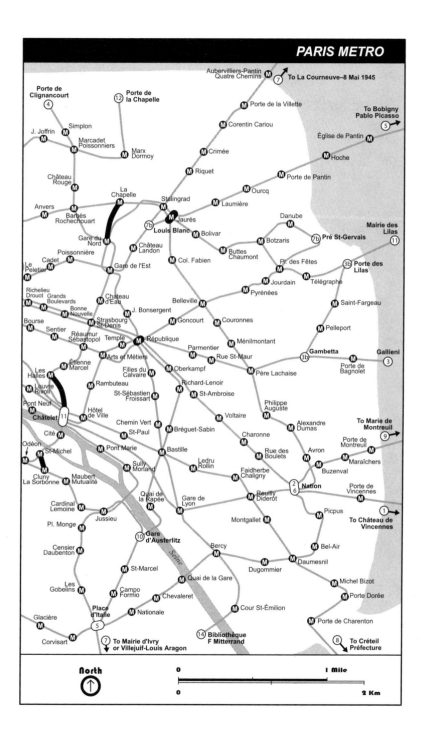

PARIS METRO